MW00966801

The
Butterfly
Experience

The Butterfly Experience

Healthy Transitions in Athletic Hirings

Beth Bass and Betty Jaynes

with Jana Hunter

Foreword by Jean Lenti Ponsetto

B & B PUBLISHING

Lilburn, Georgia

Copyright © 2010 by Beth Bass and Betty Jaynes with Jana Hunter

All rights reserved. No portion of this book may be reproduced, stored in a retrieval system, or transmitted in any form or by any electronic or mechanical means—including photocopying, recording, scanning, or other—except for brief passages in a review or article to be published in a magazine, newspaper, or on the Web without prior written permission of the publisher.

B & B Publishing
4646 Lawrenceville Hwy.
Lilburn, GA 30047
(770) 279-8027 x101
bettyj@wbca.org

Printed in the United States of America.

Cover, illustration, interior design, and layout by TwoJay! (Keri Evans and Jody Roginson). Copyediting by Laura Hambly.

A significant portion of the proceeds from the sales of this title will benefit the Betty F. Jaynes Internship Program at the Women's Basketball Coaches Association.

ISBN: 978-0-615-34911-4

In honor of my parents, Bob and Hylda Bass,
who—from "the greatest generation," as Tom Brokaw called it—always
asked how I was treating Betty whenever I talked about work.

~ B.B.

CONTENTS

Acknowledgments viii

Foreword ix

Preface xi

Introduction 1

Transitions 3

Chapter 1
MAKING A CHANGE: The Metamorphosis Begins **9**
Deciding to Go 10
Breaking the News 19
Wrapping It Up 33
Bridging the Gap With Players and Staff 36

Chapter 2
GOING IN MOTION: The Hiring Process **42**
Taking Preliminary Steps 42
Identifying Candidates 43
Interviewing the Candidates 50
Arriving at "Yes!" 56
Announcing the Decision 66

Chapter 3
SMOOTHING THE PATH: First Steps After the Hire **69**
Relocating 70
Administering to Needs 73
Attending to Priorities 80
Meeting People 100

Chapter 4

PASSING THE BATON: Momentum Is Key............................ **107**

    Communicating 109

    Honoring 125

Chapter 5

PROGRESSING WITH CLASS: An Intentional Effort......................... **141**

    Leading From the Top..142

    Focusing on the Student-Athlete.............................147

    Taking Care of Self 156

Chapter 6

PREPARING FOR GREATNESS: Young Head Coaches **160**

    Moving Up From Within 160

    Mentoring and Being Mentored 163

    Managing People, Places, and Things.....................167

Chapter 7

UTILIZING A LONG-TERM INTERIM COACH: A Dialogue **172**

    Birth of a Unique Situation......................................172

    The Plan...173

    Everybody Wins...174

    Interim Seasons...176

    The End and the Beginning 178

About the Authors 182

ACKNOWLEDGMENTS

Many thanks to the transition teams for their time, transparency, and trust in this project; to the external reviewers who provided valuable feedback along the way; and especially to Francie Dalton of Dalton, Inc., for giving us the encouragement and motivation to write the book.

FOREWORD

The primary purpose of college athletics, in my opinion, is not to make money, win games, or draw attention to a university. The intent is to create environments and experiences in which coaches help college students graduate, develop their character, and grow into adulthood.

But the student-athletes aren't the only ones in position to learn from their involvement in college athletics. When approached with an open mind and an open heart, the opportunity for continued development is equal among players and staff, and it can be just as vital at the beginning, middle, or end of a career.

At this stage in the development of women's athletics, the lessons to be learned by coaches and administrators take on added significance. Fans and media shower teams with more attention than ever before. Athletes display skillful performances that players in the previous decade could only dream about. But perhaps most importantly, the jewels of the women's coaching profession—the frontrunners who have mentored so many—are in the twilight of their illustrious, influential careers. The sincerity and diligence with which we capture their knowledge and wisdom, the style with which we apply it, and the manner in which the next generation of coaches works to keep sports on its upward trajectory will be primary factors in whether we're able to sustain the phenomenal growth of the past two decades.

This book is an invaluable tool for that endeavor, and I can think of no pair more qualified to teach us to navigate those paths than Betty Jaynes and Beth Bass of the Women's Basketball Coaches Association (WBCA). Since 1997, they have demonstrated that delicate balance of honoring the past while moving forward to an even brighter future, each exuding a seemingly effortless grace in leading the organization through a transition that could have divided the sport but which instead produced its most successful decade.

But they didn't stop at simply sharing only their ideas in *The Butterfly Experience: Healthy Transitions in Athletic Hirings*. They also gathered the insights of 28 others who serve as wonderful examples of how to change well-established leadership on a team or in an organization without disrupting its foundational stability, integrity, and support.

As a long-time advocate for student-athlete welfare, I recruit coaches and administrators to our department who have integrity, who respect the foundational purpose of intercollegiate athletics, and who communicate and interact with others honestly and respectfully. The message of this book is based on those same concepts. Every athletic administrator, every collegiate coach, and every person considering entering the field of athletics would do well not only to read *The Butterfly Experience* but to be guided by its principles.

Jean Lenti Ponsetto
Director of Athletics, DePaul University

PREFACE

It was not supposed to work. People in their right minds could see that from all across the country.

In 1996, Betty Jaynes was drowning in her own success. After serving 15 years as the only executive director of the Women's Basketball Coaches Association (WBCA), Jaynes was directing operations, executing new initiatives, consulting with coaches, managing staff, and planning for the future—all while traveling 20 days a month serving on more than three dozen boards of directors and liaising with other organizations.

Popularity of the women's game had just begun to take a significant upward turn, and the future teemed with the possibility of a real explosion of growth. Jaynes was running ragged trying to stay ahead of the curve that she had spent her life, really, creating.

Then-WBCA president Sylvia Hatchell, head coach at the University of North Carolina, recognized that Jaynes needed help and that the organization and game needed a marketing expert to pounce on the ripe opportunities. On a trip the two took to the Nike headquarters in Oregon, they encountered a well-known women's basketball face in Beth Bass, who had spent most of her professional career as a sports marketing executive for Converse and Nike.

Afterward, Hatchell hatched her plan: create a CEO position for Jaynes and bring Bass in as executive director. As Jaynes recalled, "The big hitch was that neither one of us would report to the other. We would report directly to Sylvia. And that's the part where my friends told me this would probably be the craziest thing I would ever do, because nobody could survive with a two-headed monster."

The resulting growth and effectiveness of the WBCA amazed people in and out of the game. Not only had they tamed the two-headed monster, but as Jaynes moved out of the CEO position and into a consultant role in 2000, they flourished in the complex undertaking of changing leadership when the outgoing employee is a legend. As they watched similarly weighted transitions in the women's basketball community struggle to varying degrees, causing programs to backslide and threatening the continued growth of the game, they began to recognize the significance of their own.

They also saw a predicament looming. That first generation of truly powerful and influential coaches and administrators of women's sports and especially of women's basketball—who endured life before the passage of Title IX in 1972, who kept their collective foot on the pedal of progress even when it was not popular, and who finally have reaped a measure of benefits for their undying efforts—were nearing the age of or inclination toward retirement. The attrition is natural after 30- to 40-year careers, but the implications nonetheless remain. Although much progress has been made, equality in opportunities, attitudes, and finances in women's sports is not nearly complete.

Two strategies during these inevitable shifts in leadership will position women's sports for continued progress. First, a respectful, cooperative transition keeps the momentum moving forward. A slide in success can be mistaken for a lack of interest or ability and can lead to cuts. Second, just because the outgoing coaches or administrators are moving out of their positions doesn't mean they are no longer needed. They understand the history—what's at stake—and have invaluable experience and wisdom to teach the rest of us. Bass refers to it in her world as "women's basketball intelligence."

Ceal Barry moved into administration after her coaching career at the University of Colorado knowing that her situation (Kathy McConnell-Miller filled the coaching position while Barry stayed in the department) could pave the way for similar transitions.

"It happens all the time in men's sports," Barry explained. "Men's coaches are transitioned into administration out of football, basketball, baseball, wrestling, and other sports all the time. In women's sports it's fairly new, so you're under a microscope a little bit: 'Are they going to be catty?' It's important for women that we pave the way and be role models and show that it can be successful—that a female can transition out of a high-profile position, a young coach can transition in, and they can work seamlessly together."

Jaynes and Bass decided they couldn't just sit back and see what happened. The outcome was too important. So they hand-picked 10 high-profile, successful transitions in or closely related to Division I women's athletics, including their own. They asked the outgoing employee, the incoming employee, and the key administrator in each transition to share their experiences: what they did, when they did it, what they didn't do, and how they handled certain situations.

What follows are their wisdom, their guidance, and their stories, all of which carry direct application to all of collegiate athletics.

INTRODUCTION

Just like people, balls, and buildings, transitions come in all shapes and sizes—primarily because people, balls, and buildings are involved.

Each participating person—the administration and athletics department personnel, the student-athletes, the outgoing and incoming staffs and their families—adds a distinct element to the situation that will never be replicated. The group's collection of sundry skills, experiences, personalities, ideas, biases, needs, and desires at that particular moment in life plays conscious and unconscious roles in each stage of a transition.

Inherent in each ball—or sport—is a community, a culture, a history, and a timeline that is unique to that sport. Available candidates, acceptable hiring timeframes, challenges of the hiring process, requirements of coaches, expectations of staff and student-athletes, and the policies and opportunities of the all-important factor of student-athlete recruitment represent only a few of the ways a transition can differ significantly from one sport to another.

Buildings also figure prominently in transitions, both in the literal and figurative senses. The structures on a university campus help create the school's ambiance. The competitive and practice facilities can foretell the importance of athletics on campus in general and that sport within the department in particular. All play a part in the final decision of who fills the open office. The figurative buildings, representing the collective administration operating within them, are an even more important piece of the puzzle. Their philosophies, policies, and priorities immeasurably influence what day-to-day life will be like in the open chair.

Clearly, because no two transitions are alike, no two implementations of transitions will be alike. This should come as no surprise. As the basketball coaching pioneers quickly discovered, there is more than one way to win. Some swear by the press. Others favor an up-tempo game. Traditionalists hang their reputations on a controlled half-court offense. But every one of them won hundreds of games because of the commonalities of dedicated preparation and precise execution by personnel for whom that style matched.

The same is true with successfully navigating transition in key positions within athletics departments or organizations. In talking with these very successful and respected coaches and administrators, it became obvious that their tactics outside of competition differ as much as they do within it. When is it time to move on? How involved should student-athletes be in the interview and selection process of their coach? To what extent should the outgoing employee be involved in the program? Does the outgoing coach continue communicating with still-eligible players?

What remains the same is their focus on and attention to fundamentals. In basketball, that's moving your feet on defense, boxing out under the basket, following through on shots, and pure hustle. In transitioning, it's leadership, communication, selflessness, respect, and a commitment to the welfare of the student-athletes. It comes down to treating people honestly, considerately, and fairly. This unanimous sentiment among the interviewees is seemingly obvious but not necessarily commonly implemented. "It's all about relationships," summed up Judi Henry, senior associate athletics director at Texas Tech University.

The term "butterfly" began as a code word for the book, but soon it became clear that the metamorphosis of a butterfly parallels the phases an employee passes through during a job or career transition.

An egg is laid. An employee decides to move on.
A caterpillar emerges and sheds its skin. A candidate braves the hiring process.
The cocoon is spun to protect the insect. An employer assists the new hire.
The butterfly's wings are readied for flight. The outgoing supports the incoming.
The butterfly soars. An employee progresses with grace and integrity.

The first five chapters move through those stages—making and communicating the difficult decision to leave a program as honorably and aboveboard as possible and then taking care of the two parties (student-athletes and staff) left in the aftermath; filling the vacancy according to fit and policies, and in the case of the incoming employee, considering the important factors; setting the new staff off on the right foot in the first days, weeks, and months; maintaining the momentum as the outgoing and incoming employees interact; and keeping the transition on the right track after the initial dust settles.

All transitions are unique, of course. However, just as the pigs in George Orwell's *Animal Farm* declared of themselves that "all animals are equal, but some animals are more equal than others," some transitions are "more unique" than others. The final two chapters cover mentoring young or first-time head coaches, since they often are the ones who find themselves following a legend, and eavesdropping on conversations with the University of Southern California trio that thrived throughout a planned, two-year transition.

With that conceptual backdrop, following are the tangible nuts and bolts—the specific, implementable game plan—of how to make your next transition a smooth one.

TRANSITIONS

ATLANTIC COAST CONFERENCE

Outgoing: **Bernadette McGlade**
Former Position: associate commissioner for women's basketball operations and senior woman administrator, ACC
Tenure at ACC: 1997-2008
New Position: commissioner, Atlantic 10 Conference
Date Hired: June 2, 2008

Incoming: **Nora Lynn Finch**
Former Position: senior associate athletics director and senior woman administrator, North Carolina State University
Tenure at N.C. State: 1977-2008
New Position: associate commissioner for women's basketball operations and senior woman administrator, ACC
Date Hired: July 7, 2008

Administrator: **John Swofford**
Position: commissioner
Tenure at ACC: since 1997

UNIVERSITY OF COLORADO

Outgoing: **Ceal Barry**
Former Position: head basketball coach, Colorado
New Position: associate athletics director for student services and senior woman administrator, Colorado
Date Hired: April 1, 2005
Tenure at Colorado: since 1983

Incoming: **Kathy McConnell-Miller**
Former Position: head basketball coach, University of Tulsa
Tenure at Tulsa: 1999-2005
New Position: head basketball coach, Colorado
Date Hired: April 26, 2005

Administrator: **Mike Bohn**
Position: athletics director
Tenure at Colorado: since 2005

GEORGE WASHINGTON UNIVERSITY

Outgoing:	**Joe McKeown**
Former Position:	head basketball coach, GWU
Tenure at GWU:	1989-2008
New Position:	head basketball coach, Northwestern University
Date Hired:	June 9, 2008

Incoming:	**Mike Bozeman**
Former Position:	assistant basketball coach, GWU
Tenure at GWU:	since 2006
New Position:	head basketball coach, GWU
Date Hired:	June 24, 2008

Administrator:	**Jack Kvancz**
Position:	athletics director
Tenure at GWU:	since 1996

UNIVERSITY OF ILLINOIS

Outgoing:	**Theresa Grentz**
Former Position:	head basketball coach, Illinois
Tenure at Illinois:	1995-2007
New Position:	vice president for university advancement, Immaculata University
Date Retired from Coaching:	April 17, 2007

Incoming:	**Jolette Law**
Former Position:	associate head coach, Rutgers University
Tenure at Rutgers:	1996-2007
New Position:	head basketball coach, Illinois
Date Hired:	May 11, 2007

Administrator:	**Ron Guenther**
Position:	athletics director
Tenure at Illinois:	since 1992

UNIVERSITY OF SOUTHERN CALIFORNIA

Outgoing: **Lisa Love**
Former Position: head volleyball coach, USC
Date Retired
  from Coaching: March 24, 1999
Next Position: associate athletics director, USC (1991-2005)
Tenure at USC: 1989-2005

Interim: **Jerritt Elliott**
Former Position: assistant volleyball coach, USC
Tenure at USC: 1995-2001
Next Position: interim volleyball coach, USC
Date Assigned: June 23, 1999
New Position: head volleyball coach, University of Texas
Date Hired: April 18, 2001

Incoming: **Mick Haley**
Former Position: head volleyball coach, United States Olympic Team
Tenure with USOT: 1997-2000
New Position: head volleyball coach, USC
Date Hired: June 23, 1999
Date Arrived: October 1, 2000

Administrator: **Lisa Love**
New Position: vice president for university athletics,
                                Arizona State University

Tenure at ASU: since 2005

TEMPLE UNIVERSITY

Outgoing: **Dawn Staley**
Former Position: head basketball coach, Temple
Tenure at Temple: 2000-2008
New Position: head basketball coach, University of South Carolina
Date Hired: May 7, 2008

Incoming: **Tonya Cardoza**
Former Position: assistant basketball coach, University of Connecticut
Tenure at UConn: 1994-2008
New Position: head basketball coach, Temple
Date Hired: July 1, 2008

Administrator: **Kristen Foley**
Position: associate athletics director and
                                senior woman administrator

Tenure at Temple: since 1995

UNIVERSITY OF TEXAS

Outgoing: **Jody Conradt**
Former Position: head basketball coach, Texas
New Position: special assistant to the director of
        women's athletics, Texas

*Date Retired
    from Coaching:* March 12, 2007
Tenure at Texas: since 1976

Incoming: **Gail Goestenkors**
Former Position: head basketball coach, Duke University
Tenure at Duke: 1992-2007
New Position: head basketball coach, Texas
Date Hired: April 3, 2007

Administrator: **Chris Plonsky**
Position: director of women's athletics
Tenure at Texas: 1982-1986; since 1993

TEXAS TECH UNIVERSITY

Outgoing: **Marsha Sharp**
Former Position: head basketball coach, TTU
New Position: associate athletics director for special projects
*Date Retired
    from Coaching:* February 24, 2006
Tenure at TTU: since 1982

Incoming: **Kristy Curry**
Former Position: head basketball coach, Purdue University
Tenure at Purdue: 1999-2006
New Position: head basketball coach, TTU
Date Hired: March 30, 2006

Administrator: **Judi Henry**
Position: senior associate athletics director and
        senior woman administrator

Tenure at TTU: 1980-1995; since 1997

VIRGINIA TECH UNIVERSITY

Outgoing:	**Bonnie Henrickson**
Former Position:	head basketball coach, Virginia Tech
Tenure at Virginia Tech:	1988-1995; 1997-2004
New Position:	head basketball coach, University of Kansas
Date Hired:	March 29, 2004

Incoming:	**Beth Dunkenberger**
Former Position:	head basketball coach, Western Carolina University
Tenure at WCU:	2000-2004
New Position:	head basketball coach, Virginia Tech
Date Hired:	April 6, 2004
Previous Time at Virginia Tech:	1988-1997

Administrator:	**Sharon McCloskey**
Position:	senior associate director of athletics and senior woman administrator
Tenure at Virginia Tech:	since 1984

WOMEN'S BASKETBALL COACHES ASSOCIATION

Original:	**Betty Jaynes**
Former Position:	executive director, WBCA
Tenure at WBCA:	since 1981
Next Position:	CEO, WBCA
Date of Change:	September 1, 1996
New Position:	consultant, WBCA
Date of Change:	March 1, 2000

Incoming:	**Beth Bass**
Former Position:	category manager for women's basketball, Nike
Next Position:	executive director, WBCA
Date Hired:	December 1, 1996
New Position:	CEO, WBCA
Date of Change:	March 1, 2000

Administrator:	**Sylvia Hatchell**
Position:	WBCA board of directors president (1996-97), women's basketball coach, University of North Carolina
Tenure at UNC:	since 1986

Chapter 1
MAKING A CHANGE: The Metamorphosis Begins

There is rarely a good time to leave a coaching position.

When the program is on solid ground—when the coach and team are beloved in the community and the wins far outweigh the losses—the assumption from student-athletes, recruits, staff, administration, fans, and the coaching community at large is that the coach will remain at the university forever. Everyone is happy in the land of Utopia, so there is no need for a change.

If only wins are missing from the equation, or if an unexpected or atypical issue arises, most coaches want to work through it, just as they tell their student-athletes to work through tough times in order to emerge stronger on the other side.

Scenarios that often bring about expected change—strife within the team or department, mounting losses, and unmet expectations—certainly are not good times.

But coaches do choose to leave programs at good times, for good reasons. Life happens. Perhaps their drive for some or many aspects of the all-encompassing job diminishes and they decide to retire. Maybe a spouse is transferred to another city. It could be they accept an offer to coach another team or leave the profession altogether.

Administrators within athletics departments or organizations often face the same conundrum. They become entrenched and respected at a university or in an association. They feel a loyalty to their employer or staff. Their optimistic natures keep them thinking that next year will be *the* year they'll see their hard work come to fruition, or they may not want to leave if an especially challenging year is on the horizon.

The decision is often difficult but always momentous—the first stage of a personal metamorphosis akin to the single egg laid on the underside of a milkweed leaf that morphs into a monarch butterfly. That individual conclusion, like the lone egg, represents new possibilities, a new life certain to change shapes in the following days, months, and years. It also is the first in an infinite collection of effects and actions encompassing how that decision is reached and communicated and how the outgoing employee and key administrators proceed from that point. It affects virtually everyone related in ways great and small to that person's professional and personal life.

Coincidentally, the result is similar to the butterfly effect, which states that small incidents or variations can substantially impact the end result in ways not imaginable or even quantifiable. In other words, the nature, timing, and perception of each subsequent decision, deed, and word by the employee or administrator—no matter how seemingly minor or insignificant—can profoundly influence the success of the transition.

DECIDING TO GO

One of the more gut-wrenching decisions coaches and administrators make is to leave their current position. The resulting emotional impact is usually far-reaching. Even when the change is self-directed, the employee is not immune from the seven stages of grief. It causes teams and colleagues sorrow or confusion at best, pain or anger at worst. The ability and willingness of coaches to look at the situation from multiple perspectives, to recognize the world will continue turning if they leave, to consider the consequences to all parties, and to be prepared to empathize with each one will make the first ripple predictably smooth.

Theresa Grentz, who retired from the University of Illinois in 2007, recounted a lesson she learned as she struggled with her decision to leave her post as a sixth-grade teacher at Our Lady of Fatima School in Secane, Pennsylvania, for the nation's first full-time women's basketball coaching position at Rutgers University in 1976. The school had waited for her to learn whether she received an admissions position at St. Joseph's College, where she had a part-time job as head coach. When she didn't get the job, she committed to returning to the elementary school. The Rutgers opportunity arose just as summer wound down.

In her anguish of feeling disloyal, she drove straight to the convent. "I told Sister Thomas Michael, IMH, who was principal of the school, what had happened. She said, 'Theresa, you have chosen a field where you will have to move several times to reach the level of success you aspire to. You need to understand something: In a job, you are *always* useful. You are *never* necessary.'"

> *"Sister Thomas Michael said, 'You need to understand something: In a job, you are* always *useful. You are* never *necessary.'"*
>
> ~Theresa Grentz

C. Vivian Stringer, current head coach at Rutgers, several times has professed that her, her team's, or a colleague's "steps are ordered." Jolette Law, Stringer's former associate head coach who followed Grentz at Illinois, said it another way. "If you can come out of self and be able to realize your time [in a particular position] has run out, and it's time to move on and do other things, everything doesn't have to be about a negative. People said, 'Wow, something must have been wrong at Rutgers for you to leave.' No, it was time. My purpose at Rutgers was done, and God wanted more from me."

RETIREMENT

Some people have jobs, finding their life's work in family, community activism, spirituality, or hobbies. Some people pursue careers that provide them with more meaning, more satisfaction, and they dedicate a great deal of time to their work.

And then there are coaches. For the lifers, coaching finagles its way into the bloodstream and becomes part of their being in a way most in society simply cannot understand. A few become singly focused on their teams and programs, mentoring the student-athletes, searching for the perfect recruits, and devising new ways to win more contests. Many manage to juggle families and outside interests, but the hold on their hearts of the student-athletes and competition remains as critical to their lives as air and water. Not surprisingly, the decision to retire is not an easy one. As former head coach at Colorado Ceal Barry conceded, "It's hard when you make a decision to not do something you were kind of born to do."

The immediate aftermath can be difficult as well. "The first year is the hardest," shared Texas Tech University senior associate athletics director Judi Henry, remembering the experiences of Marsha Sharp and others. "You're so accustomed to a certain lifestyle, and that's your identity. Then all of a sudden your identity is gone. It's not like people aren't still going to walk up to you and clamor for your autograph and say what great things you do, but it's not the same. What was important to Marsha was having an impact on young lives, and so to not have that connection was hard."

Sharp also struggled initially for another reason. "I had known for two to three years that the most difficult things about deciding to be finished were not about me," she said. "It was about everyone else it was going to affect: coaches, families, kids, a lot of folks who are within that inner circle. Their lives are going to be drastically changed no matter what happens. That's the toughest part to me about making that decision, because it affects so many people besides you."

WBCA CEO Beth Bass remembered hearing C.M. Newton, former athletics director at Kentucky and former USA Basketball president, once say, "Leave when they're in love." That adage sounds great on the surface, seemingly boiling the life-changing decision down to a specific point in time that is filled with happiness, prosperity, and, of course, wins.

"It's good to know when to pass the torch," Bass said, "but then know what you can still contribute." In other words, when it comes right down to it, you still have to find that thin, faint line that separates a lifetime of passion and work from an unknown world of freedom or new interests. To walk away too early can lead to regret for not leaving everything you have on the court or field. But to retire too late is to risk overstaying your welcome, so to speak, and not putting the health and welfare of the program first.

"Women's basketball in particular doesn't recycle well," Bass asserted. "We don't build that mind capital. Robert Neyland [former football coach and athletics director at the University of Tennessee] once said he'd have been a better coach *after* being an administrator. Amy Ruley at North Dakota State University said the same thing after she retired from coaching and became an associate athletics director. But we have some ageism preventing women from getting those later-in-life opportunities."

Gut Instinct

Ceal Barry transitioned at Colorado from head coach to assistant athletics director for student services in 2005 before eventually becoming associate athletics director for student services and senior woman administrator. She said she began considering a change as early as 2002. "These coaches coming in now are getting their head coaching jobs when they are 37, 38," Barry reflected. "I got mine when I was 23. Having been a head coach that long, I began to have an internal argument about how much I love it and how much I'm willing, at my age, to give."

By late 2004, she decided if the opportunity arose for a second career, she'd pursue it. Within weeks the position opened, and she committed to it. "I just didn't want to keep that pace up until age 56, 57, 58."

"When you pursue your passion, I think you just operate a lot on gut feeling and instinct. I was starting to feel that I needed to step aside, to have some free time."

~Jody Conradt

As Ohio State University's former athletics director Andy Geiger put it when he announced his retirement after an extremely successful but embattled tenure, "I'm just tired, just bone tired. Not the kind of tired that a good night's sleep fixes."

Jody Conradt, the second winningest coach—male or female—in Division I basketball history for the University of Texas, also played it by feel. "I don't think I can give you a concrete timetable, because I never operated with one," she explained. "When you pursue your passion, I think you just operate a lot on gut feeling and instinct. I was starting to feel that I needed to step aside, to have some free time."

Theresa Grentz at Illinois described an unsettledness and feeling that another opportunity was in store, sharing the intuition only with her husband and spiritual director during a two-and-a-half year period. "There was something else in my mind that I knew I needed to do, but I wasn't sure what it was," she said. "You think you're coming to the end of your career and it should be calm and it should be easy, but mine wasn't. I was very restless."

That something else wound up being vice president for institutional advancement at Immaculata University, where she first arrived in the fall of 1970 and became a cornerstone of the foundation of modern women's basketball. She led the Mighty Macs to three straight Association of Intercollegiate Athletics for Women (AIAW) national titles beginning in 1972, the year Title IX was passed.

A Few of the Signs

Girls' and women's sports across the spectrum have benefitted since the passage of that landmark bill, and women's college athletics has changed phenomenally since the mid-1990s especially. During that time, the United States took second in the 1995 Women's World Cup, dominated women's team competition at the 1996

Olympic Games in Atlanta, saw the formation of the American Basketball League in 1996 and the Women's National Basketball League in 1997, and then captured the world's attention by winning the Women's World Cup in 1999 in striking fashion.

Those successes in turn increased the number of opportunities, improved the quality of those opportunities, and dramatically amplified the attention given to women's sports. But the ramification of those developments has created an even more intense, nonstop rat race and ever-changing landscape: compliance concerns with university, conference, and national policies; saturation of media bringing greater scrutiny; recruiting that is both broader in scope and more pervasive with regulations; escalading staff size and expectations; and technology advances allowing—yet sometimes demanding—more connectivity and more immediate access, often creating additional static and less intimacy in life. There comes a point at which the wins evoke only a sense of a relief yet the losses excruciating pain.

"If you look back to 1976, I think we only had three to four tuition scholarships," Texas's Jody Conradt pointed out. "Off-campus recruiting was not legal, and nobody knew anything about women's basketball. When I retired, there was no time off. In the summer you had three to four weeks of camp, plus more than three weeks of recruiting. I also had a sense that the recruiting part of it is, in some ways, distasteful, and I don't think it is a positive part of our sport for the most part. It was very time-consuming, with no time to regroup or refocus. If you did take a day off, you felt tugged that somebody else out there was outworking you."

Not only has the structure of the job changed, but so has the culture and intention. "Yes, it was about winning in the beginning, but I think I can honestly say that wasn't my number one priority," Conradt explained. "It was about providing opportunities for young women to enjoy being part of a team and to strive for excellence, and to build public awareness and appreciation of how talented women are in basketball and other sports. And now over time it has become more of a winning business. That doesn't mean that's a negative or a bad thing, just that it's expected. Some of the other groundwork has already been laid.

"The interaction with the athletes, the day-to-day practice—all of that really continued to be a lot of fun," she continued. "Over time, the practices became more rewarding than the games. I can't really explain that. I would get up on game days and think, 'Oh, I wish I were able to just choose my own agenda and how I would spend the day,' so there was a tug to move away, and all of that just came together at that point in time."

Lisa Love transitioned from two full-time jobs to one when she relinquished her duties as head volleyball coach at the University of Southern California to focus on her duties as associate athletics director, seeking to invigorate her professional life. "I retired from coaching volleyball with tears streaming, I loved it so much," she said. "But I knew in my heart that I was ready to focus on another career at that time. I felt like I was ready for a new calendar, I was ready for new information, I was ready for a fresh body of work. I'd been coaching for 21 years and was ready for a fresh approach to my year, to my month, to my day. And that's what led me to finally make a decision. And I have enjoyed my management career as much as I enjoyed my coaching career."

Leaving the student-athletes in such varying stages of progression and maturity is the most difficult aspect of walking away for many coaches. Whether it's a player who is exceptionally talented, one who epitomizes what the program stands for, or one for whom the coach feels a greater responsibility toward mentoring, there are always at least a few on each team who make leaving especially tough. Furthermore, most recruits expect that the coach will remain at the school throughout their playing careers, so a sense of unfaithfulness or abandonment on the part of the coach, the student-athletes, or both further complicates the situation.

"I still have some tugging at my feelings about not being able to fulfill what I considered a commitment to the players who are here," Jody Conradt admitted. "That's just part of the recruiting process. They all ask you—and they probably asked me more than most toward the end of my coaching career—'Are you going to be here?' And I honestly said, 'As far as I know I'm going to be,' because I didn't have a timetable. I didn't mark a day on the calendar. It wasn't anything concrete. But there's always going to be a time when you leave in the midst of players' careers. It's not like they all graduate at the same time."

Chris Plonsky, women's athletics director at Texas, recalled, "As Jody publicly stated over time, there's never a right time or a wrong time to leave coaching. It's difficult. But I do know that she cares more about young people and the University of Texas than anything, and that includes herself. She's easily the most principled person I know, and that's saying a lot. I work around a lot of great people, but Jody stands on truth, she stands on fairness, and she stands on just making the right decision."

Dawn Staley goes a step further on the recruiting trail, first for Temple University and now for the University of South Carolina. "I don't tell them I'm going to be there for four years, because I don't know. In this business, you never know. You could be fired within those four years. An extenuating circumstance could occur. I focus more on the process and principles my coaching staff follows and the outcome and rewards on and off the court the players will receive if they work hard."

Help From Administrators

Administrators can play a valuable role in helping employees work toward and through the idea of retirement by providing vision and a trustful presence. Lending an ear, a slightly removed perspective, wise counsel, and unwavering support can guide the successful, authoritative, and often prominent public figures in talking through the possibilities and ease into the next phase of their lives.

Ron Guenther, athletics director at Illinois, remembered the conversations with Theresa Grentz as she neared the end of her tenure with the Illini. "I told her that when she's ready—and it will hit her—the day will come when she'll want to take a look at something else."

When the retiree is an icon in the sport or community, the stakes are high. The higher profile the individual, the more peripheral people have an opinion about when the "right" time to leave arrives. The administrator's role is to quiet the surrounding chatter and listen to the heartbeat of the program and the employee to do what is best for the student-athlete. By relying on a keen discernment of the situation and an ability to lead the employee toward the optimal end, the external focus can stay where it should be—on the legendary employee—rather than on the missteps of those involved.

"We'd talked in generalities before, saying maybe it's a year, maybe two," Guenther said. "But when you start thinking about when the transition time is going to happen, as I told her, 'It's always better when it's your decision versus my decision.'"

Plonsky agreed. "When Jody and I talked about her decision, and I've stated this bluntly myself, she was going to make this decision. She had earned the right to make the decision herself and on her own time. Even though I am her supervisor, I never believed that was a give-up of power or authority, because it was more the trust that I have in that employee and that person to do the thing to be beneficial not only for herself in terms of timing but also for the university's sake. I always knew that Jody would do what I call the right thing at the right time, because there's not any situation in her life that I've known her in professionally that she hasn't done exactly that."

That trust and deference from Plonsky was a gift to Conradt, who indirectly credits the opportunity to come to the decision on her own with making the transition in peace, because "I was ready to do so, ready to have free time," she said.

Administrators face a difficult task in expressing their opinions in such a way that the employee always feels valued, safe, and cared for. Sylvia Hatchell understood the importance of the concept when she served as president of the WBCA in the 1996-97 academic year and formulated the plan to provide executive director Betty Jaynes with another executive to ease her workload. Jaynes understandably needed to feel comfortable with the intention and execution of her transition to CEO and the hiring of Beth Bass as executive director at an organization that Jaynes essentially had given birth to, nurtured, and led since 1981.

"A big key when you make changes is that people don't feel threatened," Hatchell explained. "After a while Betty realized we had her best interest at heart, and this was what was best for her and for the organization to grow. She loves that organization so much, and I think she started feeling good about it. It became sort of a relief that she could still do what she enjoyed yet have some help."

The key phrase to remember in that quote is "after a while." Such a dramatic shift in identity, as Texas Tech's Judi Henry mentioned earlier, does not happen overnight. It takes several conversations, not one edict. Mandates do not make for smooth transitions.

But even administrators need support, which Henry sought when preparing for Marsha Sharp's final year of coaching. "One of the things I did do in trying to set the stage for that transition was talk to people who had been through it," she said. "Every institution is different, but I just tried to think of everybody who had been through a high-profile transition. You really have to be careful with that, though, because you can show your hand when you don't want to. You have to think about the people you can trust in trying to determine your plan."

A Plan Helps

Some student-athletes feel most lost when graduation day looms. They're about to strike out on their own for the first time in their highly structured, dictated lives—and they have *no* idea what to do next. They haven't found jobs, they have nothing on their calendars: they are facing a gigantic blank page on which to begin composing their adult life stories. The prospect overwhelms and intimidates them.

If retirees aren't careful and deliberate, they can face the same challenge. What to do after a lifetime inundated with a sport or career? The specific answer matters less than simply having a sense for those ensuing steps, according to Ceal Barry at Colorado, Theresa Grentz from Illinois, and Marsha Sharp at Texas Tech.

"It's important to have a plan about what you want to do next," Sharp advised. "It doesn't have to be specific, but there have to be some things that give you purpose to walk to. Otherwise you just look back too much, and that's not going to be good for anybody.

"I had a few months to calm down a little bit and take a deep breath, but I was fortunate to find some projects that I was pretty passionate about," she continued. "It's important that more than anything else, something gives you purpose every day. We all have to have that, but especially after being in that whirlwind of an all-consuming, all-day, every-day, 24-7 job. I don't think golf will do it. It may help a little bit, but I don't think it will be everything you want."

Athletics director Ron Guenther said listening to Grentz early in her contemplation period showed that she had a plan for her final years at Illinois and would have a plan when they were over. "It became apparent that she began talking about what was left on the plate that had to be done here," he recounted. "It also became apparent that there was life after coaching with Theresa. She didn't retire. She retired from coaching."

Negotiations

When employees decide to retire, there is more to discuss than their last day on the job. Will they continue to have a role in the department? Do they have a strong opinion about their replacement? How will the remaining staff be handled?

Taking the steps to secure the staff's future should happen before the change if possible, given the outgoing employee's greater leverage at that time. "One thing that I would like to do over again is make some really strong agreements that couldn't be broken before I finished," Marsha Sharp acknowledged. "I didn't take care of that as well as I should have, and I really regret that happened."

It was clear the late Kay Yow wanted longtime associate head coach Stephanie Glance to take the reins of the North Carolina State Wolfpack. Yet in classic Yow fashion, she said if the administration wanted to move in a different direction when her tenure ended, then something better must be in store for Glance.

Sharp settled early with the Texas Tech administration on how summer camp would be handled. "I felt like it was a fair thing to do to let my staff and me do our camp in the summer, because we had already worked on it so much. And I think it helped Kristy [Curry] too, because she could say, 'I don't have to worry about camp this summer. They'll do that, and I'll get everything put together and take it the next summer.' It also gave her a chance to watch us do camp, and she was involved some and did an elite camp for high school kids who we thought may be recruitable. That was going to be important for those kids, too, to be around the staff who would coach them if they decided to come. I think those are the questions the media ask and that people who'd signed up for camp also wanted to know. You need to have an action plan in place for when it happens. One of the things we did, probably that next week, was to notify those kids who'd already sent in their money that I was still going to be involved and do those camps."

SNAPSHOT: A Look Inside the WBCA Transition

Sylvia Hatchell, University of North Carolina coach, described the events and conversations leading up to the transition of Women's Basketball Coaches Association's longtime executive director Betty Jaynes into the organization's newly created CEO position and the hiring of Beth Bass as incoming executive director in late 1996.

"When the WBCA was being formed, the board wanted someone with coaching knowledge and experience [to lead the organization], and they asked Betty. She left a tenured job at James Madison, but that's how much Betty believed in it. She started it, took the ball and ran with it, and it just grew and grew and grew. It got so big—so many committees and so many responsibilities and so many more on staff. They had to keep adding people because the demands of the job were just tremendous.

"When I got in there as vice president, I just sat back and listened. I didn't really talk. I was like a sponge, absorbing information. The next year I was the first vice president, and that's when I realized that Betty was doing the job of four or five people. She needed some help big time. She was just trying to be all things to all people and wearing all these hats. She was spread so thin, and it was affecting her health. As I was coming in to be the new president, some of the charter board members—Jill Hutchison, Billie Moore, Pat Summitt, Kay Yow—were all saying to me, 'Sylvia, we're concerned about Betty. She's almost burned out she's working so hard. You have to do something to fix this situation and make things better.' And they kept saying the most important thing was to take care of Betty. I kept thinking we needed to spread some things out. I had a great board of directors, and I kept them informed of what was happening and what we needed to do and new ideas to implement.

"I remember sitting down with Betty and talking about her health and how she was working so hard and doing so much. I said, 'We need to get you some help.' At first it was, 'Oh, this is OK. I can do all of this.' I said, 'Look, don't be a martyr. Everybody knows all that you've done here and appreciates it, but it's time to add some more staff, restructure this a little bit.'

"We didn't want to actually take her title away, and here's the thing: there are some things Betty does that she's so good at, and she's the only one who really knows the background, the history of the organization. All the committees and legislative stuff, the history part—no one knows that like Betty does. She loves that, and she's so good at it. So I said, 'Betty, let's let you continue to do what you enjoy doing and bring someone in with your approval.' We really changed the whole flowchart, because it needed to be done.

"I had several conversations with her, and after a while I think she wasn't threatened by it. She was good with it. I said, 'Nothing will be done without your approval.' And as she felt comfortable with it, she started talking to me about retirement, which was good. She said, 'I'm looking at retiring or starting to phase out in maybe five years. Can we work that into the plan?' 'By all means we can. We'll let you be CEO three, four, five years and phase out as you want to. It'll be your decision.' And so she was on board from the beginning. The main thing was, I communicated with her."

NEW OPPORTUNITY

Of course, retirement isn't the only way to go, but it probably is the easiest to explain. Choosing to leave for another university or organization stirs up more negative emotion and reactions in those left behind: betrayal, inferiority, worthlessness, anger, hatred.

Yet one of the hardest lessons to learn in life is it's rarely about you. In this case, the person leaving isn't doing so because of something someone at the current school has done but because the new opportunity makes sense at that point in time. It may be that the new university or program fits the coach perfectly. It may hinge on personal or family considerations. But it's very rarely out of spite or vindication.

Dawn Staley tried to explain that to her Temple team—understandably distraught with the news that the icon of their program, city, and sport was leaving—when she took the job at South Carolina in 2008. "I told them about my mother's health, about my professional challenge, where you can stay comfortable in your environment or go out of your comfort zone and challenge yourself in other areas of your life."

Kristen Foley, associate athletics director at Temple, concurred. "It was an opportunity for her to go back home, and she wanted to see what she could do with another challenge. She did so much in her eight years [at Temple] but wanted something new and was very open and upfront about that."

New opportunities often arise when a larger or more affluent university snatches a rising star from the galaxy of another, which is what happened to Virginia Tech University in 2004 when Bonnie Henrickson left for the University of Kansas. "It was almost a matter of time," senior associate director of athletics Sharon McCloskey conceded. "She was a good young coach, so I knew it was going to be difficult to hang on to her. We just couldn't compete with the money that was being offered to her. At that time, we were not in the ACC. Had we been, I felt that we might have been able to hang on to her. But she basically got an offer that she couldn't refuse, and we understood."

Even though it's painful, making a move can sometimes be best for the program. Mick Haley, who left USA Volleyball after the 2000 Olympics for Southern Cal, explained. "Sometimes you have to switch coaches to get to the next level because the administrators don't often understand the scope of what you have to do or that if you do [something] for one sport you have to do it for the other sports. But when you switch coaches a lot of things change: salaries, money for the program. Those kinds of changes worked to everyone's advantage: the coaches and the program and the school."

Staley voiced a similar thought. "Sometimes as a coach you need to go outside of your comfort zone, interview, see what other people have," she said. "That's not to say you're going to make the jump unless something really intrigues you, but I think it's important that you make yourself available, see what other people have and maybe take back from that trip what changes could be made to better your program or your situation."

That doesn't mean moving on is always easy. Despite the draw of the new opportunity, coaches feel they're leaving a part of themselves—shedding their skin like the growing caterpillar—after exerting such significant effort and enthusiasm for a team. "It was just kind of an eerie feeling," described Joe McKeown, who joined Northwestern University in 2008 after two decades at George Washington University. "You're kind of hollow because you're leaving something you did for 20 years. You're leaving a city you really like. My family's in Philadelphia, my wife's family is in Washington and Maryland. So it was an eerie, hollow time and bittersweet experience."

BREAKING THE NEWS

Communication may be to transitions what location is to real estate. The message and its timing set the stage for how the department, the team, and the public perceive the key personnel involved, and it paves the path to a smooth future. Reactions of invested parties cannot be completely controlled, of course, but the chances of people reacting favorably increase with a well-crafted and well-coordinated message.

Having an established plan in place helps keep everyone on the same page. That plan will change somewhat depending on specific scenarios, but the model centers on a hierarchical pattern of information dissemination within a short period of time. The specifics of the plan will be as varied as the number of scenarios: head coach retiring with or without fanfare, head coach hired by another program, assistant coach moving into head coaching role, interim situations, administrators retiring or moving on. The timing will vary depending on the sport. But while there is no one right way to break the news, the key is keeping the welfare of the student-athlete at the forefront at all times.

TIMING

When and how information is released is extremely important to the transition. How the department, team, and public react to the change, survive the interim period, and accept the incoming coach depend on when and from whom they hear about the change. When staff hears about it from the grapevine, or team members learn about it individually rather than collectively, the transition begins on the wrong foot. The fox is already in the henhouse, as the saying goes.

Texas's Jody Conradt didn't make her final decision to retire until the last game of the 2007 season, and she broke the news five days later. "I pretty much knew before the Selection Show that we weren't going to be selected, and I had communicated with Chris [Plonsky] beforehand. I had planned to tell the players prior to the show, which I did. The media were already there, so it was an opportune time [to make it public]. I wanted it not to be the kind of thing that was dramatic: 'Tomorrow at X time we have a press conference,' and you have all the speculation and everything going on. So I really think it worked about the best it could under the circumstances."

Transitions in college athletics take place very fast, as coach Joe McKeown can attest. His surprise move from George Washington to Northwestern mid-summer meant he wasn't able to tell his former team before the news went public, but he did meet with them as soon thereafter as possible.

"This thing happened so quickly," he said. "The president [at George Washington] knew, because I spoke with him about Northwestern. Mr. [Jack] Kvancz, the athletics director, and the vice president knew, because I'd been in contact with them on a daily basis. When I came back Friday night from Chicago, I had to make a decision that weekend. My press conference was going to be Monday. I hadn't talked to the players at that point, because I hadn't made a decision and I didn't want them to hear rumors. I wanted to keep it very low key. On Sunday night I told Jack, 'I'm taking the job and will fly there tomorrow and have a press conference.' I came back from Chicago that night and met with the team at GW the next day or the day after. And they'd watched the press conference. These kids today with the texting and technology—they probably knew more about it than I did."

Beth Dunkenberger also had a very narrow window in which to talk with her team at Western Carolina University before the press conference at which she was named Virginia Tech's coach in 2004. But she inconvenienced herself to squeeze it in. "I had to meet with them at seven in the morning in the locker room and let them know we were leaving, then had a press conference in Blacksburg that afternoon. So we literally met with them, got in the car, drove to Blacksburg, freshened up, and went to a press conference."

LEAKS

The erosion of ethics and the ranking of speed over accuracy in our society has penetrated the media, with reporters at times skipping due diligence in an effort to break a story first. The bad news is, leaks are part of high-profile athletics, and they cannot always be prevented. The good news is, their presence in women's athletics indicates a growth in visibility and interest. Ceal Barry at Colorado and Marsha Sharp at Texas Tech both had to deal with leaks about their retirement from coaching.

Containing Barry's news was difficult because she was moving to another position in the department, meaning several people across campus had access to the information. Her plan was to wait until the season was over, but when word of the leak reached her, she and her team were preparing to play Texas in Austin in the penultimate regular-season game.

"The director of media relations called me about four o'clock and said, 'The *Boulder Daily Camera* has it that you're retiring from coaching. You're going to need to tell your team.' I was concerned it would be on the radio and a parent would text or call one of my players after the game."

Barry's strategy was well-grounded on two points: make sure the staff and team hear the news firsthand before they hear it through the media, and tell the staff before the team whenever possible. But the pressure of feeling rushed to beat the leak resulted in a less-than-optimal outcome.

"I made a big mistake and told my staff before the game," Barry admitted. "I overreacted, and it impacted the game. They were not into the game, and the kids knew something was wrong because the assistants were, frankly, more concerned about their futures than the game. But I was going to take care of them and help them. They all landed on their feet, every single one of them. They're all in coaching right now.

"But that was a mistake I made. Given the same set of circumstances—we were getting ready to play Texas on the road—I probably would sit on the information. I probably would wait until after the game to tell everybody. And whether that would be in the Texas locker room or in our locker room at one o'clock in the morning, I don't know."

Sharp had made the decision to retire the previous fall and, feeling compelled to be up front, "told a few key people around me that it would be my last year." She had to deal with a leak with two games left in the regular season and made the best of the circumstances.

Senior associate athletics director Judi Henry, true to character, found the bright spot in the situation. "I understand that's a big story, because she was a pioneer in women's basketball and a leader and had won the first national championships for this university, but I never understood why it made a difference if they did it 12 hours later. We just had to scramble to accommodate the media at that point. But there were some things that weren't all bad about it. All along, people wanted to have a chance to thank her and acknowledge her, and obviously that's not what she's about."

SNAPSHOT: Texas Tech University's Communication Strategy

When Marsha Sharp informed upper administration in the fall of 2005 of her intention to resign at the end of the 2005-06 season, she set in motion a very well-formed plan to make sure the news reached the right people at the right time so that attention remained on the team until the end of the season. A zealous media outlet prevented the implementation of the original plan, but forethought, preparation, and teamwork allowed Sharp to execute a remarkably coherent audible with only a couple of hours notice.

What follows is Sharp's description of how the announcement and surrounding events unfolded, starting with her sense of obligation to recruits.

"I really felt responsible for those kids and the decisions they were going to make that would affect their entire college career. I think any time you're over 50 in the women's game, parents ask you in their homes, 'Are you going to coach the entire four years?' That's a difference between men's and women's coaches, because a lot of those men's coaches don't get their jobs until they're 50. But you know, if you've had the job since you were 28 or 29, they think you've been there a long time, so it's always a question.

"When I knew I wasn't even going to be there for their freshman year, I didn't want to communicate that to them, and so basically, after we signed our early recruits, I just didn't spend a lot of time recruiting that last year for that reason, although my assistants did. I didn't do a lot of that simply because I didn't want to have to face that question.

"My inner core group—my coaches—knew in November or December what the plans were, and they were terrific. We kept it among ourselves and did business as usual, knowing what we were going to do. Beth [Bass, WBCA CEO] had known since about December, because I had just finished being the president of the WBCA.

"All the way through I continued to say I really wanted the season to be all about the players, particularly for our seniors, and not about me. I told Gerald Myers, our AD, and Judi Henry that I really didn't want to have a farewell tour through the Big 12. I really wanted to finish the season before it happened, and the *Dallas Morning News* made that impossible. It came to my attention Friday morning before we played our last two games there was a leak somewhere and a reporter from Dallas got a hold of [the story]. He was going to print it with or without a confirmation from me. I felt a real loyalty to our local reporters here, because they had probably heard things and had kept it under wraps the entire time, and I didn't want them to be hosed because they were trying, out of respect for me, to do what they thought was right.

"So I said, 'We'll call a press conference this afternoon and just do it.' If I had not gone public with the story that day, they were going to print it anyway. So it was incredibly rushed. My whole deal was, I wanted that season to be about [seniors] Erin Grant and LaToya Davis and Chesley Dabbs. I really was adamant that the focus should be on them. I did not want it to turn into a circus, where it became the focus of the game every place we went, because that didn't seem right to me. But it didn't quite work out that way. Looking back on it now, the one thing I would probably change is I would not have any hint of being finished until the day I made the announcement, because I think there were a lot of dynamics that were hurt.

"Having thought about what was important for me to say and people I wanted to make sure were in that loop, I was really busy that morning. I had already talked to a few individuals, former staff and some folks I really didn't want to hear it on TV. Obviously my family knew, and some key people to me were involved. I called some of our former assistant coaches and a few individuals who had been really close to our program before I did the press conference.

"That morning I got all of [my staff] together. There were about 20 of them in the room. It was about eleven thirty in the morning. I think the press conference was at two. I had the entire group, from media relations to trainers, strength and conditioning people, all of our marketing folks, as well as our coaches and [administrative assistant] Marcy Phillips. We just sat down and talked through it and talked about the unfortunate timing of it. At that point, I was trying to give them some instructions about how much I wanted them to not worry about where I was or what I was doing that day but that we take care of those kids—that the team was protected, taken care of, that the media didn't get involved in a lot of things they didn't need to be thinking about because we were leaving the next day to play Texas.

"Then we called our team together. It was our regular practice time, so it didn't seem that unusual to them, but I talked to them about it for about 30 to 45 minutes before I met with the media. I think the worst thing somebody could do is make a statement to the media without your assistant coaches and players knowing what's going on.

"We held them in the dressing room while I did the press conference. They actually watched it on TV. I didn't want them to be bombarded by all the media who were there to try to get, as they say, the scoop. I had incredible help from our media relations people at Tech all the way through our coaching staff and our support staff that was around us. They did a really good job.

"It's important to prepare everyone around you to deal with the media, because they're going to get all kinds of questions. I don't think people really saw it coming, so the media were trying to fill in the blanks. It's a difficult situation for players and coaches, and we really tried to batten down the hatches and say, 'This is our statement, and we've got more things right now to think about and work on. We don't have time to be involved in that too much.' But no matter how it happens and when, it's crucial to prepare particularly your players about what would be the right response, because they don't really know. They want to protect you and maybe be emotional, and absolutely they should have a right to do that, but they shouldn't have to speculate on what's going on or what needs to be talked about. If the media asks them, 'Why do you think she's leaving?' you don't want their feeling or response to be, 'I don't know. Maybe she doesn't like me anymore.'

"I called our two recruits [after the press conference] and talked about my decision and that I really felt like Tech was still the place for them. That's a really big piece of it—to spend the time to do that—and it's tough, because that's not what you want to be doing right then. You know it's what you want, but you're pretty emotional. I will never forget when [assistant athletics director for special projects] Russell Warren said, 'Coach, are you ready?' We were walking across the hall to make the statement, and there's so much of you that wants to turn around and walk back and not do it. And then when it's done you'd like to be able to just go and reflect and take some time, but you feel a real responsibility to folks who have been part of your life for so long, and that's everybody from kids to staff to fans and your own personal support group. There are a lot of people impacted.

"We sent our ex-players an e-mail right before [the press conference], because there was no way I was going to get to them all. It said something like, 'At two o'clock, I'm going to resign as the head coach of the Lady Raider basketball program.' I talked about what they had meant to me and the program, and that I thought we had done some really special things together that I had a lot of pride in and I hoped they did. I said I wanted them to continue to be involved in the program, that I was going to be, and that we would continue to stay in contact.

"I sent another one to some coaches around the country who were my colleagues who I really felt close to. I made sure they understood how much I respected them and what they'd done, and how much I embraced their friendships. That's a really close-knit group when you get right down to it. I mean, you recruit hard against each other, but there's probably nobody who understands what you go through on a day-to-day basis besides them. I felt that way particularly about Big 12 coaches. Most of us had gone through some pretty important things involved in the formation of that conference, and so we had collectively fought some wars that were important to all of us. In the days after the press conference, I talked with my fellow coaches at Texas Tech.

"Then I thought it was important that we end [the season] as well as we could. The team handled it great. They went to Texas, and Texas was terrific. They did a presentation and talked about my career a little bit down there, and Jody and her staff were outstanding. But it did let me know I'd made the right decision about not announcing it earlier, because I think that becomes a distraction for your team. It becomes about something else everywhere you go. I thought they played great against Oklahoma here. I think it caught up with us a little at the conference tournament.

"The only regret I had about [the timing of] the whole thing is what it did to Erin Grant and LaToya Davis's senior night, because it should have been about them when we played Oklahoma and it became a much bigger spectacle than what just should have been their night. But we tried to honor them first, and then I tried to thank our fans and tell them how much I appreciated them. What I tried to say that night is, 'This is something we've all collectively done together, and it's really a special thing.' I still to this very day, if I have a chance to go out and speak to a group in Lubbock, the first thing I do is thank them for that, because it's the way I feel. They did some amazing things for us, so it was important for me that they knew.

"That's basically what we tried to put in place. Russell—who did all of our marketing and was in charge of my TV and radio shows—and I spent some time in January and February putting contingency plans together in how we wanted to do some things and what needed to happen. All of those things need to be thought out ahead of time if you have that luxury to sit down and say, 'Who is it important for me to tell myself, and how am I going to reach the most people?' Obviously, if you try to call all of your ex-players, it would take you a month, and the ones at the end are probably going to hear it from someone else.

"I think there's a really specific way, and everybody needs to decide for themselves, but I do think you have to have a plan. I don't think you just decide one day you're going to make an announcement and not realize how many people's lives are affected by that—your current players, your future players, your former players, everybody on your staff. In some ways I was probably the least affected. The day that I walked away from that, there were 12 people who also had to change jobs besides me, and some of it was very difficult. That's a tough thing. You know it's right for you, but it's not just you that's affected. A lot of other folks are affected, not to speak of the kids. Not only are they losing you as the head coach, they're losing that entire support staff who recruited them, coached them, took care of them."

TO SUPERVISORS

As uncomfortable as it may seem, keeping "the boss" in the loop when making decisions about retiring or interviewing for jobs breeds respect, loyalty, and trust. Few things ire administrators more than hearing through the media that one of their employees is meeting with officials from another university about a job opportunity. They understand that changing schools is part of the business, but employees who don't have the integrity to share their plans create a rift that is difficult to repair.

"Dawn was always great about that," associate athletics director Kristen Foley remarked of Staley's communication with Temple administration. "Anytime anybody was interested in her, she kept our AD in the loop with those conversations. They were on the phone, and she was very honest and upfront about it."

When a long-standing employee is retiring, the conversations can start months or even years ahead of the fact, as Jody Conradt at Texas explained. "I had talked to Chris [Plonsky] several times, even the year previous, expressing to her my feelings about how I felt—that I wasn't going to do this forever—and that she needed to start to think about what Plan B was going to be. It wasn't anything I dropped on her. We'd had conversations about it even three to four years previously. There is no real time to say, 'OK, when this happens, on this day, I'm going to step aside,' but I did tell her I was thinking about it. And she had in turn spoken to the administration."

Theresa Grentz and athletics director Ron Guenther at Illinois had been discussing the idea of her retirement for a couple of years, knowing it was approaching. But the moment it hit her, as Guenther said it would, she went immediately to his office.

"When I finally made my decision, I was at my desk and I said, 'This is it. Today's the day,'" Grentz reflected. "I got up, walked over to the AD's office, just popped in, and said, 'Just want to chat with you.' He was shocked. It was Good Friday. He said, 'I don't think you want to do this.' I said, 'Naw, I think this is what I'm going to do.' I had made my mind up, and from that point I was very relieved. Even afterwards, people said, 'Oh my, she looks 10 years younger.' And that was immediate. Because it was something I'd wrestled with for two-and-a-half years."

Volleyball coach Lisa Love encountered the same resistance from Southern Cal athletics director Mike Garrett when she finally decided, after being talked out of it a couple of times, to concentrate only on administration. "One day in March I asked to see Mike in his office. We had a long face-to-face conversation. He objected, and I told him, 'No, Mike. I'm really done.' He looked at me finally and said, 'You really mean it this time.'"

Tonya Cardoza and Jolette Law immediately called their head coaches when positions opened for which they wanted to apply. Geno Auriemma at the University of Connecticut and C. Vivian Stringer at Rutgers, respectively, provided their support and wisdom, helping guide their tutelages through the interview process (at Temple in the former's case) and the process of choosing the right opportunity (Illinois in the latter's).

When applicable, employees then have the responsibility of alerting their supervisor(s) of the change or potential change. The higher profile the employee on the move, the higher up the chain of command the news should travel. Late Monday of the Selection Show, when it was clear Texas's Jody Conradt planned to tell the team, Plonsky spent time on the phone. "I had to do some administrative work behind the scenes with the president's office and even to the regents to not have them blindsided."

TO STAFF

"The people who often are overlooked in transitions are the staff," commented Texas Tech senior associate athletics director Judi Henry, referring to the assistant coaches and support staff such as operations and administrative personnel, athletic trainers, and strength and conditioning coaches. "Their whole lives are completely and entirely changed, too. And you focus so much on the head coach that it's easy to overlook things and not understand their concerns first. They possibly are affected more in many ways than anybody else."

Considering they often have no input on when, where, or if the head coach moves on—and that their jobs are not secure once that change happens—support staff indeed can suffer from an uprooted life of someone else's doing, and at a moment's notice. To not give them the courtesy of explaining the ramifications of the transition on their short- and long-term futures is disrespectful at best and callous at worst.

"All of a sudden you walk in the office and everyone asks, 'What should we do? Should we clean out our desks and go? Should we stay? How long are we going to be paid?'" Marsha Sharp warned. "The more of those things you can have answered before the fact, the more things you're able to reassure them about, the better. They can handle that better than uncertainty."

The department at large also deserves to get the information firsthand and before the public, and it's the administrator's job to make sure that happens. The circumstances—time crunch, size of organization, time of year—often will dictate the best avenue for spreading the word. A full staff meeting may not be possible or appropriate, but an internal memo via e-mail or mailboxes can prevent confusion, the spread of inaccurate gossip, or dissent. It also facilitates any planning for formal or informal farewell functions.

TO THE TEAM

The coaches almost unanimously agreed that the hardest part of a transition is breaking the news to their teams. Coaches and players develop such a strong bond, forged through the intense highs and lows that come with wins and losses, competition and extreme experiences, common goals and togetherness. Coaches become like parental figures at times, or at least mentors, with players relying on them for wisdom, discipline, and emotional support during such a pivotal time in their lives. Then that person, that rock around whom the world has revolved, is suddenly and often unexpectedly departing, leaving the athletes reeling. But just as in relaying other types of information to the student-athletes—playing time rationale, scholarship decisions, praise, and corrections—the delivery manner, message, and timing make a world of difference in how they hear, process, and digest the news.

"I remember telling my boss that the most surprised people on earth were going to be that group of young ladies, and that's why it had to be very silent until that bracket was announced," Chris Plonsky said of Jody Conradt's retirement. "Jody was always up front with those kids, and they had to hear it from her."

Joe McKeown recalled the difficult conversation with his team when he made the surprising decision to leave George Washington after 19 years. "When you leave, it's like a light switch goes off and they go, 'You're not my coach anymore. Why?' Sometimes I wish I had a better answer. It hurt. You love these kids because you've helped mold them into who they are, and you also know they look at you as someone who walked out on them. And I understand that, especially at a school like that where nobody thought I'd ever leave. When I recruited them I said, 'Well, I've been here 18 years. I'll be here another 25. I'm going to be your coach the next four years.' So when I left it was a shocking thing for a lot of people."

The best time to reveal the information can be tough to determine. "The hardest part was going back and telling my players at Connecticut that I was leaving, because I didn't warn them at all that I was interviewing," Tonya Cardoza said when she took her first head coaching job at Temple. "They were blindsided by it, but I didn't want to say anything beforehand, because I didn't want it to be an issue at the time. I just wanted to do the right thing."

Communication will take on a number of forms based on circumstances. When school is still in session, gathering a team is not difficult. It's a matter of course for them. But during summer or holiday breaks, it becomes more of a challenge to touch base with each player personally before news spreads among them. Although technology makes it feasible to reach each player simultaneously, e-mails, text messages, instant messages, or social networking sites are not the best venue for imparting such personal and potentially distressing news. And while a coach may feel he or she has exhausted the message during the team meeting, it's naïve to think that will satiate the entire team. Some players will need one-on-one time to ask questions and process the change, and giving that gift to them is a luxury that should be afforded whenever possible.

"It was in May, and most people had gone home before summer school," Illinois's Jolette Law recounted of her departure from Rutgers. "We had a meeting with our staff. Then I called some of the players who lived close and had one-on-one conversations with them, and then I called the other ones. The most important thing was to have those one-on-one connections with them, to hear it directly from me, and to tell them good-bye and let them know how much they meant to me."

One of the more critical points to emphasize is similar to that which divorcing parents impart to their children: "It's not about you." Gail Goestenkors, so synonymous with Duke University, was coming off a last-second, gut-wrenching loss to Rutgers in the 2007 regional semifinals when she accepted the opportunity to follow Jody Conradt at Texas.

"That was the toughest thing I've ever done in my life, facing those kids," Goestenkors remembered. "We were all extremely emotional. It was hard for them to understand. I'd been there 15 years, and we were so close. They felt like I was leaving *them*. I'll never forget Abby Waner asking, 'If we would have won the national championship, would you have stayed?' And I said, 'NO!' It would have been easier to leave, because that was the unfinished business. I wanted to make sure they understood it was not anything they did or did not do. It did not have to do with them. If it was just about them, I'd love to stay there forever. But they move on. They leave after four years, so they're continually leaving *me*!"

> "I wanted to make sure they understood it was not anything they did or did not do. It did not have to do with them. If it was just about them, I'd love to stay there forever."
>
> ~Gail Goestenkors

Marsha Sharp focused on the same message in her rushed meeting with the Lady Raiders immediately before the press conference once the rumors began to fly. "I wish I'd have had even more time to explain to them that day that it didn't have anything to do with them. It had to do with me. It was just time in my life to make a change. I'm not running off to go coach another group of kids because I didn't like this one. It was just time."

After two years as interim volleyball coach at Southern Cal, Jerritt Elliott relayed the opposite message to the team when he left for Texas in 2001. In his heartwarming and characteristically unselfish way, he expressed that it *was* about them. "I tried to keep it quiet. I asked that no press releases be done, and I went back and had a team meeting, but I think at some point they may have gotten wind that I was going. I basically broke down and told them the reason I got that job was because of them: the things they were able to accomplish on the court, the way they were able to represent Southern Cal, and their day-to-day stuff. I hoped they could see that the opportunity they created for me in this profession was something that was remarkable. They were upset, which you can't blame them, and sad, and I'm sure they went through all those emotions. But now they're starting to realize the impact they had on my life and how they created something that was very special for me."

Another upstanding point in the message is holding the university and department in the highest regard. Bashing the administration or bringing up any challenges or issues does little else than taint the outgoing coach's reputation by leaving the players and the program in turmoil.

"I shared with those women that the situation had presented itself, and it was an opportunity for me and the entire staff that I couldn't turn down," said Bonnie Henrickson, who left Virginia Tech for Kansas in 2004. "That's the gut-wrenching part, the worst part of it. And I said, 'Just because I am leaving doesn't mean there is anything wrong with this place. It's a great place. They'll take care of you.' The most important thing was there was not an ounce or hint from me or my coaches that this was a bad place, that they needed to leave or come with us. Our whole message was all the positives, like the recruiting pitch when we tried to get them to come [to Virginia Tech in the first place]. I promised those kids on the front end that they would hire someone who would take care of them."

"I said, 'Just because I am leaving doesn't mean there is anything wrong with this place. It's a great place. They'll take care of you.'"

~Bonnie Henrickson

The more specifically and certainly coaches explain why they are leaving, the easier it is for student-athletes to grasp. While it's unlikely each team member will immediately understand and completely accept the change without emotional turmoil, an open, honest conversation will play a constructive role in their continued growth into full adulthood and, eventually, help them come to grips with the situation.

Gail Goestenkors did just that with her Duke Blue Devil team. "I had always—every day—encouraged them to step out of their comfort zones," she explained. "So I talked to them about that: 'You hear me all the time saying, step out of your comfort zone. Sometimes growth is a little painful and a little scary, but you have to be willing to do that to grow. So for me not to take this job, I feel like I would be a hypocrite. This is about me stepping out of my comfort zone and doing something very scary, but I know I'm going to grow because of it.' So when I put it in those terms, they understood. It still wasn't easy, but I could see the recognition on their faces, and they got it."

Both Theresa Grentz and Jody Conradt moved beyond the explanation of their decisions and began setting the stage for a successful transition for the next coach. "When it came time to talk with the players," Grentz said, "I told them it was a pleasure and an honor to coach them and be with them, but I wanted them to please respect my decision at this point in my life to move on. At the banquet I told them, 'This is the last directive you're going to get from me: There will be a new head coach. It could be a man, it could be a woman, it could be someone sitting in this room. Whoever it is, make sure that every one of you gives that coach 110 percent cooperation. Don't find fault. Don't separate yourself. If you do, you will negate the chance to ever get the championship you're looking for.' One of the traits of a good leader is that you teach them that even if you're not there, they still go forth and do things the way you would have wanted them to do. They'll look at that and say, 'What would Coach Grentz have wanted us to do, and how would she have wanted us to do it, and let's do it.' That's a good leader, and I would like to be thought of as that."

Texas women's athletics director Chris Plonsky reminded the players that Conradt had told them the same thing. "You heard what Coach said in the press conference: 'What you guys need to be doing is getting yourselves prepared so that whoever comes in here, you're going to be the best player you can be. Rather than concentrating so much on who we're hiring, concentrate on what you're doing in the classroom, with your basketball, with your physical preparation, so that when whoever does get hired and walks in here, you're ready to go.' And most of them heeded that call. But it was emotionally distressing for them."

Ceal Barry at Colorado had to deal with the ripple effect of the leak. Not only did she feel pressured to tell the team on a road trip, she also was forced into the challenging situation of explaining why she would continue to work in the department in a different capacity. "I had a lot of individual conversations with each one of them," Barry recounted. "It was hard for them to come and ask me personally why I was getting out of coaching yet continue to show up and work hard for me the last couple of weeks. They wanted to know why, yet on the other hand I was still the coach."

Communication with the team encompasses recruits and parents as well. Parents can be just as, if not more, anxious about a change in coaching staff than their children, and being up front with them and alleviating their concerns will help them guide their children through the transition.

"I communicated that day with the three kids we signed and told them I was leaving but felt like it was a great place for them," Bonnie Henrickson said of Virginia Tech. "At that point I didn't know who they were going to hire, but I promised those kids they would hire somebody who was good and who would take care of them. But after that conversation, I never again spoke to them. I said, 'If your parents want to talk to me, I'll take a call.'"

Barry worried more about how the transition would affect the recruits new to Colorado than she did the returning team members. "The ones I coached, I knew they'd be fine," she theorized. "They'd gotten through a freshman year and would be OK. But the incoming ones—that was tough. On the other hand, I think it was helpful for the parents to know that I was going to be around here."

TO THE PUBLIC

Going public isn't easy either. Contending with the reactions of talk radio, rabid fans, uninformed gossips tweeting and blogging, and a population often too eager to assume the worst yet pass judgment with the best of them can make even the toughest stomach turn and surest mind waiver.

The decisions of when and how to break the news must be tailored to specific situations: large cities versus college towns, retirement versus joining another school, longtime coach with a close relationship with fans versus one with a shorter tenure, and an accurate and chattering rumor mill versus an airtight story are a few of the dictating factors. But following general principles with personal integrity will improve them all.

Communicating with the public should happen as soon as possible after the decision has been made and the university administrators, key staff, and preferably the team have been informed. That communication can come in the form of live press conferences, teleconferences, one-on-one meetings with local media, media statements, and individual exchanges with sponsors, boosters, and fans.

Ceal Barry learned that informing the public isn't necessarily a one-time event but an ongoing conversation that requires a commitment to the original message. "I'd tossed this around in my mind for two to three years," she explained of her retirement from coaching. "I was ready for my own reaction, but I wasn't ready that they weren't ready. If I had to do that over again, I'd be a little more prepared for the questions I still get: 'Are you coming back?' 'When are you coming back?' 'Are you sure you made the right decision?' I was 49 when I retired, and the perception is that I'm still young enough to do it. That made my exit a lot harder for me, because I had to make the decision over and over and over again, every time I was asked."

Marsha Sharp experienced the same phenomenon in Lubbock. "I can't even begin to tell you how many questions I've answered about how much I like retirement. That's OK. I'm glad people are interested and want to know. It's something your mind-set needs to be. You're not going to walk into a room and make the announcement and walk out and not be affected by it. People from all over are going to have questions or want to have some fairly extended conversations about it with you, the whole range, from coaches around the country to your fans to kids to everybody."

> *"I was ready for my own reaction, but I wasn't ready that they weren't ready. If I had to do that over again, I'd be a little more prepared for the questions I still get: 'Are you coming back?' 'When are you coming back?' 'Are you sure you made the right decision?'"*
>
> ~Ceal Barry

Through the Media

The natural place to break the news to the masses is in a press conference announcing the change. In the vast majority of situations, it also should be the first time the public hears the news. However, modern communication devices and patterns, combined with an ever-increasing interest in college athletics served by aggressive media, make this increasingly difficult to achieve.

The press conference should be conducted at the current school in the case of a retirement and the hiring school in the case of a move, complete with a press release that provides key details and statements by the employee and the key administrator(s). Attendees can include the athletics director, the subject of the release, media relations personnel, university administration, team and departmental staff, team members, and key boosters.

As sterile as they sound, press conferences are not easy, especially for coaches moving from one coaching position to another. Gail Goestenkors's train of thought about her introduction to the media as Texas's new coach aptly reveals her range of feelings that morning. "My press conference was probably the most delicate thing. I was so excited, and I wanted to talk about all the new things we were going to do. Jody [Conradt] was there as well, so I didn't want to put down the past at all, but I wanted to be so excited about the future. And it was webcast, so I knew all of my Duke players were watching, so if I was too excited I didn't want them to feel bad as to why I was leaving and taking a new job. That was one of the most stressful days, because I didn't want to hurt anybody's feelings, and I wanted everybody to be excited."

Determining whether a retiring coach attends the new coach's press conference can be difficult. The retiring coach's presence shows that he or she supports the hire—an inevitable question from the media—and the sooner and clearer that point is established, the better. On the other hand, in some instances the focus of the press conference can shift from the new hire to the retiree, which can create a number of additional issues.

But anyone with experience with the media knows that the questions don't stop with the press conference. It is only the beginning. A concerted effort and full commitment by all parties are essential in presenting a united front. The alternative too often results in damage control, with an ongoing story of more negative press than is necessary. By establishing a message and making sure the athletics director, key administrator, media relations staff, outgoing coach in the case of a retirement, and incoming coach know and adhere to it, the school can better control the message and keep it consistent.

Savvy athletics departments will take advantage of press conferences for drawn-out hires to inform the media about the process moving forward and use them to spread the word about the position and the program. Mike Bohn's second day as athletics director at Colorado began before 7 a.m., when the women's basketball coach that the interim athletics director thought he'd hired called to back out of the agreement. A quick shift in mind-set and strategy by Bohn turned a negative into a positive.

"We chose to take advantage of that opportunity and educate the media about our plan for moving forward," said Bohn. "We really worked hard to have a very transparent and a very candid discussion with the media to help them educate not only our fans, our faculty, and our community but more importantly coaches around the country of what we were looking for, what we were going to do, and how it was going to work. It ended up being a great opportunity for us to create some further visibility for Colorado and hopefully entice the right coaches to have an interest."

Individually

The longer a coach has been at a school and the more connected he or she is within the community, the greater likelihood that coach will want to communicate individually with certain boosters or sponsors. Making the announcement public without their knowledge can feel like a slap in the face or stab in the back to an inner circle of supporters.

The key is knowing who can be trusted to keep the confidence until the general announcement is made, and for how long. Sometimes the best bet is to make contact directly after the press conference to personally communicate appreciation for the support and friendship, and to say good-bye. Hearing the news firsthand, without the media's interpretation or instead of comments that have been misconstrued or abbreviated, can clear up potential misunderstandings and ensure the parties remain on good terms. Writing thank-you notes to a broader circle can do the same. A good coach knows the team's ardent supporters are invaluable. A classy coach goes the extra mile in communicating that to the very end.

"There were a few key people who I felt I needed to make direct contact with," Jody Conradt at Texas said, "and I did make a call to those people, either right before or right after [the press conference], just for the courtesy of talking to them personally."

WRAPPING IT UP

Moving on is a chaotic time in life, whether an employee is taking a new job across town or across the country. The number of details that must be attended to at both places mounts exponentially. Beginning to wrap up the old job before the official announcement is made feels premature, yet the expectation is that work begins at the new job immediately after the announcement. Essentially, an employee has two full-time jobs at the height of frenzy while at the same time almost always relocating to another city.

"The players cooked a dinner for all of us, and that was probably the best day there," Bonnie Henrickson described of her last days at Virginia Tech. "Then I just tried to get to as many people as possible—those I was closest to—to thank them and say good-bye as we were leaving. That was hard. I just cried for three days trying to pack, get the house on the market, all of that. Plus I was in the midst of recruiting, trying to switch gears and recruit for Kansas."

It would be easy in that situation to let aspects of the old job fall through the cracks, but doing so only hurts the team, program, and reputation of the departed. It also simply isn't professional or considerate. College athletics is a small world, and eventually such behavior will backfire in one way or another: loss of future job opportunity, difficulty in filling coaching staff vacancies, or walking into a similarly disheveled environment.

Finalizing administrative and program details is not a one-person job. The head coach or administrator must continue to lead the staff, setting the tone and delegating responsibilities to ensure everything is left in good shape. In fact, the bulk of the work likely will fall to the staff, especially if the employee must shift focus immediately to the new position. But pre-established leadership and checklists make the process smoother.

Kristen Foley and Temple benefitted from members of Dawn Staley's staff who did not accompany her to South Carolina. "Some of her staff went with her but a couple didn't, and they were great in the transition," Foley said. "It was key that we were able to communicate and close the loop on some things with Dawn before she left. Everything was in place for Tonya [Cardoza] when she came in because Dawn wanted it that way."

ADMINISTRATIVE AND PROGRAM DETAILS

An outsider or casual fan may assume that 90 percent of coaching is on-floor teaching and game strategy and only 10 percent is administrative. Insiders know that is far from accurate. Documentation for national and conference governing bodies, university paperwork, human resource procedures, managing staff, staying connected with various constituents, and creating and organizing electronic and paper files add up to a significant undertaking before even stepping on the playing surface. Head coaches sometimes more resemble the CEO of a company, with aspects of administration, finances, and marketing taking at least as much of their time as actual game preparation and coaching. And each loose end should be tied, or at least visible and untangled, before the succeeding staff enters the office.

Since Ronald Reagan first did so, presidents have written personal notes or letters of encouragement, well-wishes, and the most pertinent advice and information to their successors. Rudy Giuliani did the same for Michael Bloomberg, who followed Giuliani as mayor of New York City in 2002. Similarly, leaving detailed lists and notes helps an incoming employee function at a higher level more quickly. A written message that covers everything from interactions with the faculty athletics representative to specific opportunities and challenges will provide the incoming something tangible to help smooth the transition.

Bernadette McGlade's diligence in leaving her Atlantic Coast Conference associate commissioner's office in excellent shape ensured that Nora Lynn Finch could keep the ACC women's basketball programs moving forward without spending unnecessary time looking for files, deciphering notes, or rushing to meet unexpected deadlines.

"I transitioned out of my job—setting things up in the office, separating things out, finishing what had to be finished in a timely manner, making notes in files for immediate, short-term, and long-term transitions, updating the timeline of job responsibilities, and cleaning up everything you happen to build up over 11 years—so that everything was laid out pretty succinctly for whoever came into the job," McGlade said, epitomizing professionalism. "I embarked on that right away so that it would be left in good order."

Items that are more directly related to the student-athletes' well-being and the sport aspects of the program also lengthen the to-do list: student-athlete files and academic progress, equipment inventory and orders, practice and competition schedules, recruiting and scouting information. And in the flurry of activities, capturing personal files and information off computers, cell phones, handheld devices, and cameras—and then sanitizing the technology of the data—must take place before turning them in.

"It was a quick turnaround for Dawn [Staley]," Kristen Foley remembered. "She wasn't here a lot after she made that decision [to leave], so we really had to tighten

CHART 1.1: FINAL CHECKLIST

ITEMS TO RETURN

_____   Keys

_____   Courtesy car

_____   Laptop computers

_____   Communication devices

_____   Video and still cameras

_____   University-owned equipment

ITEMS AND INFORMATION TO ORGANIZE

_____   Loose paperwork

_____   File folders

_____   Computer files

_____   Players' academic status

_____   Practice times

_____   Competition schedule

_____   Scouting folders

_____   Recruiting overview

_____   Recruiting files

_____   Recruiting videos

_____   Camp files

PAPERWORK TO COMPLETE

_____   Compliance—university

_____   Compliance—conference

_____   Compliance—national

_____   Final invoices

_____   Human resources

ADDITIONAL TASKS TO COMPLETE

_____   Verify upcoming season schedule

_____   Verify upcoming class schedules

_____   Verify academic tutor meetings

_____   Organize and inventory equipment

_____   Order equipment

_____   Make sure locker room is in good order

_____   Make sure office is in good order

_____   Capture personal content on communication devices and computers

_____   Sanitize communication devices and computers

_____   Change and share pertinent passwords

_____   Deactivate e-mail address

_____   Write letter to successor

some things up right away: recruiting, scheduling, making sure kids in the program were OK academically, equipment inventory and order, making sure practice times for the fall were set. All those little things she took care of. It was only about a week— four or five days—where she was able to do these things."

GOOD-BYES

Saying good-bye to teams and longtime colleagues can be heart wrenching—"It's like losing a spleen," WBCA CEO Beth Bass said—but it is a healthy part of the process of making a change. Of course, each person's philosophy on if, when, and how to say good-bye varies. Temple had a formal good-bye party for Dawn Staley, making it easy for her to speak directly to many more people than she otherwise would have had time to do.

Jody Conradt was adamant that she not be thrown a party. "I just didn't need to. It was over. It was done. They needed to move forward. I really felt that was the right way to do it, and I'm really glad they followed through with my wishes on that."

On the other hand, the large gathering with which North Carolina State honored Nora Lynn Finch after her 31-year tenure helped calm her after the emotionally tumultuous decision to accept the position at the ACC.

"Kay [Yow, the late women's basketball coach at N.C. State] and her staff gave me a most fond going-away party," Finch reflected. "We had about 300 to 320 people there. It was a light time, a time when some people at the university very publicly spoke about where the women's athletics program was and how it got there. What that allowed was fans and parents of players and former players and people involved in the sponsorship program and others—I had a chance in one night to see all of them and remind them how much I love them and appreciate them and for them to do the same. So it gave me a formal closure. Had I left without having had a very special night like that, I would not have ever felt that closure. Kay knew that, and she is the one who made sure that happened. Don't ever underestimate how emotional a move like this is, from having been there so long."

BRIDGING THE GAP WITH PLAYERS AND STAFF

Telling a coach good-bye wreaks emotional havoc on student-athletes. On top of sadness, they may feel discarded, angry, bitter. Then, when the new coach arrives, the players find themselves competing anew for their place in the pecking order, for attention, for praise. But the interim period—"purgatory," as Chris Plonsky at Texas put it—can test the young adults like no opponent ever will.

Some players are, of course, rocks, steady as they were before. A few crumble from the emotional distress. Others are like wild adolescents going off to college, out of their parents' jurisdiction for the first time. Their lives up to that point have been very structured and controlled, with the head coach serving as the chief taskmaster. When that figure is gone, so too is their restraint. It's as if the coach moves off with the players' common sense, discipline, and maturity.

Staff members can feel just as lost. Perhaps they didn't get chosen to join the head coach in the new venture, or their perception of what made the coach leave in the first place leaves them bitter with the school. They may not yet know what their futures hold in the short-term (how long they will get paid) or long-term (where their next jobs will be).

The exact date and time of each transition is rarely known, but the reality that transitions occur is as predictable as sneakers squeaking on a gym floor. Administrators would be wise to plan their approach concerning both student-athletes and sport-specific staff during the scary, uncomfortable, and emotional period when both groups are without a direct leader.

Players and staff can have complex relationships with the head coach, on the one hand at odds with the coach because of heavy discipline and high expectations, yet on the other hand completely reliant on the coach's tough love and predictable attention. Parents aren't necessarily any steadier, what with the sometimes suffocating shield they place between their child and any discomfort or difficulty. The more an administration can serve as an interim leader for the team, recruits, immediate support staff, and parents—delivering news, listening to concerns, and insisting on consistency—the more stable a bridge for the incoming coach to cross.

BOLSTERING STUDENT-ATHLETES

Former NFL defensive tackle Joe Ehrmann once said, "One of the great myths is that sports build character. Sports don't build character. Coaches do." When that coach leaves, whether abruptly or not, players usually struggle.

"The people who are caught in the transition are your current student-athletes, and how that is handled is important," Illinois athletics director Ron Guenther said. "As much as young people choose their institutions for the institution, they're so tied to the coaches who attracted them to the institution. We were very careful with that."

Adults are responsible for protecting the children in their care, a necessary and admirable practice. But when protecting drifts into sheltering, and the children edge into adulthood, the outcome is more damaging than helpful. Collegiate student-athletes run the gamut of maturity, some just removed from asking permission for a cookie to others functioning virtually on their own. But part of the educational process of college is dealing with issues like an adult, and keeping players in the dark regarding their past and future coaches only deprives them of a valuable learning experience.

> *"The people who are caught in the transition are your current student-athletes, and how that is handled is important. As much as young people choose their institutions for the institution, they're so tied to the coaches who attracted them to the institution."*
>
> ~Ron Guenther

"Whatever is best for the student-athlete should always drive what you do," Texas Tech senior associate athletics director Judi Henry advocated. "You can't protect them, because you have to tell them the news, but you have to think about the support you have in place."

As with almost any other aspect of life, communication reigns. The more all parties involved discuss the situation—establishing expectations of both players and administrators during the intervening days or weeks, outlining the timeline, and passing along appropriate information—the more comfortable and reasonable they will be. And lest anyone forget, only one-half of communication is talking. Spending the time to listen to their concerns and ideas is a key component to keeping student-athletes feeling valued and part of the process.

Mike Bohn at Colorado had an especially difficult message to the players on his second day on the job. "The first time they met me was when I let them know that a [previously hired] coach would not be joining them and that we'd be searching for another coach," Bohn began. "They were looking at me thinking, 'Who is this guy, and how do we know if he knows what's best for us?' We were concerned about the welfare of the existing team and returning players. They had just gone through an emotional time of losing Ceal [Barry] as their coach. To learn who their coach was and begin to get comfortable with that, and then to be told that he would not be coming—it was emotional for them.

"I tried to spend as much time as I could with them informally as well as formally, to see them in their normal daily lives," Bohn continued, "whether it was the academic unit or in the training room or in the arena, to just talk to them about what was going on. We spent a lot of time trying to inspire those athletes to feel good about the process and where we were going, and Ceal was an instrumental piece of that."

Student-athletes usually don't have the practical and emotional experience to grasp the situation quickly and understand the various factors involved. Compounding the matter is the sudden absence of their leader.

"They're used to going in and talking to their coaches every day, and all of a sudden those people are gone and they don't know where to go," Virginia Tech's Sharon McCloskey pointed out. "I thought it was important to let them know that my door was open, and they did come in. We met them whenever they had concerns. I think that helped calm them down a little bit, saying, 'Hey, we're not just going to run an ad in the local newspaper. It's a high-profile position.'"

Providing the team with additional audiences besides the administration can help the players put the transition in perspective and comfort them by hearing the same message from multiple sources. Fran Dunphy had made the cross-town move to become the men's head basketball coach at Temple after 17 years at the University of Pennsylvania two years prior to Dawn Staley's departure. When he spoke to the Temple women's players, they knew he had relevant experience to impart.

"Everyone gave a little of their time and sat down and talked quite a bit," senior woman administrator Kristen Foley said. "Coach Dunphy was involved in that process as well. He wanted to make sure the players were OK, and he was a tremendous support for them. It was just another resource for them to hear about the process he went through, and they were very appreciative of that."

Keep Them Informed and Involved

Philosophies about how much to include student-athletes in the interview and selection process vary greatly. One extreme places at least one player on the selection committee. The other keeps the team completely in the dark, with stops on the continuum including meeting with candidates and providing input about optimal characteristics of a coach.

The administrator's model of leadership, the university's policies, and the situation's details will influence the approach. "We wanted to engage them as much as possible," Foley offered, "but at the same time you don't want to give them too much. Our biggest thing was to get them all in a room together and tell them we were going to bring somebody in who would continue to do the right things, keep this program going, and certainly be a great leader and motivator for them. And we engaged them in what kind of coach they wanted."

George Washington and Colorado allowed student-athletes to be very involved in the process, either as official members of the selection committee or by meeting each candidate during the on-campus visit. Like Temple did, Illinois and Virginia Tech engaged the team in a discussion about the qualities they would most appreciate in their next coach.

"The kids were not necessarily informed of candidates, but in all of our transitions we make an attempt to keep the team together—to keep them informed and keep them upbeat," Ron Guenther at Illinois said. "We had several meetings with the squad and then with the captains. It was an open-door policy, and I think they had opportunities to bring names of people they wanted considered. Some of them had suggestions, and we were open to that. At the same time, I gave them a timeline of when I expected to have the hire made."

McCloskey and Virginia Tech took a similar approach. "I met with the players before we started the search," she explained. "One of them wanted to be on the committee, and I said that's never going to happen because of the confidentiality factor. But I did say, 'Get together and think about what kind of qualities you want in a coach. Put them down on paper,' and they did that. They were very, very mature about it. I think that was helpful. Even though they weren't a firsthand part of the process, they felt they were part of the process."

Keep Them on Track

Maintaining close contact with the student-athletes meets only part of their needs. Their requirement for supervision outweighs their desire for it, but keeping close tabs on them will ward off potential trouble socially and help ensure they fulfill their daily responsibilities athletically and academically. Research shows that athletes perform better in the classroom during season than out of it; sustaining that controlled environment is key.

Colorado's situation was unique in that Ceal Barry remained employed by the athletics department. She and her staff continued mentoring the student-athletes during that transitional time, staying in their offices and moving the team forward as they always had until the new staff arrived.

"I think the best thing we did was transition the athletes," Barry said. "It's important to keep them on a schedule, keep the structure in their lives. There are a lot of areas where they could go off, particularly in March and April: exams, they're out of practice, nobody's watching them, and they're used to having supervision. I felt it was better for me to stay there, be with them, answer their questions, and get them involved in a spring conditioning program—business as usual—rather than leave them without any direction, particularly academically. Just because we weren't going to coach the first game the next November didn't mean we couldn't put them through a good spring workout and keep them going. They didn't miss a beat. They never felt abandoned."

Beyond the Players

Bolstering student-athletes means bolstering their parents, too. Teams function as a family unit, and keeping their immediate families knowledgeable and positive about the change will help keep the players themselves upbeat. Otherwise, if parents are working off second- and third-hand opinions and suppositions—or if they hear the news only from the viewpoint of their children—they can develop a skewed perspective and lead their children down poorly informed paths.

Touching base with recruits is equally critical. They rarely have developed solid relationships with anyone on the team or at the university. The rug has been pulled out from under them, and leaving home for the unknown may have just gotten scarier. Further, they may wonder if anyone still cares if they join the squad or not. Sharing with them and their parents the plans and timeline, making them feel welcome, reinforcing their value to the team, and answering their questions can alleviate some of their qualms.

"We'd signed five kids, and I talked to and wrote all five parents," athletics director Jack Kvancz at George Washington said of his first steps after coach Joe McKeown left. "They should at least know what we're doing. So I told them the whole thing: 'We have four candidates coming in. We have a selection committee. As soon as I can make a decision on that, I will, and then I'm going to have that person get a hold of you and let you know what's going on. And if your parents have any questions, tell them to call me.' And the truth is, it solved a lot of problems that probably would have been a pain later, but I took that on as soon as Joe left."

Local AAU, club, high school, and junior college coaches also have a vested interest in the hire. Communicating with them can keep hearsay down and relations positive for the incoming coach, ensuring the recruiting channels remain open.

SUPPORTING STAFF

Assisting the coaching and support staff also is a two-part assignment. First and foremost, the staff should be informed about the ramifications of the change as it relates to them. When will they know if they will be retained? How long will they be paid? When should they clean out their desks and return their equipment? What should they do during the time being?

"The day after Jody's announcement was Take Care of Texas Day," detailed women's athletics director Chris Plonsky, who operated a sort of staff triage that day to stop the emotional hemorrhaging when Conradt retired. "I wanted to spend all day Tuesday hopefully helping assuage the fears and the concerns of the other people, because there was no [warning]. I was nervous about them, because purgatory isn't fun for anybody. That goes right down to the managers and basketball operations person. When you lose a leader, it's trepidation for everybody. I was making sure we had HR policies in place for adjustments for the people who were going to continue on payroll. A lot of it was behind the scenes and in quiet individual conversations, but that was a priority for me as an administrator to especially comfort people. Just hearing that payroll conversation was essential for them."

The second task is delegating remaining responsibilities among the staff. As Plonsky explained to the remaining assistants, "There was a process we had to go through and establish a search committee, but that number one we needed to take care of the kids."

Ron Guenther at Illinois made sure not only the assistant coaches but also the support staff remained heavily involved with the team. "We had staff members still holding conditioning," he said. "In these transitions, it's important that the support people—the academic services people, the strength coach, the trainer, the people who are surrounding the program in a different kind of way—are talked to as well. That has been helpful in holding the team together. When they saw attitudes of concern, such as talk of transfer, we had those kinds of questions brought to me and senior associate athletics director Terry Cole, who oversees basketball."

Removing the head coach from the equation can make it difficult for assistant coaches and support staff to carry out their roles. The leadership void can create a consequence void—or at least the perception of one by the student-athletes. "The academic responsibilities fell to the director of operations, which was part of her job during the year, but now she had to make sure they were going to class and tutor appointments," Kristen Foley at Temple remembered. "That was tough because there was no head coach involved to mandate they do. What was the punishment if they weren't going to go to class? Bill [Bradshaw, Temple athletics director] was great about that when he met with the kids: 'Even though Dawn's not here, you still have to go to class and those things.'"

***

Everything changes, whether noticeable to the naked eye or not. The Grand Canyon appears to be an example of permanence. Yet its shape and ecology—from water temperature and sandbars to driftwood and wildlife—shift daily even though it takes centuries for those alterations to become discernable. Claude Monet, the famed impressionist, painted a series of 31 canvases of the Rouen Cathedral façade in northwest France over three years. Though the subject remained the same, Monet captured the variations in its appearance and mood based on climate, time of day, and light.

A clever bumper sticker reads, "Change is good. You go first." Beth Bass of the WBCA professed, "Change is hard, but it is a prerequisite to personal growth—the path to our personal equilibrium. The compost of our lives is decay, but compost is what causes the best growth."

While transition is a great impetus for change, the goal should be that those involved have an effortless experience, just like that of a monarch's metamorphosis.

Chapter 2
GOING IN MOTION: The Hiring Process

Filling a high-profile position within an athletics department or organization takes research, fortitude, and a little luck—for both the employer and candidate. It's rarely as simple as plucking a person or job out of the air. When Joni Comstock was athletics director at American University, she once said, "Sometimes you back into your best decisions." Even when it appears clear-cut—when the dream match is obvious and advantageous for all involved—a great deal of effort goes into making it official.

After an employer reevaluates the vacated position, from its structure and responsibilities to its reporting lines and support staff needs, the next steps for the administration include posting the job opening, researching and consulting with others to identify candidates who fit the position, conducting the interview, and making and announcing the decision, all while adhering to human resource policies. The candidates must evaluate the preliminary proposals, prepare for and go through the interview process, and then consider the offer from a number of angles before accepting it.

When a tiny caterpillar first hatches out of the egg, it is barely visible to the naked eye. It is immature, wingless, and in constant need of nourishment to fulfill its sole purpose of growing as quickly as possible in preparation for its transformation into the next stage of life. The hiring process resembles that caterpillar's reality, a critical period which requires an openness and vulnerability by the administration and potential employee that can be seen not only as a weakness but also a liability. In addition, it demands of both parties a voracious appetite for information when evaluating positions and people.

As the caterpillar's body grows, however, its exoskeleton does not. Instead, it sheds its skin up to five times during the larval stage. Similarly, when employers and candidates embark on a new direction, they shed their previous allegiances to teams, colleagues, and staff—the layers of the professional onion, if you will—as they grow into their new roles.

TAKING PRELIMINARY STEPS
Laying the groundwork before launching into a job search only makes sense. It's also the law. All universities and organizations have policies and procedures that must be followed, some of which are state and federal mandates. Even if the perfect

candidate is right around the corner, rules about where, how, and for how long a job opening must be posted dictate how quickly public institutions can move forward with a hire. The human resource departments within athletics and the university both exist to assist with the hire and ensure the processes are followed.

But before the job description can be posted, it must be finalized. Transitional periods are perfect opportunities to make changes to a position that have been discussed or at least mulled during the previous months or years. The job may have grown beyond the original vision, requiring an increase in salary to attract qualified candidates, additional staff, or a change to the organizational chart to reflect alternative reporting lines.

"We talked about restructuring my job very quickly in the beginning," said Bernadette McGlade of her position as associate commissioner for women's basketball operations at the ACC. "The position I was leaving got restructured before hiring anyone. That was a benefit for the position and good for the people who were applying. We'd already had the revised job description written before I even had my press conference for the Atlantic 10."

In most cases, the job also must be officially posted based on organizational, state, or federal regulations. Public institutions will have more hoops to jump through than private ones, but all have at least internal procedures that must be followed.

IDENTIFYING CANDIDATES

Identifying potential employees takes more than making a list of the most successful applicants, and it should be an ongoing mental exercise for administrators. Transitions can happen at any moment because of standard, unique, or tragic circumstances. The makeup of the ideal candidate will change based on the circumstances of the departed, the landscape of the sport, and the aura of the athletics department, but administrators who keep the possibilities in the backs of their minds are able to react more nimbly.

In short, identifying candidates is not a passive component of the process, as Mike Bohn at Colorado described of his first week on the job during which a coach backed out of the position. "We resurrected our search trying to rebuild the pool after an exhaustive process that occurred prior to my arrival. All the work that went into the preliminary round obviously now was in a different phase. We spent a lot of time being very active in recruiting candidates, pursuing coaches from across the country, talking to marquee coaches and getting their feedback. We worked really hard to do a great job of gleaning information from numerous constituents to help us. It wasn't simply, 'Let's just put an ad in the newspaper and have this national story go out there.' We were very active in trying to pursue the best coach for Colorado."

DETERMINE IMPORTANT TRAITS

Searching through the dozens of appealing characteristics that a collection of top employees possesses and homing in on the ones that are most critical to a specific position is like an ice cream aficionado trying to choose a flavor of the day. Any number of them would be good, but one or two will rise to the top of the list after careful consideration. Matching traits in the areas of fit and familiarity to the needs of the position, the culture of the department, and the location of the organization takes patience and focus, but the result is worthwhile.

Fit

"It's a simple word, but 'fit' is critical in positions," ACC commissioner John Swofford said. "It's not always easily defined, but more than anything else I look for the right fit, not only in the particular skills for the position, but the individual—what she's all about, how she would fit into the role and with the existing organization, what she would bring to it, what potentially might be a problem. Some people would be great at a particular job at a particular place and might not be the right fit [in the same job] in another place or another position [at that same place]. If you spend the time and energy and focus on finding those individuals who are the right fit, that's how you build a quality organization."

> *"If you spend the time and energy and focus on finding those individuals who are the right fit, that's how you build a quality organization."*
> ~John Swofford

Fit should be considered within three realms: personal fit, institutional fit, and environmental fit. Illinois athletics director Ron Guenther explained the first two as he and Jolette Law each considered the opportunity to work together. "You're looking for a personal fit, at least I do. I like to hire people who I like to be around. Then each of our institutions has an institutional fit. It's not just a basketball job. It has to be a basketball job that fits her."

Jack Kvancz at George Washington places significant importance on a person's character when filling any head coaching position. "I want to get a good person," he said, displaying the common sense that at times seems to be lacking when seeking someone around whom players and staff are comfortable and who is committed to helping student-athletes grow off the court as well. "Are you able to talk to that person? Are they going to be understanding? Or are they going to be aloof? I personally don't want that type of person. And because of the school we're at, that's important. I want you to graduate. I want you to have as good a life as you possibly can, and for that you need people to talk to and people who will try to help you."

A person's stature within the sports community can boost an organization's reputation, as Bernadette McGlade did at the ACC when she joined the conference as its first commissioner of women's basketball in 1997.

"Bernie brought a tremendous amount of credibility, energy, national awareness," Swofford recalled. "Her presence and the fact that we'd established that position sent a loud and clear message not only in our own league but nationally that the ACC was very serious about women's basketball."

McGlade also brought with her a number of personality traits that Swofford valued highly. "She was aggressive, but in an appropriate kind of way," he continued, "and she and I had an excellent relationship and were on the same page fundamentally. When you hire someone of that quality and whom you trust so much, and who also understands the parameters of the league and where we can go and what her role is, you can give her a great deal of freedom."

In transitions that involve retiring legends, protecting the outgoing person's legacy, livelihood, and emotional well-being should be either an underlying or overt priority. The history of the game, the momentum of the program, and the integrity of the people involved are on the line. It takes the right replacement to accomplish that. Sylvia Hatchell, then-president of the WBCA, knew the transition at the WBCA involving Beth Bass and Betty Jaynes would work because of the personal fit.

"Betty was so good at running the organization and the behind-the-scenes work, and Beth—with her marketing savvy, her personality, her relationships with so many coaches, her lifelong involvement in the game—could get out there and build relationships with sponsors and corporate people," Hatchell remarked. "Those two had chemistry from day one, and they have it now. And the way you have chemistry with people is you treat them the way you want to be treated. That's a big key to their relationship, and from that chemistry, you've got a tremendously successful organization."

Institutional fit matches a candidate's personality, experiences, and expectations with the style and vision of the department and organization. Environmental fit adds to the equation the culture and flavor of the community. Factors such as size of the department and university matter, as do whether the institution is public or private, the program is a perceived underdog or perennial favorite, and the setting is a small college town or a trendy urban area. Every university is different, but adjusting to too many factors at once is difficult on a personal and professional level.

Temple University is a unique setting, and the administration found a good fit in Tonya Cardoza to replace Dawn Staley in 2008. "Tonya had some of the pedigree Dawn did at Virginia and what it's like to recruit in a city, and she's from the city and loved it," associate athletics director Kristen Foley noted. "A coach needs to embrace this type of campus and atmosphere in the city of Philadelphia, and Tonya wanted that. It's important as administrators to find coaches who want to be at Temple and want to be here for not only the athletics but the academics and the city, and Tonya embraced all of those things with enthusiasm. It also was absolutely key that we find somebody who didn't have to build success, but knows how—once it's built—to keep it going and get to the next level."

A snippet of Kristy Curry's opening comments when she was introduced as the coach to follow Marsha Sharp at Texas Tech illustrated perfectly that the fit was right on all levels. After thanking several people and in the midst of paying homage to Sharp, Curry interrupted herself to confess, warn, and appeal: "...believe me I am not Coach Sharp. I will be Kristy Curry, and I pray that will be good enough." Her authentic Southern drawl, her straightforward admission, and her genuine reference to her spirituality all captured the culture of Lubbock, Texas, in two short sentences.

Similarly, senior associate director of athletics Sharon McCloskey knew the value of finding a coach the community would embrace when the beloved Bonnie

Henrickson left Virginia Tech. Given that Beth Dunkenberger had previously spent several years at Virginia Tech as an assistant, including a few on staff with Henrickson, McCloskey said, "I knew she was someone the fan base would accept."

Women's athletics director Chris Plonsky at Texas had the arduous task of finding someone to fill Jody Conradt's gigantic shoes. "We very quickly identified Gail [Goestenkors] as the individual who we felt was the best match for the University of Texas," she said. "At the time, she had a very good job. She had established a very similar foundation and indeed had put her mark and probably had her love for that place at a very high level. But Gail is a very gutty and courageous person. It takes great courage to step into a high-profile, high-pressure atmosphere when you don't absolutely have to." Of course, that same courage must be available in truckloads to coach at a university with such impassioned fans and ambitious goals. As Beth Bass noted, "At Texas, you have to be number one or better."

John Swofford took seriously his responsibility of finding a woman of prominence to replace Bernadette McGlade at the ACC, and McGlade was grateful for his commitment to push the position forward. "Oftentimes in this business, when a senior female makes a move in intercollegiate athletics, that female is replaced by someone who could be very much her junior. It's one of the barriers that isn't talked about but is very real. When you see a senior-level male leave a job for another job, I'd venture to say that 90 percent of the time that job gets replaced with another equally senior male. That's a tremendous credit to the ACC and to John Swofford's decision-making. We need more leaders in intercollegiate athletics who do that. At the same time, you have to have more senior women willing to move."

Kevin White, athletics director at Duke University, touched on that quagmire at a National Association of Collegiate Women Athletics Administrators (NACWAA) convention. Men, he noted, will move their families around the country, chasing the next position on their way up their professional ladder. But women are less willing to uproot themselves or their families. Culturally it is less acceptable, and women and organizations miss out on valuable opportunities of fit.

Familiarity

Knowledge and understanding of the pressure and expectations at that level of competition, the individuals and opponents associated with the position, and the most meaningful cultural traits of the organization are key to transitioning without encountering significant surprises. Incoming ACC associate commissioner Nora Lynn Finch talked at length about the advantages of such familiarity.

"I have enjoyed multiple unusual benefits in making this transition," she recounted. "First, I already knew the great majority of staff at the conference office, so I didn't need people wearing name tags and explaining what they do. There were interns and some people who work in specific areas I would not have overlapped with [while at N.C. State], but for the most part I already knew everybody, and that was enormously helpful.

"Second, I knew the people at the 12 schools very well—athletics directors, senior woman administrators, many of the senior associates, their faculty reps—so I'm not having to learn their names and what schools they belong to and what their views of the ACC, the NCAA, and college athletics are. That's enormously helpful.

"Plus, Bernie [McGlade] and I had talked over the years about philosophical issues. My having chaired the women's basketball committee and her having chaired it, we talked often during her chairmanship about the NCAA issues, and we talked a lot about marketing for the ACC tournament. We just enjoyed exchanging ideas about our vision for not one school but rather the whole league. I had great benefit in knowing her and knowing pretty well how she thinks so that when I came into her office it wasn't difficult to see how she organized her files."

RESEARCH POTENTIAL CANDIDATES

Armed with a clear picture of the type of employee who would best fill the open position, the administrator then must delve into the nitty-gritty of the sport to develop a list of candidates who each embody that collection of traits. Getting a handle on the climate of the sport—from where it is on a local, regional, and national level to who's who at the top and in its governing bodies—involves sifting through pages of information as well as utilizing all connections within the sport.

"Part of my job is to make sure I have a slate of coaches [to consider at any time]," Ron Guenther at Illinois explained. "I have our associates doing the same thing. You have one level of successful head coaches. Then you have another level of assistants who, for the most part, are coming out of very successful programs who you think are ready. I try to keep it within a working number of five, but it changes."

Determining who should be on that list requires research, which comes in several forms and from multiple sources: utilizing networking tools such as LinkedIn and the National Association of Collegiate Directors of Athletics (NACDA), reading *Sports Business Journal*, browsing media supplements, studying news coverage, scrutinizing RPI and academic progress reports, and talking to internal staff and external contacts. Of course, when working on a specific opening, those discussions must be with trustworthy parties who will keep the conversations confidential to maintain the integrity of the search.

Beth Bass at the WBCA marvels at University of Oklahoma athletics director Joe Castiglione's hires. "He does a masterful job of getting the right person for the university," she marveled. "He has a knack for making unique hires that people might not see on the first go-round, but he met them on different walks of life in the sports industry. His staff is always a mosaic of individuals who make a colorful yet coordinated department."

Information Sources

Hidden nuggets of information can move a search forward in valuable ways when the unexpected facts unearth a dark horse candidate or reveal how to convince a front-runner to take the job. Studying biographies, results, and interviews of candidates can reveal possible connections to the department, university, geographic area, or other commonalities that otherwise go unnoticed.

Is the candidate or spouse from the region? Did the candidate work with a key department or university administrator at a previous job? Do results indicate success against opponents in the conference? Does the candidate seem to have a pipeline to recruits from the region? How does he or she come across in the media after key wins and losses?

Such research is well-suited for a member of the media relations staff, since they deal with that type of information on a daily basis. Again, take care to assign the task to a trustworthy staffer. The last thing a search needs is an internal leak.

Internal and External Sources

Well-informed decisions are based on a variety of sources, and starting with internal experts can uncover excellent intuition while breeding staff loyalty and teamwork. Members of the department or university administration, members of the sport's remaining coaching staff or support staff, and members of the media relations office can be gold mines of insight into who might—and might not—be wise choices.

Job searches are one of the prime reasons for developing an extensive network of external contacts. Athletics directors or key administrators from other universities, conference offices, coaching association executives, championship committee members, media, personnel in the professional ranks, coaches or officials in the sport, direct supervisors, former players—all can shed light on a side of the candidate that otherwise might be undetectable. The sport's national championship is an ideal place to find a ripe collection of knowledgeable people. Attending the men's Final Four when searching for a women's basketball coach makes little sense.

In the case of internal candidates, avid boosters also may offer a unique perspective. "I talked to some key season ticket holders and got how they felt about Mike [Bozeman] in particular," Jack Kvancz at GWU said. "We'd been to the Sweet 16 the past two years when Mike was an assistant, and they went, so they had an idea of who he was. They didn't know him as an X-and-O person. They knew him as a person, and I appreciate that. It's good to know he's a good person."

Outgoing Employee's Perspective

Of course, the best resource very well may be the outgoing employee. Who better would know the intangible requirements of the job and the most up-to-date and insider information from the sport or that slice of the industry?

"When people leave, I always like to hear their thoughts on who they think might be a good replacement," John Swofford at the ACC said. "I don't involve them in the process, but I do like to get their input about who they think might be a good person to fill their role, and why."

Outgoing employees, however, are wise to replicate Joe McKeown's mind-set on the matter to avoid inflated expectations and a deflated ego. "When you leave a job—even when you've won 500 games and they put a banner up with your name on it—they're going to make their own decisions and do what they think is best. That's when you realize you're not in charge of the program anymore."

Even though Kvancz held the final decision, he tapped into McKeown's experience with and perception of the finalists. "He was a sounding board for me, but he never said, 'Hire this person,' or 'Hire that person.' I would ask, 'What are the strengths or weaknesses of this candidate and that one, including Michael? If I hire X, what am I really going to have to be concerned with? What are their weaknesses?'"

When administrators do solicit the outgoing's thoughts, whether it is to submit names to consider or provide insight on those already on the list, the outgoing should respond professionally—which is to say dispassionately and honestly. Depending on the situation, an overzealous recommendation could actually backfire and hurt the candidate.

If the outgoing candidate is remaining with the organization, as did Lisa Love at Southern Cal, the most comfortable role might not be in the thick of the search. It helps avoid awkward situations in which the highly admired and well-known person must be in the position to relay difficult messages. "Because I was so close to the volleyball world, I asked not to be the point person on the search, and that I be what you might call the internal expert consultant."

On the other hand, administrators are advised to avoid blatantly discounting the outgoing employee's ideas and, perhaps worse, leading them during their final years to falsely believe they will have a hand in choosing their successor if that is unlikely.

"Transitions go poorly when the outgoing coach isn't involved, as long as it's a good departure," Beth Bass at the WBCA theorized, "or when they thought they were grooming a former player or their assistant for the job. That's unfortunate. It's important for people to feel that they were valued. Getting a legend's input, even informally, is very savvy and valuable.

"I like to say that every employee is brightest and most enlightened in the exit interview," Bass chuckled. "They think they have all the answers, the keys to the kingdom. But there is a way to balance that. I was flattered that when I left Converse, the president and senior VP just wanted to pick my brain to see where I thought the sport and industry were heading, even though I was going to Nike. They respected my opinion. Having those conversations shows people that they are important to what you're doing even if they're leaving."

The outgoing coach also can play devil's advocate. Jody Conradt's thought process shifted back to what was required of her when she was UT women's athletics director when Chris Plonsky considered contacting Gail Goestenkors. "She asked me, 'Why would she come?'" Plonsky recounted of their conversation. "'Look at her situation. She's loaded with players, she's got recruiting going, they're doing a great job, she's in a league she can win. This is a brutal league. Why would she come?' That really helped galvanize me to say, 'OK, that could very possibly be what Gail is thinking.' I immediately began a process of preparation that would enable Gail hopefully to see why she should and would come."

INTERVIEWING THE CANDIDATES

After whittling down the list of possible candidates to a few finalists, the process of filling a vacancy has really only begun. The preparation for and execution of the interview itself will result in a new employee—quite a significant outcome. The goal is to arrive at that conclusion with all parties fully informed and excited about the new possibilities, and it can become a reality with forethought, perseverance, and attention to detail while keeping the big picture in mind.

The laundry list for planning, conducting, and concluding the interview process is still long: determine who on staff will be integral in the process and define each person's role, establish a timeline based on an optimal hire date, officially ask permission to interview the finalists, coordinate visits, conduct the interviews, allow for the time and space both sides need to make a decision, and then make the announcement. The more consideration each task or phase is given from all angles, the more comfortable and productive the process will be—and the better the chance that the best candidate for the position will accept the offer.

PLAN

Anticipating and then planning for the scenarios that will lead to the best result is easier said than done, but the benefits are immeasurable. Flying by the seat of the pants may work well in some situations for some people some of the time, but not for anyone all of the time and certainly not surrounding an important hire. Thinking through the possibilities and the details with the end goal always in mind not only will make life easier and less stressful during that critical window. It will make a great impression on the candidates, who should be evaluating the position and organization just as intently as they are being evaluated.

"When you have good policies and procedures day-to-day, it shows during the interview process. You don't have to change into your Sunday clothes during the interview. People know fake versus real. The day-to-day is very important, because you never know when a change is going to occur."

~Chris Plonsky

The best organizations are perpetually prepared to put their best foot forward, even for unexpected transitions. Chris Plonsky at Texas intimated that by establishing the desired departmental culture and working to maintain it at all times, the candidate will recognize the authenticity of that organization. "When you have good policies and procedures day-to-day, it shows during the interview process," Plonsky said. "You don't have to change into your Sunday clothes during the interview. People know fake versus real. It didn't matter who was in the chair, Gail would have heard the same thing. The day-to-day is very important, because you never know when a change is going to occur. We didn't know when Jody was going to retire. With Bev Kearney [women's head track and field coach who suffered severe injuries from an automobile accident], getting through that spring was tough. It wasn't a natural progression. It was very hard. But if you stay true to what we are and do, you can weather even shocking transitions by doing due diligence."

Committee

Gathering the search committee is high on the list. Committees come in a variety of sizes, influences, functions, and formalities—as individual as the administrators who put them together—but placing the right people at the table is strategic. It's not only critical to consider who can best evaluate the candidates and whose perspectives matter most, but also who the candidates would most enjoy and profit from meeting: who can make the biggest impact, provide the most important information, or simply make them feel at ease and welcome.

In addition to the key administrator, members may include the sport supervisor, senior woman administrator, senior staff members such as the compliance or marketing director, sport support staff, student-athletes, university officials, faculty, and key boosters or longtime fans. The possibilities are extensive and ever-changing, with no one combination being right for every hire. It is only fair, however, that the committee remains the same throughout a single hire.

"A lot of people use search committees in different ways," Plonsky said. "Ours are for the purpose of being the sounding board for the AD. The AD makes the hire at Texas, with the blessing of the president and the regents. But the search committee is very important in the process, because those people had a chance to meet with Gail. I had a search committee that represented a great cross section of our university and Austin community: professors, donors, other staff members, a former student-athlete."

Timeline

Another element of planning is establishing the timeline for the hiring. The optimal schedule takes into consideration the timing of the opening as it relates to the sport's recruiting and competition schedules, the academic calendar, the ability of the committee to convene, any natural marketing avenues such as spring golf tours, the level of tumult surrounding the position, and the complexity of the hire. When the opening is for an administrator, keep in mind any conferences, conventions, league meetings, and important decisions the employee should be involved in when creating the timeline.

A few searches have taken all of a day; others two to three months or more. A temptation may be to move very quickly in order to minimize the confusion and questions surrounding the open position. That may be the best course of action in some situations, but often a more deliberate approach pays off in the long run. Certainly the closer the next critical responsibility of the position looms, the more urgent it is to act quickly, but the fundamental objective should be to complete the hire as quickly as possible while still taking the time necessary to make the best decision.

The longer a search drags on, the more speculation and negative press can become an issue, as Kristen Foley at Temple admitted. "We couldn't get the committee together because of their schedules, so that delayed the process a little. By the time we got everybody on board, there were so many rumors. That's something we would try to correct next time."

Coaching searches, especially, can move at lightning speed, not unlike the pace of the profession itself. Oftentimes a coaching position will come open immediately after the regular season, but the most desired prospects lead their teams deeper and deeper into the playoffs. Courtesy and common sense dictate that an administrator wait until a target coach's season ends before making direct contact.

"In coaching, the hiring process happens so quickly," Gail Goestenkors said, remembering the whirlwind of Texas's courtship with her in 2007. "We [Duke] lost in the regionals on Saturday, and it was a heartbreaking loss. I spent Sunday at home, and Chris Plonsky called me on Monday. They had to move forward. They had been patient and waited for me to end my season. I met with my AD at Duke on Monday, met with the president of Duke on Monday early evening, then flew to Texas Monday night and was there Tuesday and Wednesday."

Beth Bass at the WBCA sees a trend toward faster hires. "Because of media scrutiny, there's a faster timeline. I hear of athletics directors making quicker decisions and maybe not doing their due diligence because of the media frenzy and the pressure to get something done. When Nell Fortner was hired at Auburn, reporters were sequestering the Auburn plane flight plans. When Plonsky let Goestenkors leave campus after the interview without giving her an answer, she was skewered by her male counterparts. They thought she let the fish get away, that she didn't close the deal. The speed with which things happen in men's athletics is much quicker, although they don't usually have the details nailed down like women tend to. But with the increased media attention and brighter spotlight, I think women's athletics probably will have to learn to quicken the pace, even though more and more hands—upper administration on campus—will be in the pot."

Permission

Before Plonsky talked with Goestenkors about the opening, she first phoned Duke athletics director Joe Alleva. "I would never pick up the phone and call the coach directly," Plonsky declared. "That protocol is something that is not always followed, and it's very disrespectful when it's not. I wanted to be sure that I called Gail's direct boss to ask permission to speak to her. Joe and I had a very cordial conversation. He just asked that he be allowed to give Gail that word at his discretion, and that I not talk to her while Duke was still playing."

Professional courtesy then dictates that the administrator alert the employee of the impending call. That reveals to the employee the recruiter's manners, it eliminates the question of whether the call has been placed, and it strengthens the level of trust between the current administration and employee, especially if it appears the search will take several weeks or more.

"I would have never embarked upon the process had John [Swofford, ACC commissioner] not been very aware of it and involved in it with me," Bernadette McGlade said of her hiring experience with the Atlantic 10. "And that's from mentorship as well as building bridges and loyalty to the organization, which is really critical. A commissioner's job is not like a coaching job, which happens really quickly. It's a much more methodical process because you have many more steps of checks and balances and presidential involvement and board involvement and background checks. So it's a long process."

The internal communication also gives the recruited coach a heads-up about the upcoming conversation, which Nora Lynn Finch appreciated when her athletics director at N.C. State, Lee Fowler, told her that Swofford had inquired about her. "Lee called and told me what they had discussed," Finch said, "so I'd had a few hours to think how I would respond when John did call, and I was glad to have had that time."

There are times when inquiring about a person's interest is best done through indirect channels, which enables employers to gauge how appealing their opening is to potential candidates without getting everybody on both sides stirred up in the process.

Parameters

It is important to spell out any parameters regarding the search and hire at the very beginning. Communicating general procedures, timeline, expectations, and restrictions will help prevent missteps and misunderstandings down the line that can harm relationships and the outcome. For example, Ron Guenther at Illinois has a very clear directive regarding a candidate's relationship with the media during the search.

"For the most part, we've said to every candidate before we start talking, 'If your name appears [in the media], you're automatically out of the pool,'" he explained. "I've found that some candidates who maybe don't have as much interest love to get their names out there to help get a better contract where they're from. We've done a pretty good job of handling that situation. I also think that once their names are out there and they don't get the job, it's so unfair to the candidates. At some point, if they're up for two or three jobs, then their own jobs become tainted or they become tainted."

Setting and Itinerary

The setting and itinerary of the candidate's visit should reflect the goals and resulting needs of the search. The administrator's personality and management style, the candidate's familiarity with the institution, the makeup and nature of the search committee, and the importance of staff interaction with the position play a sizeable role in formulating the itinerary.

Regardless of the setting, an itinerary detailing the trip should be provided to the candidate prior to arrival that includes, at the minimum, flight and accommodation information, schedule, and the names and biographical sketches of each person involved in the interview. This provides the candidate details of the visit and allows him or her to get a jump start on pairing names with positions. It also prepares the staff involved, giving them an overview of the trip so they can tailor their questions based on the candidate's other meetings.

On-Site

Most interviews take place on-site, allowing the candidate to tour the facilities and offices, meet the staff, and begin to get a feel for the culture of the organization. It gives them a chance to start forming a bond with the town or city, meeting with a realtor, exploring neighborhoods, and discovering local businesses.

On-site interviews can take on a number of personalities. Will candidates primarily meet with a few people individually, with several groups, or a combination? Will they bounce from one office or building to another every hour, or will the interviewers come to them? Will the visit last several hours or a couple of days? Without careful scheduling, the trip could begin to resemble a seven-day, country-hopping tour of Europe in which the traveler becomes disoriented and exhausted without absorbing the key aspects of any one place.

Even the setting of each appointment is important. Meeting people from campus or the department on their own turf helps the candidate contextualize that person or group within the fabric of the organization. Chris Plonsky, for instance, arranged for Gail Goestenkors to meet key members of the Texas faculty for lunch in the faculty club.

Beth Bass learned a great deal about the dynamics of the WBCA board of directors and staff on her interview for the executive director position in 1996. "I remember walking in and seeing the search committee. I knew them all. These were friends and colleagues and individuals I knew in the sport. It was a V-shaped table, and the board was all around. But when I interviewed with the staff, they were all lined up like a firing squad, like a debate setting. I remember thinking, 'Oh, boy. Y'all have been way too empowered because Betty's been off doing other things.' The staff's questions and reactions were very insightful. By the end of it I thought, 'They better hope I don't get the job.'"

Off-Site

Off-site interviews are rarer in women's sports than men's, but they sometimes are necessary logistically to speed the search along and are likely a growing trend for that reason. Lew Perkins, athletics director at Kansas, interviewed Bonnie Henrickson in St. Louis. "I had a couple of phone conversations with them, and then I flew out there because the men's team was playing in the Sweet 16. I met with Lew, the chancellor, and met the men's staff while they were watching film that night in the hotel."

Guenther had a different reason for spending a day interviewing Jolette Law in Indianapolis: privacy and focus. "It's not as evident in a women's basketball search as it has been for the men, but the media have a tendency to get involved in all of this and speculate, and that can be very cumbersome," he noted. "I don't think it's fair to candidates if those names become public. And I've never used a run-'em-through-the-campus-then-choose kind of selection process. Jolette actually took this position, as did any number of other coaches I've hired, without being on the grounds. The key there is that she has a really good feeling of who we are," he continued. "For that to happen, I think it's important for her to meet some of her colleagues who are going to be working with her so she could ask as many questions about what Illinois is all about."

EXECUTE

The interview itself is fairly straightforward: make sure the candidate feels welcome, keep the visit on schedule, and be ready to adapt as the day(s) progresses. Yet attending to the intangibles will improve the process, boost the employer's reputation, and possibly land the number one choice.

One sometimes overlooked fact is that the candidate has an equal role in the process. At times it appears that one party has the upper hand, but in fact both must agree to a deal before it transpires.

"It's important for the candidates to understand they each have a play in the game," John Swofford at the ACC pointed out. "I've always looked at hiring as a two-way street. It needs to be good for the organization doing the hiring and it needs to be good for the individual coming in. When we are in a hiring process, I encourage people interviewing to ask as many questions about us as we ask them. The fewer surprises either direction, the better the transition."

Bernadette McGlade, Swofford's first hire at the ACC, is cut out of the same cloth. "I felt like I needed to find out as much information for my purposes as they needed to find out for their purposes, because I was in a truly remarkable environment at the ACC, with great people I enjoyed working with every day, great coaches, and having had a lot of success building the special thing we were able to build."

Another detail to consider is the quality of the interview sessions. Administrators should mentor staff on interviewing techniques and tips so that the time spent will be valuable for both sides. Younger staff, especially, may not have experience conducting interviews, and they unwittingly could throw a session off kilter with inappropriate questions or tangential comments.

When legendary figures are being replaced, arranging for the candidates to meet them can make a tremendous difference in the feel and direction of the transition. The subtleties of the departure, the character of the people involved, and the nature of the hiring process all play into whether a meeting is possible, but the benefits are far-reaching.

"Gail wanted to spend time with Jody and talk through the issue of replacing a quote legendary figure," Plonsky said. "They went to lunch and had an evening at Jody's house that was a very social setting with one of Jody's former assistants and me. Gail lightened up during that time, relaxed a little bit. Jody told her, 'Gail, I want *you*. I want you to have this program if you want it. I respect you. I think the job you've done is tremendous. I know you love the game. I know how good you are to young people. You pay attention to the academic side. You are a great representative for women's basketball.' Not blowing smoke, but person to person being very consistent with the types of things that are important for both of those programs to succeed."

Kristy Curry communicated a similar sentiment about her meeting with Marsha Sharp at Texas Tech. Although they discussed the team, the program, the department, and the university, it was Sharp's permission, if you will, that Curry most sought. "I was concerned that, surely there had to be a great former player…," Curry acknowledged. "I just wanted everybody to be OK with it, most importantly Marsha. It had to be OK with her or I was not going to do this. It's like getting your dad's blessing before you get married. I just wanted her blessing. That meant more than anything anybody could say, any amount of money, any amount of anything."

Sometimes execution can be difficult. Just as an opponent can disrupt a team's game plan, external forces can create obstacles to or deviations in the flow of the interview process. Despite Duke's gut-wrenching loss to Rutgers in the regional semifinals in a year it appeared the Blue Devils could go all the way, Goestenkors knew she had to shift gears very quickly when Plonsky invited her to Austin. Recognizing Goestenkors's pain and commitment to the process, Plonsky provided her with a charter flight.

"I could just tell from her voice that she was in pain. I was in pain for her," Plonsky said. "So I called my colleague DeLoss Dodds and said, 'I really feel like I need to get Gail on a private plane to get here.' I just didn't want her walking on a plane and people recognizing her and saying, 'Oh, sorry for those two free throws.' I'd rather put needles in my eyes than think about doing that to someone we're pursuing. I knew it was going to be expensive, but I don't think the media or anybody had any idea she was on campus by that night.

"That was sort of a fortuitous situation, because we got a head start before the pressures of media coverage began in force," Plonsky continued, though the media caught up, of course, on an elevator in the athletics administration building on campus. "The guy said hello to Gail and didn't say hello to me," Plonsky recalled. "We got off on my floor and I said, 'Who was that?' 'Oh, it was the beat writer from Durham.' I started cracking up."

The importance of including—or at least offering to include—a candidate's family in the interview process cannot be overstated. It's not just the candidate who should be recruited, but the entire family. Many times their comfort with the new community plays a significant factor in the decision. When an administration proves the importance of family with an expenditure of time and money, the gesture reaps both immediate and long-term dividends in excitement about the initial move and when support during challenging times is crucial.

ARRIVING AT "YES!"

Election day for both sides has arrived. The campaigns are over: tours completed, platforms revealed, hands shook. In some respects, the rest is up to the voters—in this case the administration and the candidate. The employer must consider and then decide to whom to offer the job. The candidate must consider the offer and then decide whether or not to accept it.

In addition to the difficult decisions, both must also play the waiting game. Like watching a close playoff game, the drama and suspense increase with each possession, and the protracted pace can be painful. But the final buzzer hasn't sounded, and how each party handles that juncture still can sway the outcome.

Beth Bass at the WBCA calls this phase the "discovery period" for both parties. "I like to use the acronym S.W.O.T.—Strengths, Weaknesses, Opportunities, and Threats—when making or evaluating an offer. You consider everything about the position or candidate."

MAKE THE OFFER

Hiring is more art than science, and some art takes longer to produce. Arriving at the decision requires some science, as discussed previously in this chapter, but it's in the final decision that the art takes center stage. Getting a strong, settled feel for the candidates and how they might fit together with the people and community is largely instinctual even though it is based on facts.

As with the rest of the process, the decision stage—especially the degree of involvement of those in the interview sessions—varies based on the administrator's style. Balancing the input of others with the administrator's inclination is a test of the administrator's leadership skills.

In the best cases, the feedback from the committee or advisers lines up with the administrator's gut feeling, as Jack Kvancz experienced when deciding who would replace Joe McKeown at George Washington. "We interviewed four people," he said. "Then I asked the selection committee to give me, in no rank order, their top two. In that case, Michael [Bozeman] came out ahead of everybody, and I agreed."

In other cases, the weight of the decision rests entirely on the administrator in charge of the hire, as Sylvia Hatchell felt with the WBCA transition. "We spent the whole day interviewing in Atlanta at the airport," she recalled. "When it was over with and the board voted, there was a tie and I had to break it."

Betty Jaynes wisely abstained from voicing her opinion about the candidates. "Sylvia asked who I preferred, and I said, 'I really don't care. I can work with both. Either one is fine. I just think the executive committee has got to make that decision, and I certainly don't want to be the one who makes it for you.' I think if I would have chosen one, I'm not sure they would have absolutely listened to it, and it could have changed the whole dynamics if I had not chosen the one they gave the job to."

CONSIDER

The factors to contemplate when offered a job can feel utterly overwhelming. Individual people, places, and things jumbled up in the mind can seem to multiply like a fifth-grade math whiz. Organizing and prioritizing the influences can distill thoughts and enable the brain to assign appropriate values to each factor.

Further complicating the matter, the weight given each factor—the communities, the program or position, and the personal considerations—is not consistent. Not only is it different for every person, but that person's perspective and priorities will change depending on the professional opportunity and individual life circumstances. In short, one formula does not fit all.

What is consistent is the advantage of gathering as many facts and experiences during the decision-making stage as possible, and then negotiating a fair package based on those factors. Nora Lynn Finch and Bernadette McGlade, respectively the current and former associate commissioner for the ACC, both made concerted efforts to maximize the amount of information they had on which to base their decisions. ACC commissioner John Swofford led by example and word when Finch was weighing the pros and cons.

"I called him several times and asked him what I'm sure many people would have thought were rather frivolous questions, but they were not to me," Finch admitted. "And he wanted me to talk with Karl Hicks, who is the associate commissioner for men's basketball at the ACC. He wanted me to talk with anybody in this office I wanted to talk with and get as much firsthand information and knowledge as I could."

Program and Position

Every program or position has a natural draw. It may be its prestigious history, its stacked roster, or its great support from the administration and fan base. Of course, that same opening also will present a challenge or two: a team that recently has struggled on or off the court, a difficult university to sell to recruits, overly empowered or disinterested support staff, an administration too comfortable with mediocrity. Knowing what to look for in each aspect of the opportunity will help the candidate make the best decision.

Team

Evaluating the team involves more than checking the win-loss record from the previous season. While inheriting a team that has achieved success on the court seems like an obvious benefit, using that barometer alone can be misleading. Worse, it can mask underlying issues that could prevent the long-term growth and success of the program.

The character of the players individually and the attitude of the team collectively matter more than their recent success. Tonya Cardoza valued the "winning tradition and winning attitude" in the team Dawn Staley left at Temple. "The kids she left behind are all hard workers and kids who want to win and grow and be better."

Jerritt Elliott was familiar with Lisa Love's final volleyball team at Southern Cal, given that he was an assistant coach on her staff. He, too, placed more emphasis on the quality of person on the team than the fact that it was a top-20 program, although he also attributed their on-court skills for the success he had in his two seasons as interim head coach.

"Lisa left it in very good standing in terms of the right kind of student-athlete, the right kind of personality," Elliott affirmed, "and the athletes we had were very strong—in two years we made it to the Final Four. So obviously there was a very good base that was left for me to inherit and try to tinker with a little bit so we could get to a point where we could be very successful."

Theresa Grentz counted "plenty of scholarships and balance in the classes," in addition to their appearance in the championship game of the Big 10 tournament, as reasons she felt good about the shape of the Illinois program. A team unbalanced in experience and classification can make steady growth and improvement in the first few years difficult.

As Grentz alluded to, recruiting is such a significant aspect of a successful program. Recruiting is made tremendously easier when the coaching staff recognizes and embraces the selling points that will attract players who fit into their system, program, and community. Not every athlete wants to move to a large city, or stay close to home, or be part of a rebuilding process, or attend a huge state school. Discovering a program's niches and then finding great people and athletes for whom those strong suits are a draw will keep the program strong.

Teams tend to take on the personality of their coaches. At the least, players must buy into the philosophy and style of the head coach in order for the team to reach its potential. Every transition will be difficult as the coaches and players learn each others' personalities and expectations. But when a gulf separates their ideologies, it will take a few years to fully achieve that equilibrium, and often that only happens as new players replace those at odds with the new regime. A coach must understand and accept that challenge, knowing that improvement likely won't happen as quickly as it otherwise could.

Mick Haley, the volleyball coach at Southern Cal, joined a successful Trojan team mid-season after his stint with the 2000 Olympic team was over. He recognized that the contrast in style between him and Elliott was tremendous, so he laid low for the rest of the year. "My way was so different that I'd really have screwed it up," he recognized. "I learned that when you get the players going, you get back out of the way and let them be responsible for their team. The last thing I wanted to do with this team was try to get into the mix."

Tradition

The tradition and history of a program can matter more than its most recent results. A program with multiple championships, postseason tournament appearances, and standout performers among its alumni usually has an established foundation that will support the drive to a return to glory. The administration has a vested interest in sustaining or resurrecting that prominence. Support staff who worked with those teams know what it took to be a top program and can pass that experience along to new employees. And that tradition likely drew at least some of the current players to the school in the first place. But finding a coach who can step into a tradition-rich environment and flourish can be tricky.

"For us, the foundation was dramatic," Texas's Chris Plonsky explained. "It was everything in terms of how we approached the search. The program, from day one, has been about excellence in terms of the pursuit of stated goals. Not every team measured up to that potential, but certainly it was the plan to have teams that were of high regard not only on the court but to recruit young ladies who were team-oriented, extremely talented and motivated, took their schoolwork seriously, and then utilized the platform a great flagship university provides to develop their personal skills, especially in public presentation, communication, comportment, and learning to give back to the community and university who supported their opportunities. When you think about the standards that have to exist for all of those things to resonate over 31 years of time, which was Coach Conradt's tenure, the next coach would have to understand that the expectation in each of those areas was assumed, not something that was dreamed about."

Supporters and fans of tradition-rich programs have a clear memory of the good ol' days and a longing that they will return. Theresa Grentz built an awareness of Illinois women's basketball in the Urbana-Champaign community with her media acumen and willingness to hit the pavement. Marsha Sharp did the same in Lubbock by finding that difficult balance of making it about the individual relationships while also improving the bottom line.

"Probably the thing that struck me most about it was, she knew the importance of connecting her players with her fan base, that if it was personal they would come," senior associate athletics director Judi Henry marveled. "And she is an incredible business person. So, from the start, not only did she want to be successful on the court, and more than that successful as a role model and mentor and teacher for the players, she wanted the program to be successful from a business standpoint."

Bonnie Henrickson also worked hard at Virginia Tech to make sure the program appealed to a varied demographic by understanding the uniqueness of women's basketball, as senior associate director of athletics Sharon McCloskey shared. "The marketing department had a Hokie Kids' Club, and Bonnie and her staff embraced that. We did autograph signings with the players and the kids. At that time, with the success when they went to the Sweet 16, they had a lot of student involvement. Typically, our fan base is made up of families and senior citizens, people who enjoy the fact that they can get up close and personal with the athletes."

Another important aspect of tradition is conference history. Players are attracted to conferences that earn multiple berths in the postseason national tournaments. Coaches are attracted to schools in conferences that also distribute a large pot of money each year because of revenue from television rights and playoff berths.

Virginia Tech women's basketball had stair-stepped its way up the conference ladder during the multiple tenures of Beth Dunkenberger and Henrickson. "When we first got here, we were in the Metro Conference," Dunkenberger explained. "When Bonnie left to go to Iowa, we joined the Atlantic 10. When I left for Florida, the team joined the Big East, and then when I took back over, we switched to the ACC. So in a matter of 15 years, we've been in four conferences. It's been a bigger step each time for women's basketball."

Infrastructure

While the history provides the bedrock on which to strengthen a program, it's the day-to-day support that makes that growth possible: sound competition and practice facilities; a mature, robust support staff; a university with a strong academic reputation; and a budget that is comparable to others in the conference or region so that recruiting, travel, and staff retention don't lag behind direct competitors.

Kristy Curry depicted the Lady Raider infrastructure in glowing terms. "The program was in such great shape. There wasn't anything you could want for that wasn't in place. We have everything, the best of the best. Everything that you could possibly want or need was in place."

Even though she did not see the facilities, the offices, or the uniforms, Jolette Law described the program she inherited at Illinois very specifically. "I knew of the excellent academic reputation of the program and the reputation of the Big Ten. And I felt that the state of Illinois has long been a hotbed for high school and AAU girls' basketball."

Dawn Staley spent eight years building the infrastructure at Temple that made the program such an attractive opportunity for Tonya Cardoza. "With Dawn's image and having that foundation in the city, we were able to capitalize a little bit from a marketing perspective and use more marketing dollars," associate athletics director Kristen Foley revealed. "The program also gained a director of operations position. Things kept getting better for the university as well, because our academic support area was also enhanced. So right now there's a great foundation for Tonya."

Position Requirements

When the details of a program's current team, past tradition, existing infrastructure, and future expectations are boiled down, the opportunity's true nature solidifies. Does the program call for building or maintaining? Will the job require more steady patience or fiery passion? Does the team most need motivation, better fundamentals, or different game-day tactics to improve? Is the administration expecting an omnipresent public figure or someone who focuses primarily on the game?

Kathy McConnell-Miller pulled from two of her transitions—following Grentz to Illinois in 1995 and arriving at Colorado in 2005—to make the point. "You need to make sure the tools are in place for you to be successful," she stated. "It has to be conducive to your strengths. If you're like Theresa Grentz and are media savvy, you can take over a program that has never had media coverage because you're going to demand it and you're going to get it. If you're someone who doesn't like that, those are the things that have to already be in place."

Bernadette McGlade realized during her investigation of the Atlantic 10 commissioner position that the opportunity fit her experience and interests perfectly. "After that second interview and some extensive research and analysis, it became apparent to me that this job could be very exciting at this time in my career," she said. "I came to realize there was a great opportunity in the Atlantic 10 to provide leadership and organization doing things I enjoyed very much at the ACC—getting new programs in place, writing new policy and procedures, starting new processes."

Communities

Feeling comfortable with the people and culture of the various communities of which the new position is a part is critical to enjoying and achieving success in the new job. The microcosm of the athletics department, the overall university or organization, and the town or city in which it is set can all have their own cultures. The flavor of each can be a replica of, complement to, or in stark contrast with the others. While establishing a strong connection to every aspect of the setting isn't necessary, or even realistic in every situation, the more a place feels like home, the easier the professional and personal aspects of the move will be.

Administration

A solid rapport with the administration makes day-to-day life easier. Sometimes that connection predates the interview period, as it did between Nora Lynn Finch and John Swofford. "He knew me before he asked me to come and talk with him," Finch said. "There is great confidence in somebody asking you to consider a position when that person knows you well—not working off somebody else's recommendation or your reputation or your resume, but *knows* you."

But that assurance alone didn't get Finch to make the life-altering decision to leave N.C. State for the ACC. Swofford continued to prove that he respected and trusted Finch, and that his management style fit Finch's personality. "For someone of my experience, commitment, and principles, what John Swofford was saying warmed me in a way in which I couldn't turn it down. And he knew that. He knows what motivates me. He knows I don't want to be micromanaged, and he's not a micromanager.

"I'm going to make some slips," she continued. "But the good news is, and I talked to him about this—I said, 'I'm going to make some mistakes, John.' He said, 'Good. I hope they will be trying to do something.' Well, that was music to my ears. If I mess up, I mess up. It won't be because I'm trying to mess up or give somebody a black eye. It'll be because I am going full-speed toward something. So he planted those seeds with me when we first met."

McConnell-Miller also puts great stock in sharing a vision with her administration at Colorado. "The respect and treatment of the student-athlete is important," she proclaimed. "How well they're treated and received is important. Ultimately you go to work at a place that has the same philosophy you have, the same support, the same desire to be good, and you feel like you're working for somebody who gets you and understands you and is going to be supportive of you."

For Staley, a rapport was less critical than believing in the administration's commitment to her and the program, not only in the short-term but the long haul. "The important part of it for me was I needed the support of the administration. And anytime you're the one who's selected to take over a program, the first year is the honeymoon year, and they're going to pull out all the stops and make sure you're successful. But you also have to look beyond year one and year two and try to figure out, if you're not doing the things that were projected, how is this person going to be? How is the administration going to be?"

The opportunity to talk the game of volleyball with an expert on a daily basis is what prompted Mick Haley to choose associate athletics director Lisa Love as his direct supervisor at Southern Cal instead of athletics director Mike Garrett. "How many bosses can you go up to the office and X&O with?" Haley exclaimed. "I'd say,

'I would just never do it that way.' And she'd say, 'Well, I always did it that way.' And it was really fun, because I got a whole other perspective on how she approached things."

Department

Fitting in with colleagues in the department, whether other coaches or administrators, builds a sense of community from which to draw strength and support during the following months and years, when the valleys can sometimes seem lower than the peaks are high. Is it a large department that prides itself on business-like efficiency, or does it have a small, family-like atmosphere? Are the majority of head coaches single, just starting their families, or with older children? Are many staff positions filled by young assistants, or is the group as a whole more mature? Do the sports seem isolated from one another—operating within silos—or does it feel like one cohesive team?

Chris Plonsky knew that Gail Goestenkors would want and need that camaraderie working in the pressure cooker that is Longhorn athletics. But she also knew that before Goestenkors would feel comfortable committing to Texas in the first place, she'd need to recognize that others had made the type of difficult decision she was facing, and to good end.

"It was during those one-on-one meetings with her future fellow coaches—future family of brothers and sisters like Mack Brown [football], Bev Kearney [women's track and field], Augie Garrido [baseball], Rick Barnes [men's basketball]—that allowed her to see people who had also left tremendous jobs, who had won championships, and they could express why they had come to Texas, how their families had adjusted, what they feel," Plonsky said. "They could really share with her things that I knew were going to be real innate to her in terms of the importance of trying to consider herself in another place, another setting, wearing another color, dealing with different issues."

University and Setting

Every place of higher learning has students, faculty, and staff. Similarities beyond that are not a given. Large universities, small colleges, private schools, public institutions, sprawling campuses, commuter schools, athletics-focused student body, on-campus indifference to sports—these are but a few possible university characteristics, and the combinations can create such divergent cultures. Stopping to think about and having the insight to rank the traits will result in a better fit.

Even though many coaches tend to narrow their focus to their team and, perhaps, the university, the setting in which the university is located can make or break a transition. Small-time charm doesn't always translate well to big-city style. Uprooting a family from the South and moving them to a winter wonderland will not survive without a serious dose of adaptability. Moving across time zones can throw off internal clocks for years.

Beth Bass, CEO at the WBCA, grew up in a small South Carolina town, spent her college years in east Tennessee, then settled in Boston as she worked her way up the ladder at Converse. A frequent flyer around not only the United States but also the world, she thought little of her move to the suburbs of Portland, Oregon, when she joined Nike in 1995.

"I probably underestimated two things about living on the West Coast: the time change and being that far from 80 to 90 percent of the people I knew," she admitted. "I thought, 'If this Southern girl could go to school in the state of Tennessee and then live in Boston for nine years, I could surely go live on the West Coast.'" But when Sylvia Hatchell and Betty Jaynes met with Bass during her first year at Nike, Hatchell knew immediately that Bass was struggling. "Heck, even the ocean was on the wrong side," Bass laughed.

Kristy Curry knew the fit in Lubbock with the Lady Raiders at Texas Tech would be a match based on her own upbringing. "I don't think I could have gone to a community where women's basketball wasn't a priority. I was raised in the Louisiana Tech system, and I coached at Purdue, where women's basketball is embraced. How many people can say they've been in three of the finest women's basketball towns in America? And Lubbock has a small-town atmosphere, like Ruston and West Lafayette do. When you look at my career, I've been in neat, neat environments: Ruston and the cotton and timber farming, West Lafayette and the corn, and out here the cotton and ranching. It's small-town people who work so hard and whose values are so important to them. It's just the way I was raised. I wouldn't want to raise my children in some big, major city."

Personal

Some of the hardest factors to consider are those that are personal in nature. Driven professionals can, at times, minimize the importance of taking care of themselves, instead pursuing success, achievement, and passion at the expense of their core needs. The effect a move will have on family, on the heart, and on the soul is critical to long-term happiness and true accomplishment.

Money often sounds to the general public like the most important motive for a move, but it rarely is. Nonetheless, the financial package must be regarded. Athletics is an unstable business. A change in administration, a couple of really tough years, poor health, unexpected family crises—all are possibilities that make for tenuous job security. Often, hiring an expert to negotiate contracts that are front-loaded and include the necessary time to transition the program results in a better package and a more positive relationship with the administration than if the actual candidate is in the trenches making the deal.

Having the family on board with the move significantly diminishes the internal stress associated with changing positions. Curry talked about wanting to move closer to her family and to raise her children in a city like Lubbock. Kathy McConnell-Miller acknowledged that the move was easier because of the support of her family and her coaching staff, which followed her to Colorado. Joe McKeown's surprising departure from George Washington to Northwestern was based in large part on taking care of his family.

"There were a lot of family issues that played into it," he began. "I have a 14-year-old son who has autism, and he was not doing well. We had a lot of problems with services for him and getting him in the right schools. Everything was going great with my job and the other kids, but he just was struggling. We had to do something, and we were out of solutions. When we looked at services and schools available in the Evanston area north of Chicago, we were really excited about what they had to offer. And that was a big reason for the move."

The impact a relocation has on a family can be the most difficult aspect of a transition. But despite the lure of a new opportunity, sometimes leaving a position can be a very tough decision for coaches. "There's no question I had a broken heart," Curry acknowledged about leaving Purdue. "That was the hardest part. When you love somebody and care about them, it's not easy to walk away. I don't think people understood how difficult it was for me to leave. But you don't pick and choose. These opportunities only come along once in a lifetime."

Beth Bass had to weigh her familiarity, comfort, and stature in the corporate world with her feelings of geographic displacement and love of women's basketball when she left Nike for the WBCA. "Honestly, it was a little bit of a stigma to go from the corporate world to a not-for-profit," she confessed. "But I did some real soul-searching, talked with some of my mentors, and realized that if I truly love the sport, I have to shed the logos. I have to shed my identity of being with Converse or Nike and say, 'You know what? At the end of the day I love this sport, and where can I best make an impact, and what's my next growth spurt going to be?'"

Bonnie Henrickson also felt the tug that location can create in the heart. A native of Minnesota, the position at Kansas put her only eight hours from her family, whereas it was a 24-hour drive from Virginia Tech. Add to the fact that "it was a collective decision by all of us [her staff]," and her decision became clear.

Gail Goestenkors and Dawn Staley both were pulled by an internal compass that perpetually draws them toward challenges. Goestenkors constantly challenged her Duke teams to step out of their comfort zones, and she felt that declining the Texas offer would hypocritically be staying within hers. Staley mulled factors like her mother's health, but the idea of a new professional challenge also loomed large when she considered moving from Temple to South Carolina. "You want to move up and challenge yourself," Staley said. "I wanted to put myself in the position to coach against some different people, some of the top coaches in the country."

WAIT

Reading a candidate and getting a feel for how much time and space to allow before requiring an answer is pure instinct. Often, the higher up coaches or administrators have climbed, the more difficult a move will be, especially if they have a great job already, if they are firmly rooted in a community, or if they are nearing retirement.

Nora Lynn Finch remembered the comfort she felt in the way ACC commissioner John Swofford handled her during the difficult period in which she had to decide whether to leave N.C. State. "He called a couple of times to say, 'Don't think that because you're not hearing from me I've had any change of heart or am thinking any different. I'm giving you the time and space you need. Do you have any questions?'"

Chris Plonsky's pursuit of Goestenkors is a study of gut instinct, gender differences, honesty, and professionalism. After waiting two weeks following Jody Conradt's retirement to begin discussions with Goestenkors, Plonsky waited another six days for her acceptance—an eternity in the industry.

"I really wanted to ride back with her [on the airplane] just so we could download, because we didn't spend a lot of what I would call one-on-one time except for a couple of settings during that Tuesday-Wednesday period," Plonsky divulged. "And usually the AD wants an answer before you leave. I asked Gail, 'I'm not going to pressure you for a decision, but I'd just like to spend some time with you.' She said, 'Chris, I really don't need any more time. I know what I need to know.' I knew I would get crushed politically and otherwise by people who said, 'You let her go back home? You blew it!' because Duke was staging a Coach G rally on campus. She said, 'I'm not going to that,' and I trusted her. This was going to be her decision, and she needed some time to weigh some things. I knew she probably had a circle of friends and advisers, and she wanted to interface with them. There was a trust there that I think was professional and real, and I was not going to be talked into pressuring her to make a decision. That would have blown it up in my opinion. But it was a very interesting political landscape that rolled out."

ANNOUNCING THE DECISION

The moment both parties decide the fit is good, a predetermined and well-orchestrated plan should be put into motion immediately to keep the logistics and perception of the process on a smooth track to completion. Human resource policies abound, regardless of the institution or organization, and while the details of each announcement will differ, the critical factors are to devise a sound plan and then follow it as closely as possible unless unexpected circumstances require a deviation.

POLICIES AND PROCEDURES

Even a top-level coach has to apply for a job, though that detail sometimes takes place after rather than before the decisions have been made. Policies exist to protect both the employee and employer, and they exist at a variety of levels: departmental, organizational, state, and federal. Because each university or organization has specialized systems, assigning someone from the hiring organization's staff to guide the candidate through the process will decrease the chances of glitches and increase the appreciation the new employee feels toward the employer.

Similarly, even athletics directors have to clear hires with their bosses, who in some cases have to clear the hire with their bosses. As coaching contracts increase in value and complexity, the red tape must pass through university presidents, chancellors, and boards of regents. That step also must be figured into the timeline of the announcement.

Plonsky recounted the steps she went through once Goestenkors accepted Texas's offer to become only the third women's basketball coach in Longhorn history. "I called my administration and supervisors and indicated that this is the individual that we would like to hire," she explained. "Gail literally had to apply for the job online. We had to prepare documents to give to the regents and HR about why this is the one we had interviewed and hired, because we are under affirmative action by the university standards. There was also a BCA [Black Coaches & Administrators] document that had to be completed about the diversity of the pool, the search committee, and how things were considered. And, because it was such a high-profile hire, the regents absolutely needed to call a special meeting to approve the hire and contract terms."

COMMUNICATION FLOW

Communication plans can be no more cookie-cutter than the transitions themselves, but certainly it starts with nailing down the deal: the final contract terms, the start date, and how and when the news will be shared.

Perhaps the most logical flow of official communication would be for the candidate first to tell the new administration (after all, without this step the deal is not done) before alerting the former administration, the former team, the new team, and finally the media. The press conference isn't always the culmination of the communication plan, because many coaches and administrators want to make personal contact with close friends and colleagues, but it certainly is the ceremonial finale.

Bernadette McGlade's plan when she left the ACC for the Atlantic 10 began more personally. "I shared the news that I was going to take the job with the coaches and administrators I was closest with the weekend before the Monday announcement," she said. "I think that was important because, sometimes when you are making transitions, there are people who are always going to continue to work with you and be there when you need them, and you're also going to be there for them when they need you. But by any stretch it was not a wide circle. It was a very small circle of people. The new organization wants to preserve their press announcement. They don't want you confirming it officially in advance of the organization's announcement."

Immediately after accepting the Kansas position, Bonnie Henrickson followed the script that felt best to her. "I accepted the offer late that night after meeting with him [athletics director Lew Perkins] and a number of people administratively for several hours," she described. "Then I flew back on the first flight the next morning and went to talk to my athletics director. I shared with him that I had accepted the job and that it was important to me to tell the team face-to-face before they heard it from someone else."

Virginia Tech picked up where Henrickson left off, making sure the team's place in the line of com-

"Before the announcement was made, we met with the team to introduce Beth. We thought it was very important that they meet her prior to the press conference."

~Sharon McCloskey

munication remained appropriate when announcing the hiring of Beth Dunkenberger to replace Henrickson. "Before the announcement was made, we met with the team to introduce Beth," Sharon McCloskey said. "We thought it was very important that they meet her prior to the press conference. The athletics director orchestrated the press conference through the sports information office. The only thing that went out was that there would be a press conference at such-and-such time. With the internet these days, word is going to get out, but we tried our best to make the announcement at the press conference."

Hires in athletics can be big news, with media stalking and conjecturing, so each person must be committed to following the plan and not leaking the information for personal gain or glory. The intense media attention and speculation surrounding Gail Goestenkors's hire, the relatively lengthy process and waiting stage, and the philosophies and procedures at Texas and Duke made it impossible to achieve a tidy flow of information.

"The external communication in making the hire known was coordinated between UT and Duke, and we both had to respect each others' processes," Chris Plonsky explained. "I had to go back to my administration, Gail needed to get back and tell her team, and then we coordinated with Duke through our communications office when the news would break. I think it actually broke the night before, but because our regents were having a meeting the morning of the press conference, we could not comment. The Duke president had made a statement—the story was out—but at that point we were still following our procedures.

"The communication protocol is really custom to the situation," Plonsky continued. "This one was unusual because Duke felt it had to be forthright with their constituency about Gail's decision. So even though it was a bit unusual that by Wednesday night the Duke media were reporting that she had advised their president, and they had acknowledged that she was planning to take the job at Texas, we had to stay mum on it all day Wednesday and Wednesday night at UT. We had a regents meeting the next morning and then sent out an advisory that we were going to have a press conference at 11 a.m. So Duke's communications office and ours just had to agree to disagree, that there was going to be a difference of news reportage in both of our areas."

***

After boiling down the search for possible candidates, researching and interviewing those candidates, and reaching a decision, the hiring process really comes down to fit. Certainly the rest of the steps matter. Choosing from a great pool of candidates is better than choosing from a mediocre pool, and thoroughly preparing for the interviews reveals a level of professionalism about both sides of the table. But at the core, what is essential is fit: Does the DNA of the candidate match the DNA of the administration, department, university, and location? Only when they are in line does the transition have any hope of progressing smoothly.

Chapter 3
SMOOTHING THE PATH: First Steps After the Hire

The energy generated by a high-profile hire is palpable—ebullient because of the possibilities; frenetic because of the hit-the-ground-running mentality; chaotic in the juggling of new responsibilities, old responsibilities, and physically moving between two locations; cooperative between the support team and new staff; enticing between the community and employee.

Not all of the energy fields are positive or forward-moving, though. As excited as student-athletes may be about a new coach, or at least relieved to know who it will be, they exude a nervous energy about the change. Staff whose undying loyalties lie with their outgoing leader or colleague may radiate an antagonistic energy, whether knowingly or not. The media may have stirred up a negative energy during the hiring process.

Each intangible force is real, normal, understandable—and impressionable. The communication and, perhaps more important, the actions taken by the administration and new employee are crucial to the short-term grace and long-term success of the transition. First impressions during the interview process matter, but the first ones on the job are even more consequential.

Everyone—team, staff, community, media, and, in some cases, the nation—is watching, and most can be swayed. Some are eager to jump on the bandwagon, believing, or at least hoping, the new coach is the answer to their perceived problems. Others view the hire skeptically, watching every move with a critical eye. How are people treated? How are difficult or tense situations handled? Is the new coach warm? Intensely focused at all times? Moderate? Open-minded? Short-fused?

The responsibility of steering that energy toward the greater good of the program lies as much with the administration as it does with the new hire. Administrators may bear the greater load, because they often must support the new employee, the outgoing employee, and all remaining constituents. The better their personnel and systems, the more effectively they can provide that support.

When Kathy McConnell-Miller replaced Ceal Barry at Colorado, the department and university were in the midst of several transitions. Athletics director Mike Bohn, himself new to his position, described the perfect foundation—the one he was building—from which to facilitate such a change.

"You'd have consistent leadership at the top on campus," he posited. "You'd have continuity in your senior staff in the athletics department—the faculty athletics representative, athletics director, senior woman administrator, compliance officer—to the point where, when a new coach walks in, you have the connections, the teamwork, the chemistry, and the tools to help that coach. When you don't have some of your fundamental practices in place, it puts pressure on everyone to really establish how they can have the influence they need to help the coach."

Slowing down or stilling the mind long enough to draw a road map of the first few months on the job and paying attention to the following must-see attractions along the way may seem staggering or virtually impossible. For the administrator, that means keeping up with the various ways to support the new hire. For the employee, it means taking a zoomed-in look at the program and attending to the most pressing priorities first.

After a caterpillar molts for the last time, it moves into the pupa stage, spinning a protective cocoon around itself in which to transform. Dramatic changes occur inside the safety of the chrysalis as the insect rearranges its structure into that of a butterfly. People involved in a transition also rearrange themselves immediately after accepting a job, surrounding themselves with new people, adjusting to new processes, and developing new routines. The administrator's job is to provide the security from which the new hire feels safe to evolve into his or her new role.

But like that caterpillar, which must leave the milkweed plant to pupate, the new employee has to relocate before that transformation can take place.

RELOCATING

Packing up and moving a household, putting a home on the market, finding a new residence in an unfamiliar place, locating the myriad services a person or family has grown accustomed to having at their fingertips, becoming acclimated to a new town: the details—and stress—of a move go on and on. An administration's first priority should be to help get the new employee, family, and household to the new city as painlessly as possible. The second is to guide a new hire through the maze of city streets, municipal services, and community connections that are vital to establishing a home.

Jerritt Elliott appreciated Texas's efforts to alleviate some of his moving concerns when he joined the Longhorns as their head volleyball coach in 2001 after serving as interim head coach at Southern Cal. "They tried to do everything they could to allow me to be the coach and not have to worry with moving services and transporting my car and figuring out where I was going to live. That was very important for me to be able to get help with it so I could focus on coaching."

Throughout the recruiting and hiring process, the administrator should have picked up a sense of the new employee's needs, interests, and style in order to make better recommendations and references during the relocation stage. Is temporary housing necessary until the new employee has time to make a sound decision? Would he or she rather have a house or condominium? What type of neighborhood is preferred, and where is the ideal location? Is the family interested in public or private schools? What are the spouse's professional aspirations and personal pursuits? And remember: if a head coach is hired, new assistants and staff will need similar support.

The administrator is well-poised to offer referrals on a range of services to help with the acclimation, as Mike Bohn at Colorado described. "Helping coaches with banking relationships, with real estate relationships, with relocation of staff, with business connections and booster connections in the community, with schools and churches—those sound like little things, but they take pressure off coaches and allow for an easier transition."

Kristy Curry recognized that the work of her administration at Texas Tech during her family's relocation to Lubbock not only lifted a tangible burden from her shoulders but also touched her emotionally. "It's not just been about the daily ins and outs of the job. They've cared about us personally in so many ways to help us with the transition."

As Curry suggests, the move is about more than details that the mind must check off a list before the family is settled. Matters of the heart and soul matter, too. Lisa Love, a key administrator in Mick Haley's early tenure as Southern Cal's volleyball coach, saw the off-court value in Haley arriving mid-season in 2000 yet allowing Elliott to continue leading the team.

"What Mick was doing with his wife and children was making a very significant cultural move to California," Love explained. "His objective initially was to become familiar with Southern Cal, familiar with the volleyball program, but his primary objective was moving his family. That was his target: getting his family comfortable, getting his kids in school comfortably. After those four years, with as much as he traveled with the Olympic team, I believe he dedicated most of that early transitional period to the Haley family, which made him feel very good and right. We simply provided the kind of networking resources to help the Haley family set up house."

Joe McKeown upset his professional equilibrium largely for the sake of his family when he left George Washington after 19 years to find a better environment for his autistic son, so it's no surprise he places significant weight on an administration that expends as much effort on the family as the employee. "I think the most important thing that universities can do is make sure they take care of people's families," he said. "Coaches understand the job they're getting into. They know the work that needs to be done. But it's really difficult on your family when you move, I don't care if it's across the

"I think the most important thing that universities can do is make sure they take care of people's families. Coaches understand the job they're getting into. They know the work that needs to be done. But it's really difficult on your family when you move, I don't care if it's across the river or across the country."

~Joe McKeown

river or across the country. The biggest thing is to make sure people reach out to your family."

Becoming familiar with the political and social aspects of a city also can help a new hire acclimate. Kathy McConnell-Miller felt grateful that she could rely not only on Mike Bohn but also her agent to indoctrinate her into the inner workings of Boulder and the University of Colorado. "My agent lives in Boulder and was a former CU employee, so from an outside perspective, John Meadows has been able to enlighten me on Colorado and the history and significant people in the university and community."

CHART 3.1: RELOCATION DETAILS

____ Moving services: house, vehicles

____ Realtor

____ Housing/neighborhood advice

____ Municipal services: communications (telephone, internet, television), power, water, sewage, garbage, recycling

____ Job leads for spouse

____ Banking relationships: accounts, loans

____ Schools: public, private

____ Child care

____ Health care

____ Business connections

____ Booster connections

____ Home furnishings

____ Churches

____ Veterinarian

____ Hairstylist

____ Grocery stores: standard, specialty

____ Coffee shops

____ Bookstores

____ Vehicle(s)

____ Relocation of staff

Dawn Staley made a major cultural move when she relocated from Philadelphia, where she coached at Temple, to Columbia, South Carolina, to coach the Gamecocks. Although she went to school at Virginia, she was born, raised, and firmly rooted in Philadelphia when the South Carolina opportunity arose.

"People have gone out of their way to make me feel comfortable, because they understand that South Carolina is a lot different than my hometown of Philadelphia," Staley acknowledged. "It's just a different culture. My Philadelphia guard won't allow me to acclimate myself to how nice they are right now. We don't say, 'Hi,' to one another in Philadelphia. We just keep moving."

Regardless of how drastic the move is, coaches often are forced to act and adjust quickly, as Gail Goestenkors at Texas shared of her shift to the Longhorns from Duke. "It doesn't necessarily allow you time to adjust emotionally. You just have to jump in and be ready to go. That makes for a little tougher transition. You can't ease out of or ease into anything. And you have to be willing to jump in, too. You can't straddle. You can't have one foot in the past and one foot in the future. You're jumping, so you might as well jump with both feet."

Administrative hires at times can afford a bit more leeway. When Nora Lynn Finch decided to leave N.C. State, ACC commissioner John Swofford knew from experience the transition would be especially difficult and that allowing Finch extra time to make the move would pay off in the long run. "John was so gracious in giving me the time I needed to go through the emotional withdrawals that were inevitable when leaving a place after 31 years with the great friendships I have there. He was very wise to give me all the space and time I needed."

ADMINISTERING TO NEEDS

Once the new hire is relocated, the administration's focus should shift to providing the employee the professional and emotional support needed to function immediately and efficiently. Just as Goestenkors recommended that coaches make a whole-hearted leap, Temple associate athletics director Kristen Foley counseled administrators to help make that possible.

Foley said one of the keys to a smooth transition is "getting the new coach to feel as comfortable as possible with the policies and procedures of the athletics department—getting her comfortable with who to ask what in meetings and knowing where she needs to go to get things done—and then worrying about the university policies and procedures after that. If it takes three weeks to get a key to your office or a cell phone, that's a problem. You can't move. You can't function. You want them to jump in with both feet, and you want to give the coach the support to do that."

That involves a range of services, from helping with the various paperwork and procedures inherent with university positions to securing equipment and new athletics department apparel. As Jerritt Elliott said, "It's putting people in the right place who could help me get organized in the day-to-day operations and the different departments we needed to be able to deal with." It also entails offering encouragement and actively and continually displaying the confidence in the employee exhibited when making the hire in the first place.

EXPLAIN POLICIES AND PROVIDE EQUIPMENT

A possible perk of a transition is receiving the technological gadgets and clothing required of the job. Then again, the prospect of shuffling through a new set of paperwork and procedures ought to be enough to keep a person in a job for life, but it isn't. In both cases, the onus falls on administration and support staff to ensure the new hire follows the systems and is outfitted with gear branded with the university's logo and colors.

When Elliott was interim head volleyball coach at Southern Cal, he felt comfort in knowing Lisa Love was guiding him through his first experience heading a team. "Lisa was the one who was there making sure I was being taken care of, explaining what needed to be done, and helping me through that process."

Policies and Paperwork

Policies certainly are not a glamorous aspect of the job, but they are necessary, ranging from personnel policies (hiring procedures, benefits packages) and business transactions (getting invoices paid, knowing how to purchase large and small items) to understanding equipment contracts and facility regulations for camps. Procedures such as how to get a team schedule approved, what paperwork is required for travel, and who signs off on recruit visits can trip up new hires because they invariably will be different than they were at their previous places of employment.

A list of examples can never be comprehensive, given each organization's differences, and it's difficult for a longtime employee to recognize the details that are so familiar to them. But creating a list by talking with department heads and administrative personnel about paperwork and policies within their realms is a good place for an administrator to start. Then, asking the most recent hires about what they struggled through can round out the list and ensure the problem areas are addressed.

Meeting department heads is important, but knowing who specializes in what aspects of the operation may be even more so. Even the amount of helpful information can be tremendous, making new hires feel they must eat the entire elephant in one sitting. Start with a one-page cheat sheet of the most important people and facts. Then, a departmental contact list of staff names and titles, office and cell phone numbers, office locations, and e-mail addresses helps a new employee find the right staff member for a particular question. An organizational chart helps make sense of the department; a university and departmental map helps keep the new hire from feeling—or getting—lost; and a parking pass with a visual explanation of allowable lots will prevent irritating (and expensive) tickets. A composite schedule provides a sense of the ebb and flow of departmental activities, and a collection of media supplements from each team gives a more comprehensive picture of the department, its strengths and weaknesses, and the university.

Coaches also should be well-versed in the academic offerings of the institution in order to recruit athletes who fit the university profile as closely as they do the team makeup. For example, a student-athlete with a lifelong dream of being an interior designer should think long and hard before attending a school at which that department hesitates to accept collegiate athletes into the program.

An administrator's role will differ somewhat depending on the coach, the hire date, the sport, the university, and other factors. The administrator may assign a point person to orient the employee, divvy it up among a few people, or handle most of it personally. A comprehensive policies-and-procedures manual with easy online access to forms can be extremely beneficial not only for new employees but long-standing ones.

"She did everything for me," Tonya Cardoza at Temple said of senior woman administrator Kristen Foley's support when she hit the road for a month of recruiting just days after arriving. "From the hiring process to helping with travel and getting me business cards right away, taking care of all kinds of paperwork and stuff that either I or one of my assistants would have been doing, she definitely made it so much easier because she took things off my plate and let me focus on who I was going to hire and getting out on the road."

Equipment

Equipment is less likely to be overlooked than procedures, because it remains relatively standard from one job to the next. Each coach needs a cell phone and/or PDA, a computer, business cards, credit cards, clothing, and keys to facilities. The staff needs videography equipment (which could differ from what the previous staff

CHART 3.2: CRITICAL PROCESSES AND INFORMATION

BUSINESS

_____ Travel (pre- and post-trip)

_____ Requisitions

_____ Purchases

_____ Invoices

_____ Reimbursements

PERSONNEL

_____ Payday

_____ Direct deposit

_____ Benefits package

_____ Hiring process

DEPARTMENTAL

_____ Compliance forms

_____ Scholarships and financial aid

_____ Acceptable equipment vendors

_____ Facility regulations

_____ Contact list (name, department, title, office phone, cell phone, e-mail, office location)

_____ Organizational chart

_____ Media supplements

_____ Composite schedule

UNIVERSITY

_____ Parking permit

_____ Admissions requirements

_____ Academic assets

_____ Academic requirements

TEAM AND PROGRAM

_____ Contact information (player and family phone numbers, e-mail addresses, mailing addresses)

_____ Player information (name, birth date, major, apparel sizes)

_____ Boosters

_____ Key staff

_____ Key media

_____ Camp details

_____ Statistics and media supplements

_____ Game footage

used) and office supplies. Certain staff will be provided with courtesy cars, and administrators should keep in mind that staff may be relying on those vehicles to be available within a day or two of arriving in town, especially if they fly in before their personal cars arrive.

Foley recounted her flurry of getting Cardoza quickly outfitted to hit the road and how nuanced the process can be. "Obviously there is an orientation process and setting up some quick meetings with key people. But getting her Temple gear—there was some that Dawn left, but our women's basketball team was Nike. The other sports are Adidas. Would Nike still want to include women's basketball, and would Tonya want to stay with Nike because of her UConn connections?"

CHART 3.3: EQUIPMENT, SUPPLIES, AND TECHNOLOGY

____ Keys: office, facilities

____ Courtesy car

____ Business cards

____ Credit/procurement card

____ E-mail address

____ Passwords

____ Apparel

____ Cell phone/PDA

____ Computer

____ Camera/video equipment

____ Door nameplate

____ Office supplies

OFFER SUPPORT

Support comes in a variety of forms. The coach's personal financial package already should have been taken care of by this point, but there are still assistant coaches and operating budgets to nail down. The physical support of the move should be completed or at least underway. The technical support of teaching processes and providing equipment is ongoing.

Foundational and moral support are just as important. Clarifying the position and its accompanying responsibilities and intricacies lessens any ambiguity that may still be lingering in the staff or employee's mind. Making sure the new employee feels accepted and at ease, and that staff is excited and confident about the new possibilities will help avoid some of the emotional turmoil of uncertainty that accompanies a transition. That way the focus can stay on the orientation and details of the job.

That moral support can be vocal, communicating the administration's enthusiastic backing through a number of channels. It can be philosophical, with discussions that prove the administration is aligned with the employee on substantive issues. It also can be as simple as dropping in periodically, as senior associate AD Judi Henry did during Kristy Curry's first months at Texas Tech. "She and I had to develop a relationship," Henry said, explaining that they knew each other only on a superficial, professional level, "and I wanted to make sure she knew somebody was here for her. But more than anything else, I tried to be there for her but not to intrude."

Mick Haley cherishes Southern Cal's hands-off approach, feeling empowered with the freedom to run the volleyball program in a way that he has determined—through his long and extremely successful career—gives the team the best chance of winning national championships.

"The greatest help they gave me was saying, 'You're in charge!'" Haley exclaimed. "They just stayed out of my way. I know a lot of people think, 'They don't care.' I just think, 'Leave me alone and let me go now.' And I think that's why they hired me. They wanted someone to come in and take the program to another level. That's great support when you don't have people calling you in and saying this or that. At first I thought it was indifference, but I realized later it was just management style."

Foundational

One of the earliest key roles of an administrator with a new employee is to spend ample time laying the foundation of the position in a more detailed way than takes place in the recruiting and interviewing process. The lines of reporting and communication, the realities and expectations of the position and its perceived or real priorities, and any political or staff challenges should be presented in a fair, factual, unemotional manner so that the new hire has a fully developed picture of the job and organization, as ACC commissioner John Swofford emphasized.

"Once you find that right fit, I think it's very important to define what that individual's role is, to talk about culture, the mission of the organization, what's important from a tangible and intangible standpoint, and how important not only productivity is but also cooperation with the whole and the connectedness that you have within the culture," Swofford said. "You need to find people who are generally on the same page in terms of the values your organization has."

When Nora Lynn Finch accepted Swofford's offer and replaced Bernadette McGlade, Finch was familiar with virtually all parties with whom she would work closely, but her change in position meant a change in role and thus dynamics, as McGlade explained.

"Her persona had been as an administrator from a member school, and now all of a sudden her persona is *she's* the conference office, which is what I call the ambassador to all," McGlade described. "Nora Lynn stepped into a job for people she'd worked with for 30 years. Essentially, she moved her seat from the side of the table to the front of the table. So there are certain things, coming from her perspective, she had to readjust to. She'll probably tell you the work part of it was the easiest part of her transition."

At the WBCA, lines of reporting shifted significantly when Beth Bass arrived, given that CEO Betty Jaynes had supervised all employees and all programs since the organization's inception. When Bass took over that role, then-WBCA president Sylvia Hatchell made absolutely certain everyone—Jaynes, Bass, staff, the board of directors—understood the structure and expectation.

"Sylvia Hatchell did a great job transitioning us, explaining how to act and work," Jaynes noted. "Our responsibilities were so segmented. At first, my job was to continue serving on all of the external boards, overseeing the financial matters of the organization, and developing the programming for the convention. Beth's job was to manage the staff and programs and to improve our marketing and image.

"Sylvia laid the groundwork and rules of the staff as to what was going to be expected of them," Jaynes continued. "The staff would report to Beth, and my job was the only one that was secure, but I am an employee like everyone else, with goals and objectives to meet, annual reviews, and staff meetings. We had really rigid and clear reporting lines. Both of us reported directly to the board and not to each other, and Sylvia had the final say on disagreements. But Beth and I were committed to never let it get to the point where Sylvia had to make the decision. It would be like we couldn't handle our own house.

"Working and dealing with Sylvia during those times, I can see why her players respect her," Jaynes said. "She doesn't pull any punches with you. She tells you, 'This is what you have to do in order for this to happen.' That's how she operates as a leader. It worked well for us. If it had been another person as president, I can't tell you how it would have worked. I don't know. I can't speculate. I'm just saying Sylvia was probably the right person at the right time with the parties involved to make the transition happen and not get anybody upset."

Hatchell offered the details of Bass's assignment. "I'm a big believer in not giving people more than three things to focus on. We gave Beth the guidelines: take care of Betty, build up corporate levels and sponsorship, and explore new areas we'd like to venture into a little more. We continued to restructure a little bit and change the flowchart in a way that made Beth more comfortable."

Verbal

A huge boost to a new hire's confidence is the spoken support from the administration—a constant and comprehensive reinforcement—to the team, the staff, and the community. But it starts with making sure the hire directly and clearly hears the administration espouse his or her virtues.

Jack Kvancz and Mary Jo Warner, George Washington's athletics director and senior associate athletics director, respectively, imparted that message to Mike Bozeman after he accepted his first collegiate head coaching job with the Colonials.

"He made me feel like he had confidence in me and that I could do a good job," Bozeman said, explaining the value of such positive reinforcement. "Mary Jo made her position clear that she gave me the vote of confidence, too. Mind you, I don't know what was said behind closed doors. All I know is what they said to me. I just felt like I didn't come into the situation where they wanted somebody else and I was the settle-for choice. Now, the reality of that is, I really don't know. All I know is they did a heck of a job making me feel like I was *the* choice. I think that's one of the biggest keys—for the administration to pass along confidences to the person who is taking over the program, and that that person receives the confidence from the administrators."

Not only did Kvancz boost Bozeman's self-confidence, he also boosted the team's confidence in Bozeman by making sure they knew that he believed Bozeman was the right choice. "Jack had already spoken to the players," Bozeman said. "Unbeknownst to me, he had meetings with the players after the announcement but before I actually moved into the head coach's office. It was the proactive approach they used that really was a key."

Hatchell made a special trip to the WBCA's headquarters on Bass's first day to make very clear to the staff that Bass was now in charge of all office operations. "I introduced Beth and said, 'Look, she's the boss, and Betty's going to be her right-hand man here. They're going to work together, and this organization is going to grow. There will be changes made. Now, the faster everybody gets on board with the changes, the better.'"

Jaynes added even more detail about Hatchell's conversation with the staff. "She said, 'Betty is going to be the CEO, and she is going to report directly to me and the executive committee just like Beth is. And Betty will still have the responsibility of liaising with all of the 40 different boards that we are involved in. But I'm just telling you, Beth has the right to fire any of you any time. The only person she cannot fire is Betty Jaynes. If you have problems, then I certainly understand, and you can pack up your office and leave today.'"

Philosophical

Strengthening the philosophical connection the administration and employee established during the hire keeps motivation high for the employee to continue working toward that greater end and helps the employee feel part of a high-functioning team.

Sharon McCloskey at Virginia Tech made sure head coach Beth Dunkenberger understood they were teammates in Dunkenberger's efforts. "I just felt like it was important to visit with Beth once she was hired to let her know I was here to help her," McCloskey explained. "I don't look at being an administrator as The Boss. I look at it as we're both working together trying to achieve the same thing."

Kathy McConnell-Miller at Colorado appreciates Mike Bohn's view of an athletics department. "Mike has always been about developing his coaches and teaching what Colorado is all about," she said. "He's been great assisting with implementing a plan for Colorado and a plan for our program. He's very instrumental in supporting my philosophy with my student-athletes and with the community building a fan base."

Illinois athletics director Ron Guenther provided not only valuable background information about student-athletes on the team to incoming coach Jolette Law, especially their behaviors and attitudes during the transitional period, but also support and encouragement during the first months as inevitable challenges surfaced.

"As much as you want to hold onto all the kids, there are certain individuals on the team who are not going to buy in and feel good about the transition," Guenther stated. "What we went through with Jolette was supporting her and giving her the ability to talk to someone who would just support her during that time.

"Generally, if the hire goes the way you'd like it to go and you're excited about the hire, the athletes get excited. But there is a process that takes place during that first year. One is getting to know each other and what the new people stand for. And then there's always a player's question of: 'Does what I do fit into this system when you get to the X and O part?' But how you manage the parent and the athlete with the new staff is where the administration probably has its greatest value. We have to be in support of the new regime. If people want to leave and releases are in the best interest of everybody, those releases are going to happen. But at some point during that first year, the kids went from doubters to believers. She had to stay on track, stick with the program she put in place."

ATTENDING TO PRIORITIES

Most coaches and administrators are leaders with fix-it personalities and a certain amount of impatience to make improvements to their team or organization. New hires have dozens of great ideas—large and small—about what to tweak, alter, or overhaul to lift the program to their envisioned heights.

But the to-do list is overwhelming, with urgent details and global goals, endless tasks and mid-range needs: staffing; the program's culture; the locker room or practice area décor; a player's mechanics; the competition schedule; travel plans; recruiting analysis; league familiarity; visibility on campus and within the community.

Where do you start? Balancing the daily minutiae with long-term planning is difficult in an established position within a stable program, especially in a professional environment in which overachievers constantly fear their opponents outworking them. But in the turmoil of a transition, those dichotomous undertakings seem capable of ripping a person apart.

The priorities can be sorted into four major areas: staff, student-athletes, recruits, and ancillary program components. Their order of importance will differ depending on the people involved and the specific situation in which they find themselves. But it's clear that, as in the rest of life, work in athletics boils down to people. Jerritt Elliott implied as much when he talked about his experience moving from interim head coach for Southern Cal volleyball to the top spot at Texas. "It's being able to step back and try to think of every area you're going to be involved in, then trying to get those people—first and foremost the players, but the staff, too—to feel welcome and to understand and buy into what you're trying to do. Then have some accountability to that and really try to do a good job of evaluating areas that need improvement."

It's also important really to grasp that most people fundamentally don't like change. Forcing extensive yet largely unnecessary policy and procedural changes too quickly can disrupt productivity, dampen moods, and create distrust among the staff. Betty Jaynes, current consultant at the WBCA but CEO when Beth Bass joined the organization, acknowledged Bass's managerial skills in that regard. "Beth didn't change a great deal at first as it related to the staff. Her focus was on improving our branding while she watched and listened and absorbed as much as she could that first year. She was not into that popular measurement of her first 100 days or next 100 days. She wisely chose to watch the staff in action before deciding what changes needed to be made."

ASSEMBLE STAFF

Everything can't be done at once, and far less can be done by just one person than by a staff working in sync and toward the same outcome. But because of the excitement for and enormity of the job, it is easy to begin plowing through the pages of tasks instead of taking the time to have conversations with candidates and their references, consider the options, and set up interviews.

Because it is clear that several people can make better progress than just one, another instinct may be to rush through the hiring stage only to end up with a dysfunctional collection of individuals instead of a unified group. Beth Bass recounted a valuable piece of advice she credited to former Hewlett-Packard CEO Carly Fiorina: "If you have even two percent of doubt about a hire, live with the vacancy."

Neither postponing nor rushing staff hirings builds the strongest foundation. The best staffs are a hard-to-achieve blend of unique personalities with common ideals. Most combine the best of the new era, when the incoming employee brings along familiar assistants, with the best of the old, because familiarity with the team, department, university, league, and region can make the transition so much smoother. Either way, the administration should help guide each subsequent hire following the same procedures outlined in Chapter 2 to ensure the short-term effectiveness of the staff and a long-term and positive relationship between the staff and administration.

Marsha Sharp, the outgoing legend at Texas Tech, emphasized the ongoing theme of making sure the solution fits the situation. "It's really important to structure things the way you're comfortable—put the people around you and make the changes you need to so that it feels right to you. I don't think you can be successful unless you do that."

The concept that a particular philosophy will not fit the same person the same way in every circumstance was apparent as Tonya Cardoza, the incoming coach at Temple, described her thought process of assembling her staff. "You could go either way," she said. "You could get rid of everybody and start new with the people you want, or you may want [to keep people] to bridge the gap. Being a first-timer, I wanted someone to bridge the gap. If there was a next time, I would probably not do that. But with not really knowing everything that goes on, having someone who does has been really good for me."

Staffing Needs

Putting a staff in place may have the most far-reaching effects on the program. Identifying talent, signing the right type of student-athletes, preparing them for competition, and molding the program into a classy unit of which the department, university, and community can be proud requires more effort than the head coach alone can provide. Texas women's athletics director Chris Plonsky knew that, so she kept Gail Goestenkors focused on that task even as Goestenkors was abroad with USA Basketball.

"My immediate agenda with Gail was not so much on the court in terms of style, but getting her to understand that the next step is to hire her staff," Plonsky offered. "Because the things that brought Gail here were also the toughest to work in. You recruit in Texas, but everybody's after Texas players. All the schools are recruiting the same players, so the staff had to be agile, knowledgeable, ready to roll up their sleeves and get after it quickly. So really, the hiring process of her staff was the most critical thing."

Foley at Temple followed the same principle as she helped Cardoza through the initial whirlwind of a very fast hiring stage for Cardoza and her assistants. "Not only was she trying to get on the road herself, but she was trying to interview people," Foley said. "We have a formal process at Temple—very detailed in how we do the hiring process here, and we had to follow all the rules—so that took a bit of time, which was a little of a challenge to get the right people, in her mind, on board and out on the road so they could make a difference."

Planning ahead by the incoming employee is a common and prudent trend, both in making sure the employee and the administration have congruent ideas about who might comprise the remaining staff and in making preliminary calls to gauge interest in potential choices before being hired. When Kathy McConnell-Miller replaced Ceal Barry at Colorado, she appreciated the consent to bring her assistants from Tulsa.

"When I thought or talked about taking over a program, I always wanted to find people who were different personalities from myself. Coming from Connecticut, I thought the fact that we all were different personalities as a staff made us really successful, and I wanted to do the same thing—not just have people around me who would agree with me, but people who would challenge me and help me grow."

~Tonya Cardoza

"In a transition, you need to have the freedom to hire your own staff," McConnell-Miller explained. "A lot of times when you take over a position, you'll hear from an administration that you *have* to keep so-and-so, or they strongly recommend you look at someone. I sometimes think we're better when we have the freedom to surround ourselves with the people who we know will make us better. Just because someone made Ceal better doesn't necessarily mean they are going to make me better. I think that's extremely important."

Piecing together a staff early in one's own hiring process is a tricky proposition. To do so contradicts the superstitious tendencies of athletics personnel, not to mention increases the possibility that news of the potential hire will become public. But to not do so can leave the employee in a lurch or too influenced by the administration.

"I'm very superstitious," Cardoza admitted, "so I don't like to do something before it's actually set in stone. But recruiting started about five days after I was hired, so I had to make sure I had a staff lined up. That was something I had to do beforehand—making sure I had people ready to go as soon as I was hired—because we had to get out on the road."

Mike Bozeman did the same thing during the hiring process at George Washington to ensure his staff represented the specific experiences he wanted in them. "I had preliminary calls out. In the coaching circle they do this: 'Listen, I'm up for this job. If I get it, would you want to come?'" Bozeman explained. "But I already knew who I wanted to hire. I knew I needed somebody who was experienced, and I knew I wanted a former player who knew the landscape and could share her experiences with the six freshmen on what to expect in playing this kind of basketball."

The staff characteristics Cardoza described were less detailed but no less important. "Dawn [Staley] had set the bar really high, so I knew coming in I had to have a good staff around me," she said. "When I thought or talked about taking over a program, I always wanted to find people who were different personalities from myself. Coming from Connecticut, I thought the fact that we all were different personalities as a staff made us really successful, and I wanted to do the same thing—not just have people around me who would agree with me, but people who would challenge me and help me grow."

Beth Bass at the WBCA couldn't agree more. "You have to have that creative tension," she explained. "If I do one thing well, it is hire people who are smarter than me and with different strengths and skill sets who are going to push me and prod me and make me drill down. That's uncomfortable at times, but you have to be secure enough to keep people around who bring different things to the party."

Mick Haley, head volleyball coach at Southern Cal, made the same point when imparting advice to younger coaches, especially. "Coaches have to understand that people revere them, and so they'll say whatever they think the coach wants to hear to be in the confidence of the coach. Coaches have to be smart enough to understand that. When you hire assistant coaches, the last people you want to hire are people who are going to tell you what you want to hear all the time. If you do that, you're never going to get it right, because you're only going to hear what people think you want to hear and not what they think you ought to be doing. So you never get an alternate opinion. I think that's the thing that the young coaches need to understand. It makes you feel good when people are on your side and who rationalize the situation like you might want to, but that's not always the best thing, and you really need to hear some other views to give you a middle-of-the-road approach to whatever's going on."

> *"You have to have that creative tension. If I do one thing well, it is hire people who are smarter than me and with different strengths and skill sets who are going to push me and prod me and make me drill down. That's uncomfortable at times, but you have to be secure enough to keep people around who bring different things to the party."*
>
> ~Beth Bass

"When you hire assistant coaches, the last people you want to hire are people who are going to tell you what you want to hear all the time. You never get an alternate opinion."

~Mick Haley

Dawn Staley placed an emphasis on trustworthiness and self-direction from the individuals she chose as assistant coaches at South Carolina. "If you make any transition, you have to bring people with you who are resourceful and who are loyal. I was actually out of the office the first two weeks or so trying to get myself moved. Carla McGee and Nikki McCray spent two weeks without me in the office. When you feel comfortable enough having somebody pretty much running the program, that's important."

Having a vision of the ideal assistant is significantly easier than successfully hiring someone who closely matches that profile. Finding a compatible mix of personality, experience, philosophy, willingness to relocate, and interest in a specific job is hard enough in one person, much less two or three. A lucky few head coaches have achieved what they consider a perfect staff and then convince that group to make the move intact, as did Kathy McConnell-Miller at Colorado, Beth Dunkenberger at Virginia Tech, and Bonnie Henrickson at Kansas.

Even bringing one or two assistants helps form a nucleus that has a good chance of gelling into a cohesive unit. It also takes some management pressure off the head coach because of an assistant's familiarity with that style.

When Gail Goestenkors made the move from Duke to Texas, she knew she wouldn't go alone. "I brought Gale Valley, who has been my assistant my whole life. She knows me—she knows what I need and when I need it, and she can relay that information to other people as well. Shaida Williams came with me as my special assistant. She was in my first recruiting class, so I've watched her grow up as a player, then as an assistant, get married and have a child. I was fortunate they came with me so I had people I already knew I could trust with my life. If you can bring somebody with you, that's really imperative."

Nora Lynn Finch understood the value of a familiar assistant and was thankful she had one when she joined the ACC. "I was able to bring my own administrative assistant, because Megan Kahn went with Bernie [McGlade] to the Atlantic 10, which really helps Bernie because she has somebody there who knows how she works and how she likes things presented to her and organized for her. At the same time, I was able to bring [administrative assistant] Georgia Davis, who had been my graduate assistant at North Carolina State and who I really clicked with. That has really helped me. She knows me. She's not the least bit intimidated by me, and that's enormously important. She's been able to explain to [assistant director of women's basketball operations] Brad Hecker that I'm a coach first, so I really do want teamwork. I'm not terribly autocratic. I like to delegate. I like to involve other people. I really don't have time to do it all myself. I don't need to be the one always answering the question, because Brad and Georgia are so good at answering the questions, too."

Familiarity is one thing. Trust is another. Goestenkors reiterated Staley's sentiment that allegiance is paramount. "Loyalty, as far as I'm concerned, is the number one priority—to have people who have your back." She also understood the value of familiarity with the league as she continued describing her new staff. "I was fortunate to get [former Kentucky head coach and longtime Tennessee assistant coach] Mickie DeMoss to come out of retirement. That was a coup, really. And [assistant coach] McKale Malone was at Nebraska. I didn't know her ahead of time, but we felt that connection immediately. She's somebody who knew the Big 12, so that was helpful to our staff."

In certain situations, though, forming a brand new staff is required or makes the most sense. The pressure to develop a unified team of coaches in order to develop a unified team of players can be difficult, but it's certainly attainable, as Jerritt Elliott found when he became volleyball coach at Texas. "We brought in a new staff, so that was a challenge. There were some great staff members [already at Texas] who were really qualified. I just felt like trying to get a breath of fresh air and make sure there was new, genuine excitement for the program—there was not anything tied down to the old way of doing things—and the players knew it was a fresh start for everybody."

Jolette Law toyed with the idea of keeping assistant coach Stacie Terry on staff when Law followed Theresa Grentz at Illinois. "We'd always been friends, but it was to the point where, when you keep one, some of the kids may get upset—'Why don't you keep that assistant?'—and I decided just to do a whole new staff. Part of her wanted to stay, but part of her knew she had to move on. She was a good assistant and a good friend during that transition. She stayed until the end of June, and I'll forever be indebted to her."

Retained Employees

While it is unusual for members of a coaching staff to remain in their positions after a change at the top, wholesale changes in support personnel also are unusual. Far fewer athletic trainers, strength coaches, media relations and marketing directors, managers, and compliance officers change jobs when there is turnover in leadership. That doesn't mean they are automatically immune from the whims of the head coach, who should consider all angles before hiring a completely new support staff.

Certainly the closer an individual works with the leader or is exclusive to a particular sport, the greater likelihood his or her job will be impacted if the employee leaves. The director of operations is a prime example of a position that serves at the discretion of the head coach, while sometimes administrative assistants and secretaries struggle most with the change. But keeping consistency in these two positions can be extremely helpful to an incoming staff with little or no familiarity with departmental and university procedures.

"I kept the secretary and director of basketball operations in place," Law said. "They made things easier: the paperwork, who we need to contact. They helped my staff because we were all new and had no clue about a lot of the stuff. They were very supportive. I even kept last year's managers—one of whom was Coach Grentz's son—and they were very helpful with my transition as well. It wasn't as easy as people may think it was. It's good and now people think we were smelling like a rose, but there were many days my face was on the mat. By the grace of God we got through."

Gail Goestenkors did the same at Texas. "Joy [Fellenz, senior administrative associate] stayed on—thank God!—because she knows the ins and outs, who I need to get a hold of, how to get a hold of them. She knows how to get things done. I had a great person as my administrative secretary at Duke, but it would have been too hard to navigate this system, so it was a godsend that Joy stayed. [Director of basketball operations] Cathy McDonald stayed, and I'd say those were the two key people who were really necessary and saved us so much time, effort, energy, because they knew how to get things done. Cathy had played basketball here and graduated from Texas, so she understood even more the tradition. She helped us understand the traditions that were here, why certain things are done. Just coming from the outside, you wouldn't know. You have to have somebody on the inside who understands it. So that was really helpful."

As the women's basketball supervisor at Texas Tech, Judi Henry guided and watched the transition from Marsha Sharp to Kristy Curry with keen interest. From her vantage point, the administrative assistant figured prominently in the success of the changeover, but it wasn't easy. "I would say that Marcy [Phillips, administrative assistant] was definitely the glue," Henry explained. "That's a tough position to get caught in. You have this tremendous loyalty to Marsha, and you have this new person you want to succeed and want to support. Poor Marcy got caught between trying to take care of Marsha and the influx, plus a whole different system and style, a new coaching staff, a lot of paperwork, and a whole different recruiting style. I don't know how she managed to keep her head above water, but she did a great job. She's probably an unsung hero who isn't in the forefront, but she did some incredible things to keep it going."

Curry's attitude and manner certainly helped. "I took it upon myself to set up individual meetings with all of the support staff to introduce myself and my staff. Coach Sharp, Gerald [Myers, athletics director], and Judi explained to me everyone I had in place, and any changes I wanted to make I could have. But there were so many things that were right, there was no reason to make a change. In so many situations I have friends who say, 'Oh, no! You need to bring in your own people.' Well, I trust Coach Sharp enough to know that her people are certainly good enough for me."

Jerritt Elliott made a comparable move when he was promoted to interim head volleyball coach at Southern Cal, developing relationships with the staff in his new capacity. "I had meetings with my strength coaches and trainers to come up with a philosophy and talk about new things we would try to incorporate, and make sure my outside forces who have day-to-day interaction with the athletes knew there was going to be a change and this was the way we were going to go about it. So there was unity amongst us all. They were clear in terms of the vision and direction I wanted to have, and I really tried to make them a part of it, too."

Bernadette McGlade left huge shoes to fill at the ACC. In her 11-year tenure, she built the league into one of the premier women's basketball conferences in the country, and everyone on staff and around the conference knew generally what to expect out of her office. When Nora Lynn Finch was hired as her replacement, the transition period could have been extremely difficult. As Finch said, "We think alike, but we're very different in our management styles. I'm a guard. She's a post. I don't think people expect us to be alike."

But the combination of Finch's personality and managerial style, the retention of McGlade's top assistant, and the fact that Finch's administrative assistant came with her from N.C. State made the transition "seamless," described commissioner John Swofford. "I have a tremendous staff here, and Nora Lynn is easy to embrace. She's such a positive person who knows how to lead and fit in at the same time, and that's a gift not everyone has."

Finch embraced her staff and their strengths, didn't hide her own weaknesses, and led with energy and sensitivity in a way that almost anyone can learn from. "I listened a lot. I listened to Brad Hecker, who was Bernie's assistant director for women's basketball. I'm so fortunate that he's still here. She trained him very, very well. He was hands-on in getting a lot of logistics done. He's able to explain a lot to me because of his having so much firsthand experience. Had Bernie not had him on staff or he not been here when I came, the learning curve would have been much steeper.

"What I've explained to him is, my objective my first year is not to mess up what Bernie has set up very well. And I want to begin to adapt some of this to my management style and try to use some of my strengths. Where I'm maybe not as strong, make sure Brad is more involved. It's a great thing that his greatest strengths seem to be where mine are not, and that's just a blessing.

"In the first few weeks, I would ask Brad, 'What would Bernie have done?'" Finch continued. "He began to think I was going to copy her, and then he quickly figured out I'm not the same person. The reason I was asking the question—and I didn't elaborate with him—was there are other people who are accustomed to things being done a particular way. Now I'm not going to do everything the way Bernie did. I just want to know what other people are expecting. So I'm going to pick and choose which surprises I'm going to give them. And if it's something really sensitive, I'm going to gradually make that change, not radically or abruptly make that change. I'm trying to make sure I understand what works well so I can, at the right time, figure out if I want to keep doing it that way or personalize it a little more to my style.

"So, coming into any new position, you have to have a clear understanding of your strengths, your purposes, how you go about doing things. But you can really disrupt the existing staff and existing structure if you're not compatible with what's already in place, or if you're just determined you're going to turn the Titanic in a day.

"I depend on Brad so much, I didn't want to start throwing him curves and get him off-balance or unsure," added Finch. "I want his confidence intact. I have the confidence in him that I can say, 'Are you comfortable doing that? You know how to

"The whole power in a position is not having to use it. It's everybody recognizing where the authority is, and knowing full well that all it takes is one 'No' and we're not doing that. So the great thing about a leader is that people recognize there's authority there, but the hammer's not being swung all the time. If you swing it all the time, people try to get out of the way. When they get out of the way, they're moving away from you instead of toward you."

~Nora Lynn Finch

do that? Fine, teach me about that next week when we're not so busy.' And he'll just smile and say, 'OK, Boss.' And I'd say, 'Not Boss, we're teammates. You can call me Coach, but not Boss.'

"But his fear is I won't be hands-on enough to make sure that all the pots that are being stirred are being stirred by this office. Yet he sees that I want to empower people to be able to make decisions. So he came in to visit with me and wanted to know, 'What do you do if somebody isn't getting the job done or isn't in step with you?'

"The whole power in a position is not having to use it," Finch suggested. "It's everybody recognizing where the authority is, and knowing full well that all it takes is one 'No' and we're not doing that. So the great thing about a leader is that people recognize there's authority there, but the hammer's not being swung all the time. If you swing it all the time, people try to get out of the way. When they get out of the way, they're moving away from you instead of toward you.

"It's important to understand about teams that you're trying to get most of the people going in the same direction most of the time. You're not going to have everybody going in the same direction all the time. And if you're expecting that, then you're going to be disappointed. That's really important, because we don't all think alike all the time. I'm not going to be with you to answer every question. You have to answer some yourself. You just want to have enough basic understanding to know some boundaries of what's good and bad and to know what kind of things you need to ask approval for and which ones you don't.

"But I'd rather have people making decisions to keep the enterprise moving and that person think that he or she is doing it in a good team effort than not," Finch maintained. "I'd rather we not be stopping the train because somebody is afraid: 'What path are we going to take?' I'm not afraid of taking the wrong path. We can turn the train. There are other tracks. We've got a reverse. We can back up. But if somebody's not carrying his or her work, or if somebody's not a team player, you simply will not see those people around very much. You'll see them involved and engaged less and less until you just don't see them. That's just the way I work."

When staff members are retained, Beth Bass at the WBCA believes it is important to allow them to begin the new era without any baggage or personality conflicts they may have from the former reign. Betty Jaynes explained their tactic. "I focused on being extremely honest and forthcoming about every single thing that had to do with the WBCA with the exception of the staff, and that was a request from Beth. She asked me to take all of the personnel folders home with me. She didn't want to read anything. She never wanted me to talk about any of them. Since they were all reporting to her, she wanted to develop her own opinions. So that [first] afternoon she helped me carry all of the personnel folders to the trunk of my car. I took them home and kept them as long as the law requires, and then we destroyed them. She never knew any of their performance evaluations or anything that had ever happened. When a staff member was not carrying their weight as well as they should, I really had to bite my tongue sometimes not to say, 'That's typical.' That was hard for me to do, and I really worked on it so she could develop her own opinions."

As Bass reflected on her first months, she admitted to second-guessing her retention of a workforce that had grown accustomed to Jaynes traveling two-thirds of each month. "As Betty will tell you, the staff was way too self-empowered. It was like the patients were running the asylum. The more aggressive ones had anointed themselves chief of staff. Like coaches who inherit players often feel, I think I should have come in and wiped the slate clean. But compassionately I couldn't have done it. It's just not my personality. And it was only four months until the [Final Four] convention, so you try to salvage things and work with them. You're reluctant to let them go that early because you don't know exactly what their knowledge is. Eventually, by natural attrition or letting some people leave, you start recruiting your own people, just like coaches do.

"When I look back, I wouldn't try to save as many people," Bass concluded. "I would have made some changes. We could have subcontracted somebody to do our convention. I think I've always had a longer fuse but probably should have pulled the trigger sooner on my gut feelings. But I've always said you hire with intuition and you fire with compassion. Always leave somebody with their dignity."

DEVELOP RELATIONSHIPS WITH STUDENT-ATHLETES

Coaches coach because they enjoy the process of working with student-athletes. The competition and recognition can be addictive, but if the primary motivation isn't the satisfaction of interacting with student-athletes and seeing them mature as people, the coach will not last long in the profession.

All of the necessary detail work of a transition can be difficult to juggle for coaches who really want to be with their players. Kristen Foley recalled the first month for Tonya Cardoza and her staff at Temple, when traveling to recruiting tournaments dominated their first several weeks on the job. "That was tough for them. They were on the road for three weeks, then had to pack up [their previous homes] and find a place to live. Once they were back, it was still a whirlwind, because now you have kids visiting unofficially, practices to plan, getting everybody temporary housing and cell phones, getting cars organized and washed and everything. There was finally time in August for everyone to catch their breath and have time to do what we hired them to do, which was coach and mentor these young ladies. They did a great job."

Jerritt Elliott's primary interest when he was promoted at Southern Cal echoes that of most coaches in transition. "There are questions involved in any transition. My main priority was spending time with the team, working with the players to get them on board. We had individual meetings and team meetings before we actually got started in the gym to really start investing in those relationships."

Because of their age and typical connection to their coaches, players often have the hardest time with transition, although Jolette Law at Illinois offered a differing opinion and an excellent remedy. "I realize they get attached to coaches and don't adjust to change," Law said. "But I'm in a new place, coming out of a land of familiarity after being somewhere for 12 years. We shared our stories, and it made it a little easier. I don't think they looked at it like that: 'I know you are adjusting to different coaching styles, different coaching philosophies, different drills. But you have to get to know only four people. I have to get to know 12 different personalities. You guys know each other. You've been part of a team. You've been around each other for more than a year or two. But my staff and I haven't been around each other. We're taking a chance on each other. We don't have the benefit of being around each other for even a year.' So when we started explaining and getting feedback from them and letting them see that, 'Hey, we're all making a change here,' they started loosening up a little bit."

> *"We shared our stories, and it made it a little easier. When we started explaining and letting them see that, 'Hey, we're all making a change here,' they started loosening up a little bit."*
>
> ~Jolette Law

Even with that team-building exercise, joining a team that was put together and coached by someone else is difficult. Players worry about their value and place within a new system. Their loyalty can be tied to the previous staff, so they may not be eager to embrace the new coaches. The title "coach" does not automatically bring with it trust and respect from the players. That must be earned.

Foley was impressed that Cardoza was in no hurry to make cosmetic changes to the women's basketball areas, even though Staley's name, face, and accomplishments were prominent. "Tonya said, 'We'll get to that stuff. Right now my concerns are the kids in the program, recruiting the best athletes, and making them better students and better players. We'll worry about those little things later.'"

Inheriting Players Takes Sensitivity

Just as Beth Bass described the difficult decision to retain or release staff, coaches face the same dilemma when taking over a team. "This is one area where people's philosophies are very different, but inheriting players is a very sensitive issue," Kathy McConnell-Miller at Colorado began. "It's a difficult thing to do. How you handle it is very important to the perception of your program, of how you're going to treat your student-athletes, and ultimately of how successful you can be. Philosophies range from one end of the spectrum to the other. Do you run everybody off and try to get your own players, or do you teach and engage and develop the players you have and bring in players more to your style and your philosophy gradually? It's a fine line, and it's a very tough thing for coaches.

"My philosophy is, that's somebody's daughter, that's somebody's sister, that's somebody's player, that's somebody's friend," she continued. "I am just not in the nature of running people off. I never, ever view the people I inherit as not being my players. Maybe they weren't handpicked by me, but these are my players now. I always have been careful not to say, and I will tell you Ceal [Barry] has never heard out of my mouth, 'Wait until I get my own players in here,' because I have such great respect for what she's done."

Elliott followed suit with Texas volleyball. "My biggest message to the team was, 'Everybody here still matters. Just because the coach previous to me resigned or was dismissed doesn't mean you're not important.' The concern they had, I felt, was I didn't recruit them. They didn't know who I was. They didn't know their value. So I just told them they did have value. Some of them were going to have great roles and some would have different roles, but I tried to build that confidence with them that we weren't just going to throw them out or take away their scholarships.

"I also tried to get an understanding of, did they want to be there? If not, that's OK, too. But I wanted people who were there 100 percent in an effort to turn the program around and do it the right way, and get them to buy into it as well. That was their biggest fear in talking to me: Was I going to come in and clean house? How was I going to make them feel important, that this 10-18 team that didn't have an opportunity to be successful is still worthy?"

But it's not always smooth from the outset. Kristen Foley knew any coach would struggle to follow Dawn Staley at Temple because of the team's attachment to Staley. "We knew the team was upset that Dawn left. She was such a big part of their lives as a mentor, and they really didn't want somebody new. It didn't matter who it was. So that was the biggest challenge for Tonya [Cardoza], to have the team embrace her as the new coach. There was going to be change, and the kids did not want that, whether it was a change of practice drill or time of practice or how they started or different film work or different accountability for going to class. Tonya came in with great enthusiasm and energy, but the kids really didn't embrace her or her philosophy right away just because it was different."

Regardless of a coach's philosophy, though, some players will feel the need to leave the team. The best of intentions does not always lead to a perfect outcome, and

> *"Inheriting players is a very sensitive issue. How you handle it is very important to the perception of your program, of how you're going to treat your student-athletes, and ultimately of how successful you can be. I am just not in the nature of running people off. I never, ever view the people I inherit as not being my players."*
>
> ~Kathy McConnell-Miller

the perfect outcome is not always that the entire team remains intact during a transition. All of the time, effort, communication, and understanding in the world won't always overcome personality, expectation, or style differences.

"Some of these kids had very strong ties with some of the previous staff, and I knew it would be a struggle trying to get them to buy into what I was all about," Illinois's Jolette Law acknowledged. "Some transferred, and that was a challenge. But with the kids who stayed, the opportunity was great because they wanted to win. They just didn't know how to challenge themselves to exceed their own expectations. That was an opportunity for me to share my vision with them and help them reach their potential on and off the court. I embraced that challenge. I knew I was going to have to convince them that they're great and that we can be a great program."

Bonnie Henrickson's arrival at Kansas disrupted the internal balance of several team members. "We had about four players leave before we got here, probably the right decision for them. It wasn't going to be a good fit—'That's not how I want to work,' and 'That's not what I expect for myself.' We wanted kids who, at the end of the day, bought in and were committed to graduating here, training to win a championship, and being great role models in the community. If you could live with those three things and could buy into that, then we'd open arms. But we got down to eight or nine pretty quick."

Building Trust Takes Time and Effort

Developing relationships with players isn't an item on the priority list that a coach can check off and move beyond. Work should begin as soon as the coach is hired, with team and individual meetings, but it belongs in the "ongoing" category because it never ends. It's a continuous, back-and-forth journey, with the coach earning the trust and respect of the players, and the players earning the same of the coach.

But the process can begin slowly if the coach is out of the office for much of the first few weeks on the job, as was Cardoza. "We immediately gave her a contact list with e-mail and cell phone numbers so she could speak to them," Foley said, explaining Cardoza's initial days and weeks. "We also invited all of them to the press conference, so she met some then, and she met the kids who were in summer school immediately. But she didn't meet everybody else until school started. Technology helps so much now, because the kids that she did meet would text or e-mail the players who were a little further away saying, 'She's great! She's doing this and that.' So it helped those guys during that tough month."

Cardoza's strategy during that initial period was a great compromise between all coaches being on the road recruiting and establishing a presence with the team. "One of our assistant coaches, Brittany Hunter, stayed back and tried to be that bridge, so they could have someone there. We tried to make sure we always had a coach in the office so they'd always have someone to go and talk to. But my interaction with them in the summer was hard because I wasn't around, and then things started happening that weren't positive, like missing classes or not showing up for appointments. So from the start I had to come in and start laying down the law and punishing people right away before they really got to know me. But now that we're able to interact with each other, our relationships have changed to the point where they know that I'm just trying to show them right from wrong."

Texas's Gail Goestenkors boiled it down succinctly. "It's all about relationships and trust and communication. To build trust, it takes time. I spent more time with these players early on. I was constantly meeting with them, trying to get to know them and know what was important to them. And they could begin to understand who I was and get to know me as well, so we could develop that bond and that trust, so that when I was telling them they had to run another 30 minutes, they would believe I had their best interest at heart.

"If you don't have that trust, you don't have a foundation for a great relationship. I'm not going to be able to help them become as good as they could be, and vice versa. If I don't trust them, I'm not going to be able to be as good for them. So we had to develop that mutual trust, and that just takes time. And I think, as you look through the course of that first season, we got better and better for a few reasons. One, they adjusted to my system, which was more pressing than they were used to, and they got better with it. Two, we got to know each other and trust each other and believe in one another. When they were getting yelled at or whatever the case may be, they knew that at the end of the day they would get a hug and they knew I loved them and we were going to be better. But it takes time for that."

HIT THE RECRUITING TRAIL

Recruiting is often called the lifeblood of a collegiate athletics program. So much energy goes into evaluating talent, identifying the athletes who seem to fit best into the coach's and university system, and then wooing those individuals to the school. And the process seems to start earlier and earlier in a prep player's career, with some ninth-graders unofficially committing to a school before the school can officially offer a scholarship.

But transitions wreak havoc on recruiting efforts. Even though a recruit technically commits to a school, most commit emotionally to the previous coaching staff who faithfully stayed in touch and convinced the player she had a bright future on the team. When that staff changes, the commitment of recruits sometimes waivers, and for good reason. Because of the complexity and individuality of recruiting, neither party may be as keen on each other.

"One of the challenges is trying to hang on to some of the recruits and to the relationships in recruiting," Virginia Tech senior associate director of athletics Sharon McCloskey said. "When you have a staff that comes in in late spring, it's hard for them. They have to immediately call all of those recruits and see what they can do to keep them—if that's what they want, if the recruits suit their style of play. One, do you still want those people, and two, can you keep them?"

Beth Dunkenberger, who followed Bonnie Henrickson at Virginia Tech, expounded on McCloskey's point. "We tried to follow up with some, but recruiting is such a personal thing. You recruit for the school, certainly, but the kids become identified with the coaches themselves. So it was hard that first year to connect on specific ties they had with recruits."

Another issue is developing a new recruiting plan based on the new school. The team personnel and personality, university profile, conference, and region all combine with a head coach's system and style to determine the type of player to be pursued. When coaches are hired well into the summer, making the monumental decisions quickly about what recruits to pursue and where to watch them play can begin to feel like a pressure cooker.

Jolette Law at Illinois felt she needed "to hit the ground not running but actually sprinting." Tonya Cardoza described the impact of her late arrival at Temple as being "behind the eight ball because the hiring was so late."

Even when the transition takes place shortly after the collegiate season ends, the nature of the process makes that first year especially difficult, as Kristy Curry at Texas Tech explained. "In recruiting, you build up those relationships so early. When you take a job in April or May, you're so far behind, especially if you have a different recruiting base. It's totally different to leave a job in the Midwest and try to recruit those same kids to the Southwest. That was probably one of the toughest parts of the transition, because the relationships I had in recruiting weren't able to benefit us in this area of the country. I feel like the class we're signing this year, going into our third season, is our first true class where we've been able to make headway and build relationships."

ATTEND TO PROGRAM-WIDE MATTERS

Once the most pressing needs of the central figures of the program—the staff and the current and future student-athletes—have been met or at least addressed, attending to secondary yet significant components of the program will rise to the top of the to-do list. Does the program's collective behavior or lifestyle need changing? Are cosmetic modifications to the team's facilities desired to reinforce the new culture? How well do the playing styles of the team and the new coaching staff mesh? Will strategies, tactics, and terminology be revamped immediately, or will a gradual migration to a new system suffice? How familiar is the coaching staff with league competition?

Culture

The culture of a program automatically will change with a new staff, whether the incoming coach feels it's necessary or not. Each coach's personality, idiosyncrasies, focus, expectations, and style significantly influence the social order of the team, department, university, and community. The result can be nothing but a unique atmosphere.

The first thing Law did at Illinois was evaluate the current climate of the team and program. "I wanted to get a snapshot of the culture that was there," she said. "I tried to establish a relationship with all parties—the kids, some of the coaches who were still under contract, the secretary, the director of basketball operations, just everybody—and talk to them about the culture of the program, seeing what the expectations were of the kids, what some of the rules were, some of the accountability, the work ethic of each kid, the trust amongst the kids, what really was going on. I knew the team was successful in the past, and I really just wanted to pick everyone's brain who was still there on what exactly had made the team successful.

"I wanted to listen and hear the positives," Law continued. "I didn't want to hear any negatives or what went wrong, but try to get my own interpretation of what was going on. You never go into a situation where you think everything is peaches and cream. I wasn't foolish like that. But I focused on looking at some of the positive things I could take from it."

Once she had completed her investigation, she set about combining what she'd learned about the Illini program and what she'd learned in her career at Rutgers to fashion and then impart a new culture that represented her intuition about the program's history and her ideals about its future.

"I didn't think the team took advantage of what they had," Law explained. "Theresa Grentz is a legend, and I know that sometimes people don't really realize what they have until it's gone. The whole makeup of the University of Illinois is a sense of pride in wearing that jersey. I don't think they really understood what it meant to be a part of this program and all the history that was there. I had to educate them on what went before. Illinois went to a Sweet 16. They have a banner up. The foundation has been established. People recognized this program. We have what it takes to compete. I'm just here to reinforce what was and how it can be, and how we can continue to take it to that next level. I didn't walk into a bad situation. There were some very good players. We just had to redirect and adjust our outlook."

Athletics director Ron Guenther offered his perspective on Law's process. "The first thing that Jolette did was to explain what she needed from the kids in terms of work ethic and commitment," he said. "It wasn't changing uniforms, it wasn't changing a lot of stuff. It had to do with expectations of what she wanted to do in the gym. I think there was some fallout initially by the players: 'I'm not sure we can do this.' But because she'd had success, both as an athlete and a coach, in a program that had reached national status, they followed. It was very gratifying for all of us to watch her at the end of the first year. We didn't have great depth, but we were a very conditioned, tough group. It took a while to get there, but in my opinion, there was a branding of Illinois basketball under Jolette Law of toughness and conditioning."

Law marveled that the most basic designation of Illinois athletics had that concept of toughness engrained in it. "We have the right name! We are the Fighting Illini!" she exclaimed. "We have to fight—not physically fight, but compete hard, with that level of pride that we will not be denied. So I had to instill that passion, that swagger, breathing life back into them. And people had an opportunity to see that during the Big 10 Championship, when those kids played for each other and for the university to bring that level of respect back into the program.

"The main thing was to establish the passion," Law continued. "Where I came from was so intense. Rutgers had a lot of pride. That was all we knew. We went out. We were soldiers. We were the Scarlet Knights. That's just what we did. A lot of people didn't understand it, but we knew. We were going to compete. We were going to play hard. The game was probably going to be ugly. But at the end of the day, we wanted to put a fear of playing Rutgers.

"I think kids think you need to win at all costs, and yeah, we want to win, but winning isn't everything. Competing to win is. It's just how you prepare. And we're not just talking about wins and losses, Xs and Os, but winning as a student-athlete, GPA, being very positive role models in the community, holding them accountable to everything from top to bottom."

Mick Haley also set about transforming the practice habits and expectations of the Southern Cal volleyball team when he took over. "I wanted to change the gym culture to be more of a training culture. I felt like if we established that culture, then we always had a chance to win. And I wasn't as concerned about the end result as I was how we approached it day to day, because I felt if we had the talent and we played the competition and we had good culture and competition in practice every day, that we always would have a chance to win.

"I also wanted more people involved," Haley shared. "I developed a performance team, which included my weight trainer, my trainer, my nutritionist, my biome-chanics person, my sports psychology guy who had a lot to do with our team building. I relied on [sport psychologist] Mike Voight a whole lot, and I still employ him long-distance to do my team building. He was very good to point out that coaches are different and you have to adjust. By not being insecure and not having to do it all myself, it helped us a great deal in that they knew they could have opinions also, and even if I disagreed they could still have those opinions."

Sometimes drastic measures are needed, as Beth Bass found out at the WBCA. "I'd read somewhere that you can judge the level of trust in an organization or company by how many doors are closed," she began. "I walked through the office, and everybody had their doors closed. So I found a handy man, and one weekend, without warning, we took off every door, even directors' doors. If I could have afforded it, I would have knocked out the walls and made cubicles. They literally came in on Monday and all the doors were in storage. I told them, 'I don't know what's going on here, but that's not the office atmosphere I want.' I didn't even tell Betty [Jaynes]! She looked at me and said, 'You took everybody's door down?' I think I might have let the directors have their doors back eventually. It became a big deal. If you were a director, you got your door back."

With Mike Bozeman at George Washington, his goal wasn't to change the culture. In fact, as he said, "The first thing I wanted to do with the team is let them know that the expectation for success was not going to change." His focus was to reunite under his leadership a team shocked by the departure of former coach Joe McKeown and provide his brand of motivation for the upcoming season.

"When they came on campus, we had a big meeting," he revealed. "I played a song called 'Victory.' The first verse says, 'I have evidence, I have confidence, I'm a conqueror, I know that I win, and I know who I am, God wrote it in His plan, my name is Victory.' So I played that song and said, 'We need to have confidence and we need to have victory in everything we do. I want you to have victory in the classroom, I want you to have victory on this campus socially, and we definitely want to have victory on the basketball court.' And I wanted to have it full circle so that when they heard us talk about victory, it wasn't just about wins and losses on the basketball court. It was about wins versus losses in the classroom, in our everyday challenges that every college student has to deal with. I thought it was important that I establish a theme for the season that we can grasp onto during tough times or uncertain times, that we all could just go back and ground ourselves for the whole theme of the year.'"

Jerritt Elliott's primary objective when he was promoted to interim head coach for Southern Cal volleyball wasn't so much demonstrating to the team his trustworthiness off the court—he'd already done that during his four years as an assistant coach—but earning their trust that he had a viable plan on the court. "The players had questions, no doubt," he admitted. "How was a 31-year-old assistant going to know what to do every day in practice? One of the first things we did was install an open-door policy where there was lots of communication, really trying to get the players to buy into what we were doing. I used Paula [Weishoff], my assistant coach, a ton during that time.

"From the first day, we made sure the environment was a tough environment, that it was well communicated," Elliott continued. "They understood the roles and responsibilities of the daily agenda of practice, and we were very organized in terms of our practice routines. I wanted to make sure they knew there was organization, positive coaching styles, positive leadership, and most importantly positive growth from the technical and gamesmanship aspects in how the game is played.

"So Paula and I spent a lot of time meeting before practices to make sure we were on the same page and really knowing what we were trying to attack to make these players better and trying to invigorate them a little, too, trying to give them a burst of energy. So it was very 'Rah! Rah!' but stern at times as well, and really trying to create an atmosphere that was high energy, so they would walk out of the gym knowing that they just busted their butts and were gaining confidence through the hard work."

Details

The devil is in the details. How much of what do you change, and how quickly? Does the style of play need to change, or the terminology, or can the coaching staff adapt to what the players already are used to? How critical is it that the locker room, practice facility, or coaches' offices get a face-lift? It could be that a new paint job would emphasize or complete the cultural makeover, or it could be the current décor works just fine. Does the new staff have specific ideas about daily routines such as team meetings, practice times, and study hall? What sort of policy, procedure, and accountability information must the team learn before the players get settled into their self-made comfort zones or mistakenly continue in old patterns?

On-Court Systems

In terms of playing style and lingo, coaches must carefully evaluate the situation. The team's collective experience in the former system and its success therein, the maturity and skill of key players individually and the group as a whole, the adaptability of the team and the coaching staff, the long-term plan of the coaching staff, and the competitive landscape are several factors that should be considered before determining the optimal level of continuity.

When Mick Haley assumed the head coaching role at Southern Cal, the volleyball team had advanced to the Final Four under Elliott with a language and a style that didn't suit his preference. But Haley felt a change would benefit the team in the long run. "Every day it was uncomfortable replacing stuff that had already been successful. But I didn't feel like I could function with the nomenclature and the system that was in there."

Beth Dunkenberger inherited a Virginia Tech team that had thrived under Bonnie Henrickson's organized, disciplined offense. Because Henrickson and Dunkenberger had coached together before, it wasn't difficult for Dunkenberger to incorporate some of the team's previous experiences.

"Bonnie and I had worked together for seven years, so in a lot of ways, fundamentally, we were very much alike," Dunkenberger explained. "We ran some of the same offenses. In making that transition, when I went to put a new offense in, our point guard was very good. She had started for two years and was a junior when I got her. When I would introduce an offense, I would say, 'Did you run this before?' And if they had, I'd change it from what I called it to what they called it. Now, sometimes I'd call the wrong offense and the point guard would laugh and call it what they called it. But I tried to make things as easy for them as possible, not making them have to learn new terminology. I would ask how they defended certain situations, and sometimes I would keep it the same and sometimes I would change it. But I would certainly be open to hearing how they'd done things in the past."

Still, it wasn't effortless for the players. Because the coaches had different personalities, their coaching styles naturally were different, as administrator Sharon McCloskey noticed. "Bonnie ran a much more controlled, almost half-court offense, always totally under control. Beth allowed the players to make decisions on the court. The transition from going from a controlled offense to more of an open offense took them some time to get used to, to not look over at the bench and have the coach call the play or determine exactly what's going to happen."

Facilities

Facility changes are a natural part of a transition, whether it's simply fresh paint in the offices, a practice facility overhaul, or something in between. "We did a little re-spiffying up at her request," women's athletics director Chris Plonsky said when Gail Goestenkors came on board at Texas, "and we did some nice things in the practice facility with a few sayings on the wall."

Tonya Cardoza knew the décor at Temple needed to be updated, even though she appreciated its history and message. She playfully set up the scene she encountered after Dawn Staley's tenure. "Dawn is one of my dearest friends, and Temple women's basketball was all Dawn Staley," she began. "I mean, kids came to Temple because they wanted to play for Dawn Staley, not because it was Temple. She's an icon—a legend—in Philadelphia, and yes, this is something that she built. I walked into the office and it's painted all Dawn Staley. It was really hard, but I said to her, 'OK, we have to take this down.' And she joked, 'OK, you can paint over it, but you have to rename the floor Dawn Staley Court!'

"But because you know that's why a lot of the kids came to Temple, it's hard to do," Cardoza continued. "You don't want to slight them in any way, and they walk around in Dawn Staley T-shirts all the time. I'd say, 'You need to take off your Dawn Staley T-shirt and put on a Temple T-shirt!' One kid said, 'Well, get us a Coach Cardoza T-shirt.' It's all in fun. But the one thing with her name on the wall, that was just something I had to take down. I mean, everyone knows who she is, but that's probably not the first thing you want a new recruit to see even though there are still pictures of her around."

Sometimes changes to facilities means actually changing facilities. Haley embraced his return to collegiate volleyball with ideas he'd collected from his years at Texas and his time with USA Volleyball, and he set about implementing them right away. "We moved where we were playing our matches to a better facility, but I took the worst gym for practice instead of sharing the best one with men's basketball. I said to our team, 'We're going to be blue-collar, and we're going to paint on the walls. Each one of you gets a four-by-four square, and I want you to paint the most stimulating thing you can paint so when you come in here every day, it stimulates you to be the best you can be.' We did a lot of different things. We just started becoming a new program, yet showing appreciation for all the past tradition that Southern Cal had to offer."

League Familiarity

One of the biggest challenges that directly relates to competitive performance is league familiarity. When a head coach transitions to another school, most often the coach will be transitioning into a new conference as well. The previous hours and days of film time and games that helped that coach develop a plan of attack against former league opponents is about as useful against the new competition as an expired driver's license. Extensive work goes into preparing for any opponent, but the amount of work increases exponentially in a new conference.

"One of the greatest challenges [in taking this position] was the Big 12 Conference," Goestenkors said. "You're walking into what last year was considered the number one conference in the country. They were all preparing for one new coaching style. I was preparing for 11. Everybody was new, every style was new, every player was new. It was a lot of hard work. But I felt so much better going into year two, because I understood the strengths and weaknesses of our opponents a little better."

Even though Beth Dunkenberger had been at Virginia Tech in the past, the program's recent nomadic league history rendered her experience largely irrelevant. "It was our first year in the ACC," she said. "Coming into the league, you have Carolina, Duke, and Maryland, who all within a couple of years had gone to the Final Four. So you're joining a league that, one, is a powerhouse for women's basketball, and two, is a very different conference from the Big East in terms of style of play. So we had to transition our game and our style of play and get used to a very fast-paced, up-tempo, athletic league.

"Not only did our coaching staff have to become familiar with entirely different opponents in terms of game preparation, but so did our kids," Dunkenberger pointed out. "They don't know anything about North Carolina or Florida State. Every game for them was new as well. Whereas everyone else in the league had one or two new teams to get ready for, we had no one with familiarity with the league.

"One factor that helped me and our team is that I was able to keep my staff intact. I had hired a very experienced, good staff at Western Carolina, and I brought them all with me to Virginia Tech. We were in North Carolina, so we saw a lot of ACC basketball on TV. We'd played North Carolina and Wake Forest, so we were familiar with teams in the league and kind of had a handle on a general overview of how the league played, so that did help. It's just a lot of initial work going into your first year to try to learn the specifics and the details."

MEETING PEOPLE

One of the special aspects of women's athletics is the relationships developed between the fans and the team players and staff. Part of that can be attributed to the natural inclination of females to be more relational. It also reflects the relative youth of women's collegiate athletics, especially in the post-Title IX era. Still technically in the grassroots stage of development, programs intrinsically cherish fan support and tend to reciprocate the appreciation.

Sharon McCloskey touched on this concept when she talked about the Virginia Tech boosters' concern upon losing head coach Bonnie Henrickson and wondering who might be hired. "A lot of them still supported the program [when Beth Dunkenberger was hired]," she said. "They just wanted to at least have the same access they had, and we let them know that's pretty much the norm across the country with women's basketball. There's always that up-close-and-personal element that you get with most women's basketball programs that you may not necessarily get with men's programs.

"We have a local restaurant where we host the coach's radio show," McCloskey continued. "They were just anxious to find out who it was going to be, but they were still planning to be supportive. They've actually chosen to support just women's sports, which we've really appreciated. So I think everybody was sort of excited and anxious to see who was going to come in and see what was going to happen."

Kristy Curry at Texas Tech echoed that thought. "That's what makes women's basketball so pure in my mind: those entities of people who support it so much."

The administration is key in helping new coaches integrate into the community. For example, Kansas athletics director Lew Perkins invited Henrickson to join him at meetings and functions. Kristen Foley said Temple's tactic with Tonya Cardoza was to take her "to football games and introduce her to a lot of the donors early in the fall."

CHART 3.4: WHO TO KNOW

SPORT AND PROGRAM

_____ Players' families

_____ Players' previous coaches

_____ Recruiting channels: summer teams, high school, junior college

_____ Conference coaches and personnel

_____ Officials

_____ Previous coaches

_____ Key donors

_____ Friends of the program

_____ Alumni

DEPARTMENT

_____ Directors and sport contacts

_____ Academics

_____ Athletic training

_____ Business

_____ Compliance

_____ Development

_____ Equipment

_____ Event

_____ Facility

_____ Human resources

_____ Marketing

_____ Media relations

_____ Strength and conditioning

_____ Student-athlete services

_____ Travel

_____ Coaches

_____ Letterwinners association

UNIVERSITY

_____ Board of regents/trustees

_____ Chancellor

_____ President

_____ Provost

_____ Student affairs

_____ Faculty athletics representative

_____ Professors

_____ Human resources

_____ Admissions

_____ Housing

_____ Student body

_____ Alumni association

COMMUNITY

_____ Politicians

_____ Business leaders

_____ Friends of the university

_____ Donors

_____ Booster clubs (all sports)

_____ Season ticket holders

_____ Special interest groups

_____ Fans

_____ Media

But coaches and their staffs must be willing to do their part, which is making public relations work a priority. The coaches must not only carve out that time but be charming and present during those interactions. The initial goal should be to meet the key people individually and get in front of as many people and groups as possible to ensure their ongoing support of the program and to build a personalized network in the process.

CHART 3.5: EVENT IDEAS

_____   Meet and greet

_____   Spring golf tour

_____   Booster group meetings

_____   Chamber of commerce

_____   Special interest meetings

_____   Receptions

_____   Departmental functions

_____   Camps

Curry was one of several who expressed not only willingness but eagerness to connect with the community when administration pointed her in the right direction. "They know if they call I'll be there whenever, to meet, greet, whatever we need to do, because I want these folks to know I care about them."

Administrators and sports information directors also should help control the integration to some degree. The flip side of appeasing rabid fans and boosters with appearances is the time factor. Coaches can't spend the bulk of their days with a single individual or group. It just isn't practical, not to mention the fact that the lack of time spent on coaching and recruiting will start a downward spiral in which fan support would wane, given the obvious decrease in success the program would suffer. Having someone well-versed in the local scene prioritizing and coordinating those appearances—acting almost as an agent to get the coach's name out in the most productive, efficient way possible while making the most impact—is necessary.

Senior associate AD Judi Henry at Texas Tech explained that balance she struck when helping orchestrate the first weeks of Curry and her staff. "We were trying to manage the communication, trying to protect them to a certain extent so they can spend what quality time they have to spend, because they're going a thousand different directions," she explained. "Some of that is driven by that person, in terms of how much they want it, but you can help set the framework for determining who the most important people for them to know immediately are, particularly in high-profile positions when everybody wants to know them."

That service of coordinating introductions doesn't pertain only to the people in the community. It also includes the athletics department, university communities, and constituents closely associated with the workings of the program. Georgia State athletics director Cheryl Levick met about 300 individuals in her first six weeks on the job.

Gail Goestenkors at Texas valued how Chris Plonsky handled her early in her tenure. "She really helped me navigate my way through who I needed to know here, who could help me in each area, and how to get a hold of them," Goestenkors recalled. "There are just so many people who work here. I was used to having one person in compliance and two people in academic support. There are about 12 in compliance here. I didn't know who to turn to. She helped with the university itself, and then the community. She knew who I needed to be in front of, who I needed to get to know early. My first 20 speaking engagements were ones she handpicked."

SPORT-SPECIFIC ENTITIES

A very important group to the health and growth of a program are the people who work with that sport in various capacities, especially at the local and regional levels. Associates such as coaching colleagues, league and association personnel, referees or officials, and high school and non-scholastic coaches can prove invaluable to understanding, connecting with, and gaining the support of the sports' local community.

Longtime Texas Tech coach Marsha Sharp used her summer camps to assist Curry in at least two ways. The popular event draws players, counselors, and coaches from across the region and beyond, all of whom had previously signed up expecting Sharp's typical involvement. Instead of breaking that commitment, Sharp directed the camps as usual but used the platform to recognize Curry and let Curry focus on acclimating to Lubbock and recruiting rather than running camp.

"There were high school coaches and kids working it, and a lot of our fans had kids or grandkids in the camp," Sharp said, "so it gave us a great place to introduce her to a lot of people who were going to be important to her from a lot of different angles."

Mick Haley used a long-term tactic in winning over club coaches in southern California. "I've always shown them the product, let the kids say it like it is, and help them get better by offering to open my practices or come to my summer camps and work," he said. "It's taken about eight years, but right now I have a pretty good group of people who are appreciative of what we're trying to do and our openness and very supportive even though they might support UCLA and some other people, too."

When Betty Jaynes began shifting the external roles to Beth Bass, she made sure the WBCA didn't lose ground on the relationships. "I was on so many boards: Women's Basketball Hall of Fame, Women's Sports Foundation, NACDA, Georgia Women's Intersport Network, Atlanta Tip-Off Club that oversees the Naismith Awards," Jaynes detailed. "When Beth began to sit on the boards, I would go with her to the first meeting or two, just to introduce her and give her background about the group. She knew a lot of the coaches very well, but she didn't know the people in the athletics administrative world as well."

Similarly, while Nora Lynn Finch knew the vast majority of the people at the ACC office and institutions, there still were many pockets of people with whom she was not familiar. "While I knew the people at the top at Greensboro Coliseum, I didn't know the people who were getting a lot done. I know a lot of the Greensboro Sports Council, but there were still people that I didn't know very well: the marketing people we've worked with, the people with properties that we have relationships with such as Pepsi. I needed to get to know them, and I needed to know how they think and what they need and how Bernie [McGlade] used them and how I can expand that."

DEPARTMENT AND UNIVERSITY

Meeting people within the department and university should entail more than simply attending staff meetings, making casual acquaintances, or knowing who to call for assistance. It is establishing a rapport with those parties and demonstrating a mutual respect. Such an integration into the culture of the communities stands to benefit all parties, as any true partnership does.

In that respect, Jolette Law made sure to follow in her predecessor's footsteps at Illinois. "Once my staff was assembled, we got acquainted with different department heads, professors, and other key players both in the academic and athletics environment," she said. "We wanted to establish that we understood the value of the solid relationships that Theresa Grentz and her staff had made in the past, and that we were willing to extend our hands and try to build those relationships ourselves because we plan to be here a long time."

George Washington University has to be considered a model of how to connect coaches to all members of the university community. Athletics director Jack Kvancz spoke passionately about the importance of bridging that gap between athletics and academics on campuses in relation to promoting assistant coach Mike Bozeman into the top position.

"You're really at fault if you don't involve your students, upper administration, and fans," Kvancz started. "I think you have to expose that person as much as you can to the fans, and that includes students. If you don't do that, I think that's a mistake, because if you have some hard times, then that's tough. If they know what you're trying to do, if they know what your philosophy is, that's really important. The fans and the kids who play—and the students whose team it really is—have to understand what makes the coach tick. If you try to keep them in the back room, the team better be very, very successful, because those are the people you count on [in hard times].

"If I'd have hired somebody from the outside, I would have taken every opportunity to go visit the dormitories," Kvancz continued. "Now Mike has done that on his own, talking to the kids about women's basketball. I think all those things are important, especially if you haven't been around, because they don't know who you are if the only time they see you is the two hours you spend on the bench. You have to do more than that."

Bozeman was in the difficult situation of being recognized and at some levels known in the department and on campus because of his three years on the bench beside Joe McKeown, but the former role no longer was valid with him in the corner office. He credits the university's director of multicultural services, Michael Tapscott, with helping him break through with a new presence.

"Michael reached out and asked me to speak, in conjunction with our men's coach, Karl Hobbs, to some [university] managers about team building," Bozeman described. "I thought that was so crucial to putting my face out there to the community and then to actually have the opportunity to have a sit-down discussion. I think any mysteriousness that came with the new guy on the block could be headed off in that manner. They asked me how I selected my staff—what was important—so it turned out to be like a question-and-answer session. It was almost a town meeting, so to speak, and I thought that went a long way. So now I'm on campus and I see the director of food services, and she says, 'Hey, Coach Bozeman!' Or I went in to get my parking pass, and the manager said, 'I enjoyed talking with you the other day.'"

The other impactful gesture came from GWU president Steven Knapp. "I got a call when I was on the road recruiting, and he wanted to set up a meeting where he came over into my office and sat down and had a conversation with me," Bozeman said. "I'd met him before during the process, but we didn't have a personable conversation. I thought it was great that he wanted to come into my element and sit down with me, and I thought that was very welcoming and reassuring. He wanted me to feel comfortable, so he came to my office, and we talked for 45 minutes to an hour. He shared some stuff with me about his history, and I felt that even up to the president there was a connection with the women's basketball program."

COMMUNITY

Establishing a local presence and attending special events are what most people visualize and plan for when working to get a new hire's face and name better known in the community. Those appearances also are how the fan base calculates the coach's appreciation and approachability. An administrator, and former coach if appropriate, can indoctrinate the new hire on the various groups of supporters, be they booster club officers and members, fans who travel a great deal to watch competitions, big-time donors, corporate sponsors, longtime fans and season ticket holders, and alumni of the program.

Marsha Sharp and Judi Henry at Texas Tech sought that balance of introducing Kristy Curry, maintaining traditions, and involving the steadfast supporters while allowing Curry to be herself and develop relationships with fans who took Sharp's departure very hard.

"We tried to have some continuity from what Marsha had done, but having it be Kristy's own program at the same time," Henry noted. "When you follow such a beloved person as Marsha, there will be people who will never let that go, and you just have to understand that. It was important, too, for her to know who the loyal fans were that she needed to make a connection with. That was another example of where she wanted to carry on what Marsha had done, and she knew that was a strength. We tried to do some things with receptions to give large numbers access to say, 'I've met Kristy.'"

***

The administration should provide a new employee the same safety cocoon that the hard-shelled chrysalis does a caterpillar before it transforms into a monarch butterfly, nurturing and protecting the new hire. Once that framework is built, establishing its trustworthiness takes a dynamic effort. As Mike Bohn suggested, "The most important element of transition is high energy from people who are committed to making sure coaches feel good about what they're doing, being cognizant of the student-athletes, and really paying attention to all the little details that make a difference."

Chapter 4
PASSING THE BATON: Momentum Is Key

The practice of handing down essential information is as old as life itself, and just as critical. Lions don't force their cubs to figure out what to eat and how to get it, ensuring the longevity of the species. Bipeds have shared breakthroughs such as fire, the plow, and technology through the ages, enabling humans to continue making breathtaking advances. Nurses review charts and notes from the previous shift before starting their rounds, moving patients toward better health.

Collective wisdom prevails. Collaboration matters.

Imagine how spectacular women's sports can become if the outgoing employee communicates the wealth of information he or she has gained with the incoming employee, and the new hire esteems the veteran because of it.

The idea isn't novel, but the application in collegiate sports is rare. The concept is straightforward, but the execution isn't automatic. Certainly circumstances dictate the appropriate level of involvement between the two parties. But when all is said and done, it comes down to respect: for each other, for the student-athletes, for the program, for the sport. The new hire respects the outgoing's advances, battles, and longevity. The outgoing respects the new ideas, new era, and track record of the incoming, not to mention the administrator's decision. Everyone respects the players' dedication and effort, the program's ideals and mission, and the sport itself.

Too many times during a transition, the preoccupation with looking better than the other person fosters a culture of subversion that almost always backfires. Egos can get in the way of both the incoming and outgoing employees. The incoming can begin to feel overly important and essentially discard the outgoing. The outgoing can feel a sense of entitlement based on time with the program and demand to be involved. Both attitudes can surface easily, and both are incredibly poisonous. The more the two people take a unified approach and take care of each other—the more they handle the transition as if they're on the same team rather than feuding siblings—the better everyone will look, the more momentum is maintained, and the more polished the end product.

"To me, it was a blessing that I had someone who I respect and look up to—an Olympic coach, a Hall of Fame coach—sit down and pass the baton to me, if you will," Illinois's Jolette Law said of Theresa Grentz. "If I hadn't had those words of wisdom, that caution of those things to look for and be aware of, I probably would have taken five steps backward in my transition. It wasn't an easy transition, but it was easier because I knew what I was about to face. Some situations I encounter and think, 'Wow! Theresa Grentz prepared me for that.' So I wasn't caught off-guard."

The dangers of a disjointed transition are many: the incoming moving forward without proper regard for the foundation on which the program stands; the outgoing not accepting his or her new role out of the spotlight; both trying so hard to stay out of each other's business that their engagement is negligible.

"I was fortunate that the coach before me was more than willing to help," Gail Goestenkors said of Texas legend Jody Conradt. "She was there as much as I needed her, but she was also willing to take a step back and let me grow into this position as well."

Visualize each person's involvement creating a line. The incoming's line represents the balance between revering the past and planning a future. The outgoing's line represents being present enough to help yet not so present as to smother or wrestle for attention. The trick is to find the pathway created by the two lines, and then always to stay on that path. The trail will crook and fork as situations arise, making it sometimes hard to follow. Roots of malice will be placed by others with hopes of tripping someone up. Hidden rocks can cause the careless or inattentive to stumble.

In this case, good intentions *can* pave the path when those intentions are based on humility and admiration. Kristy Curry described the groundwork on which her transition with Marsha Sharp at Texas Tech was based.

"In any profession, there's a lot of jealousy, wanting to prove yourself, egos, selfishness," Curry said. "But throughout this process, I know Coach Sharp has been—and I've tried to be—so selfless, and that just speaks of her character. She just loves the program so much and wants us to do well. And when you have someone who has walked in your shoes every day, it is unbelievable how much difference that makes. And maybe she'd say, 'I would do it this way,' and I would listen. And maybe I'd still do it the way I was going to do it, and she was fine with it, and I was fine if I'd done it the other way. There's no competition here, and that's important."

> *"Just because you choose to use a procedure that's already in place, or you choose not to use a policy or procedure that's already in place, doesn't have any bearing on whether or not you respect the work of the previous or current regime."*
>
> ~Bernadette McGlade

Bernadette McGlade with the Atlantic 10 Conference cautions against judging a person's actions alone and recommends focusing on the motivation instead. "The mutual professional respect is so critically important. Just because you choose to use a procedure that's already in place, or you choose not to use a policy or procedure that's already in place, doesn't have any bearing on whether or not you respect the work of the previous or current regime. Having a respectful appreciation on both ends is probably as valuable in transition as anything. Because most people who step into a job are good enough to get the job done. They're going to figure it out. Again, to have that respect and not to be either departing or stepping into a situation with too much of a territorial or parochial attitude is very important."

Sylvia Hatchell believes that when others are the focus, good things happen, as was the attitude of Betty Jaynes and Beth Bass when Hatchell oversaw their transition at the WBCA. "Betty and Beth both have a tremendous work ethic, but it's not about them. I always believe you get what you want by helping others get what they want, and those two are so committed to helping other people—the coaches—get what they want, and it comes back to them 10 times."

Hatchell's instincts about people—Bass and Jaynes in particular—and leadership skills shined during that transition. So did Jaynes's trust in the foundation of what she had built and in the intentions of others.

"That took a lot of courage," Bass said. "Sylvia told us, 'Beth, the two of y'all will report to the board, and at the end of the day, Beth, you'll have final approval on day-to-day stuff.' And Betty had to have a lot of faith in Sylvia and me, because she built this baby. I knew at the end of the day I had the final call of how to run, administrate, hire, fire, direct, and market. Betty built the process, the governance, and the bylaws, and she had the courage to let go some and see how it worked."

When a monarch butterfly first cracks out of the hard shell of the chrysalis, the description of its wings sounds much like that of a newborn baby: tiny, crumpled, and wet. In the final stage of the butterfly's metamorphosis, a blood-like substance fills and nourishes its body, readying its wings for flight.

Theresa Grentz feels that the role of the outgoing person is similar to that final stage of the metamorphosis, filling the incoming with information and support—professional lifeblood—to complete that transformation. "When you mentor, you want that person who is the new leader to be able to serve and make a difference," she explained. "And it was important for me, when I left Illinois, that I did everything I possibly could to make sure Coach Law had the tools—anything I could possibly share with her—to make that difference. That was important. That's transition."

Two crucial components of maintaining the momentum in a transition are communication between the two employees, both in the very beginning and through a sustained relationship, and each employee genuinely honoring the other in specific ways.

COMMUNICATING

The depth, length, and timing of conversations initially will depend on a variety of factors—previous relationship, proximity, humility—but none perhaps more than the outgoing's future and his or her adjustment to that future. If the outgoing is a coach hired by another university and doesn't have a strong relationship with the incoming, the quality and quantity of direct interaction may not be as rich because of the time constraints and lack of familiarity with each other. Likely, other staff will relay most of the operational information.

If the outgoing is leaving the profession, conversations have a higher likelihood of being more productive. The competitive gene and natural tendency to want to get a leg up on any opponent is nullified, and time may be less of an obstacle.

But if the outgoing is retiring from the profession, capitalize! That person is a wealth of wisdom and information not only about the specific university or program he or she is leaving but about the sport, its climate, and its leadership.

What rarely varies is the value people involved in transitions place on the two parties communicating.

CEAL BARRY, Colorado outgoing: "The more communication between the two coaches the better, so there's no misperception or misconception about anything—the word on the street—just to make sure they're on the same page."

MARSHA SHARP, Texas Tech outgoing: "If I was going to pick one thing that would have to happen for a good transition to take place if the previous coach stays within the community or university, it has to be communication. There's no other way to deal with all the things that happen."

KRISTY CURRY, Texas Tech incoming: "I think the biggest factor that has kept our relationship what it should be is communication between the two of us. You've *got* to communicate."

BETH DUNKENBERGER, Virginia Tech incoming: "If there's ever an option to talk to the person who preceded you, I think it helps."

But it can't just be empty chatter. Jaynes recalled her focus on communicating with Bass. "I can't think of anything I concentrated on more than being honest and forthcoming with every single thing that we do."

With our high-tech world of cell phones, instant messaging, texting, internet, video conferencing, and methods of communication that haven't been invented today but will be all the rage tomorrow, connecting and sharing with others is highly convenient. Meaningful transitional communication doesn't have to take place in person.

"We didn't necessarily need to be face-to-face to communicate, because we both were incredibly busy," Bernadette McGlade explained of her and Nora Lynn Finch's transition at the ACC. "I was physically gone from Greensboro by the time she physically arrived, but we communicated right away. She knew that it really didn't matter what time of the day it was or if it was a weekday or weekend if there was information that was needed or files to be tracked down or just background information on this relationship with this group or sponsor or whatever. We were both experienced and confident enough to know that we didn't have to be sitting in the same room for three days to make our transition. In this world of high technology, we knew it could happen on the telephone or via the internet. You didn't have to think, 'I have to get everything from this person in three days, because then they're going to take this new job and I'm never going to talk to them again or hear from them again.' Anytime that relationship can be established between the person transitioning out and the person transitioning in, it is always a good thing."

SET UP CONVERSATIONS

Whose job is it to reach out? Like everything else, it depends. Conventional wisdom says the burden should rest on the new employee to determine the outgoing's level of involvement. In turn, the outgoing employee should reciprocate those favorable advances with warmth, openness, and maturity.

"I think it's up to the new coach coming in as to how much involvement they want [from the outgoing coach]," Barry asserted. "I think each person would be different with how much advice they want. It's individual, and it's totally within the scope of their comfort level. If they don't want any advice, I think that's fine. If they want to meet with them daily, I think that's fine, too. If they want to talk about basketball, if they want to cry on their shoulder, if they want them to go on a road trip with them—coaching is highly, highly stressful, and the inner circle can include the former coach or not, and that definitely is up to the new coach coming in, not to the old coach. The old coach, 'You had your day in the sun. Move on.' There are probably days Kathy [McConnell-Miller] wished I lived in Timbuktu, but she's been very respectful of the fact that I chose to live in Boulder. She's managed that really well, and I respect her for that. If Kathy doesn't want to talk to me about zone offenses, I totally understand that, because she's got a staff to do that, and she may want to beat the zone a different way than we did."

On the other hand, Theresa Grentz asked the secretary to set up a time to talk with Illinois incoming coach Jolette Law at Law's convenience to have an opportunity to strengthen her potential in the job. "She's going to have a thousand things to do, so I don't want to chew up her time," Grentz told the secretary, "but I wanted to help her sort out some of the necessary things. We had breakfast and talked for a long, long time. We just shared things: what I felt were the strengths of the program, weaknesses where she could correct those things or enable those things to be better served. She was not going to do those things in the first six weeks, but as she went through the process, I didn't want her to step on a minefield.

"It was, 'These are the things I think will be helpful to you. What you do with the information is your prerogative. But you need to know some of these things, and I want you be successful.' My feelings with Jolette were to sit down, give her the lay of the land, explain to her some things I thought would be helpful to know up front, and then get out of her way."

Law was extremely grateful. "I thank God daily that she reached out to me and talked to me about it. That breakfast was the most powerful breakfast that I've had, and I respect her so much for it. She didn't have to do that. She didn't share any negatives with me. She was uplifting and positive. To me, that is the definition of class. She was very classy."

But the communication and relationship can't be dictated, especially by the administration or the outgoing. Perhaps it's similar to dealing with an insecure daughter-in-law or petulant teenager. The more the elder interferes in unwelcome or overbearing ways, the more likely the younger will withdraw, resent, or retaliate.

Colorado athletics director Mike Bohn was in a situation where, as a new hire himself, he didn't have a prior relationship with either Barry, who became a part of the athletics administration, or McConnell-Miller.

"I certainly didn't want to force it," Bohn started. "Ceal's a pro. She was focused on the issues she had at hand, and I think it's important to point out that while we were transitioning through that, we were also going through a very significant financial challenge in the department. We ultimately cut the men's tennis program a year later. Ceal's transition into the SWA role was during that period as well, and Ceal took over the academic support unit for the entire athletics department. She also took a leadership role in overseeing our training table, our training room, and our strength training group, and she began to have her plate full as far as trying to learn all of that.

"Both ladies were trying to focus on the things that were important for their programs," Bohn continued. "Ceal was really working hard to get herself in position to lead those units that obviously are integral to our success, and Kathy was working hard to establish herself in the recruiting ranks and also to be active in that marketplace as well. They were both running so hard there wasn't a lot of time to say, 'Hey, what do you think?' Or, 'What about this?'

"But I think Ceal was in that professional mode of trying to give Kathy as much leeway as possible and to not be in her business but yet be there when Kathy needed her or to talk about different things. In some ways, I think they both were trying to be so professional and so respectful of each other they didn't engage as much as you might think they would to do different things. But it wasn't based on anything other than mutual respect and trying to pull all of that together."

TOPICS OF CONVERSATION

In the most successful transitions, no question is off-limits. Some answers may be more complete than others, such as Betty Jaynes not sharing personnel records and opinions with Beth Bass at the WBCA. But the incoming must feel free to ask any question that comes to mind, and the outgoing may be called upon to help the administration recruit candidates and talk openly to the candidates or new hire about the organization and team—about the land mines and gold mines and everything in between—to ensure the fit is good and the transition begins and proceeds smoothly.

Communication can take place before the interview, during the interview, after the interview, and after the hire, but placing topics in neat, chronological order is impossible. Some people will want some details sooner than others, and personal relationships between those transitioning will alter when some questions are asked and answered. But Bernadette McGlade's attitude about talking with Nora Lynn Finch in their transition at the ACC—"I think the fact that Nora Lynn and I knew and had an understanding right away that no question was too trivial"—must be embraced and adopted for an optimal transition.

Tonya Cardoza leaned heavily on outgoing coach and former Virginia teammate Dawn Staley in preparation for her interview for the opening at Temple. "Throughout the process, she was really helpful, just being able to pick up the phone and ask any question, such as what kind of questions I should ask in the interview, because she would know what exactly would tweak their interest. On my drive to the interview I was so nervous, and she just totally relaxed me. There were probably things I was going to say and do in the interview that, after talking to her about it, she told me not to. So that was really helpful."

CHART 4.1: TOPICS OF CONVERSATION

TEAM AND PROGRAM

_____   Players: skills, injuries, motivation, academics, quirks, interests, social

_____   Players' backgrounds: playing career, families, coaches

_____   Team: talent, dynamics, leaders, strategies and plays

_____   Recruiting: contacts, climate, files, video system

_____   Program: strengths, weaknesses, challenges, history

_____   Budget: opportunities, challenges, inroads

_____   Facilities: scheduling, highlights, issues

_____   Office: space, files

_____   Equipment: apparel, equipment, inventory, contracts, contacts

_____   Competition: scheduling, contracts, guarantees

_____   League: staff, dynamics, competition

_____   Job expectations: pressures, timelines

DEPARTMENT

_____   Administration: roles, personalities, interacting with

_____   Outgoing: reason for leaving

_____   Department: culture, strengths, weaknesses

_____   Support staff: roles, personalities, interacting with

UNIVERSITY OR ORGANIZATION

_____   Institution: strengths, weaknesses, opportunities, threats

_____   Personnel: administration, key professors, key department heads

_____   Academics: profile of university, requirements, class availability

COMMUNITY

_____   Fan base: key supporters, culture, expectations, hot buttons

_____   Media: outlets, key contacts

Kristy Curry at Texas Tech and Gail Goestenkors at Texas requested time with outgoing coaches Marsha Sharp and Jody Conradt, respectively, while on their official interviews. Curry then followed up with Sharp when she moved to Lubbock.

"After she had signed her contract and came back, she had a list of about 25 things she wanted to talk about," Sharp chuckled, wondering if Curry had mentioned this comedic moment. "She said, 'Do you think we could go to dinner?' I said yes, but I thought she should just come to the house, because I didn't feel we'd have a lot of luck in a restaurant trying to get things done. I said, 'I can't cook, but I will throw a couple of steaks on the grill and put on some baked potatoes. Surely I can't do any harm with that.'

"We went in and I had some things about our program displayed around the house. We were looking around and started talking about it all, and I look back outside and the grill looks like it was about on fire. I go out and take that first steak and kind of flip it up in the air, and it lands on the patio. Kristy's first thing was, 'Five-second rule! It'll be fine. I'll eat it.' And I said, 'You are not going to eat a steak I've thrown on the patio. I'll eat it.' And the other one was charred. I haven't tried to cook for her or her and [husband] Kelly or any of them since then. They'd probably be a little nervous if the invitation was extended. We did get to talk about a lot of things, but she probably had to go somewhere after she left the house and get something to eat."

Ceal Barry pointed out that in some cases, the transition team should sit down to discuss and prepare for certain scenarios. "I think a meeting between the athletics director, the new coach, and the old coach would be helpful if [the outgoing] is going to stay in the athletics department," Barry suggested, "just to talk about, 'Here are some of the things you're going to see, things boosters and ticket holders are going to ask you.' I think Kathy and I have handled it pretty well. That's not to say it's been easy. It's been a transition for her to follow me, and I'm not saying that I'm all good, but it's a transition. And it's a transition for me to exit and get behind the scenes."

Sell…But Remain Neutral

Helping an administrator convince someone to take a job you loved but just left is pretty easy, as Jody Conradt at Texas discovered when the Longhorns were courting Gail Goestenkors. "On her trip to Austin, Chris [Plonsky, women's athletics director] set up an opportunity for Gail and I to sit down and talk," Conradt recounted. "I wanted to sell the University, because there is a lot to sell here. I was hopeful it would work out. I guess in a different way it was recruiting."

Bonnie Henrickson did the same when talking with Beth Dunkenberger about the opening Henrickson's departure created at Virginia Tech. "I told her just what a great situation it was, and an unbelievable opportunity—the resources, all the positive things that I really felt as I worked there."

Dunkenberger then followed suit when Kellie Jolly Harper was considering replacing her at Western Carolina. "When she was looking to take the job, I talked to her a lot," Dunkenberger said. "I thought she would be great, and I thought the kids would really like her. The athletics director at Western Carolina was recruiting her to take the position, so I tried to help him in terms of selling the program."

But speaking the truth without commentary—without inserting abundant opinions and anecdotes to influence another's outlook—takes wisdom, self-control, and tact. Beth Bass at the WBCA marveled at Betty Jaynes's consistency in doing just that. "She would spend hours giving me a history of certain things," Bass said, "but she always presented it not to sway me but just to have the background, and that's a talent."

At Texas Tech, Marsha Sharp began her transitional relationship with Kristy Curry by setting the boundaries of what she would share. "One thing we specifically did talk about, and we made a pact from the beginning, was I was never going to extend my opinion about people or things, because I thought it would be unfair for me to predetermine her attitude about something or someone, and particularly the kids you coach.

"One thing we specifically did talk about, and we made a pact from the beginning, was I was never going to extend my opinion about people or things, because I thought it would be unfair for me to predetermine her attitude about something or someone, and particularly the kids you coach."

~Marsha Sharp

"Now, after she'd been here awhile, she'd come back and ask if I had trouble with this, and I'd say yes, because it was something she was struggling with, too. So we could then talk about it a little bit, about some things I felt like helped me find a solution to it or maybe something she could try. But to have a list of people and go through and tell her about them, whether it's kids you're coaching or people you're working for or with, I didn't think that was fair."

Dawn Staley follows that same philosophy in general and applied it to her transition with Temple incoming coach Tonya Cardoza. "I want to give people as much information so they can be successful, but you have to have your own experiences as well. I don't want to give so much of an impression that you go in not open to what you need to be open to as a coach in a different environment, but I was really honest with Tonya."

Cardoza agreed. "Once the process started, I would contact her as often as I needed, and she always was available. She gave me as much background as she possibly could, but she also wanted me to see things for myself, out of my own eyes, and not just take her experiences about what I should expect, but also to have an open mind."

Details

Kathy McConnell-Miller valued Barry's input and assistance on a wide range of questions and topics. "How do we get support from the student body? When we're dealing with recruits, who is the guy in the business office who understands the student-athletes, who wants to engage our future Buffs? How do we do this from a university standpoint? How do we do that from a scheduling standpoint? How do you deal with guarantees? What has been the history with this?'"

McConnell-Miller continued. "We talked about classes, her meeting with recruits if necessary, strength and conditioning, training table, how we make transitioning to Boulder easier for international students. I'm not trying to run out and reinvent things. She's already done all of that. [Former assistant coach] Kris Livingston was also on campus, so there was a really smooth transition about, 'Here we are. This is what we've done. Clearly you're going to do things your way, but let's just tell you how we've done this, where this has been easy and this hasn't,' from facilities to scheduling to recruiting to admissions. It was a pretty easy transition and relinquishing of everything that needed to be handed over. There has been no reservation on her part to engage or to add to what we were trying to do or assist in making my job easier."

Staley added a range of details she talked through with Cardoza. "Things that would affect your budget: travel, recruiting, away games, things like that that they should be aware of that sometimes you don't know going in. Of course you're looking out for what your salary is or your assistant coaches' salaries, but also practice times and facilities that you work out with the men's team because we didn't have a practice facility. Sometimes you have players whose schedules don't always coincide with good practice times, and that could be an issue at some point. But the men's coach is very accommodating, and we worked well together with gym space."

Sharp and Curry also touched on the Big 12 Conference in which Texas Tech plays. "She filled me in on the dynamics of the coaches," Curry said, "the recruiting and how they handle it, how hard it is to play in Ames, all the dynamics of the Big 12 and the Big 12 staff."

It's a coach's job always to push the envelope, whether it's with an individual player, the team, or seeking ways to improve the program. Any progress in making advances is invaluable information for the incoming. Beth Dunkenberger appreciated Bonnie Henrickson's disclosure of what improvements were on the verge of coming to fruition at Virginia Tech.

"Had I not known that type of support was possible, I don't know if I would have pushed for things like that. I do owe a great deal of gratitude to her for fighting for the things she fought for and then sharing all of that information with me."

~Beth Dunkenberger

"There are always things you look for and push for your program to grow so you can keep up with teams in the ACC or other teams in the nation," Dunkenberger explained. "Certain things, like Bonnie felt it should be a priority for our team to travel by charter jet during conference play so we wouldn't miss class, and it's something she hadn't had a lot of success with, but she fought for it and got close. So when I got the job, her information as to where they were in that process, and that it was something we could get, was valuable, because in fact we do charter when there is a situation where we would miss class during ACC play. But had I not known that type of support was possible, I don't know if I would have pushed for things like that. I do owe a great deal of gratitude to her for fighting for the things she fought for and then sharing all of that information with me.

"She'd also fought for money for her assistant coaches, so I knew where they were on the pay scale," Dunkenberger continued. "Coming in, our assistant coaches actually made a bump from what they were paying hers. So it was just good to know that type of thing. Virginia Tech could have shortchanged us, but they didn't. In fact, they did what Bonnie asked for before she left."

Betty Jaynes took her job of transitioning Beth Bass into the executive director position at the WBCA seriously, thoroughly covering every aspect of the organization and answering Bass's multitude of questions so that she knew not only the current details but also the history behind them.

"We'd try to spend about three hours a day the first month or so going over every little itsy bitsy detail," Jaynes reflected. "We went through every phase of the WBCA, from finances to convention programming to food and beverage to selecting hotels to publications to all the committees I served on. We went over every single corporate contract and I told her who the people were involved and why it was hard or why we did it the way we did it. And she would ask questions: 'Tell me why you do reporting lines flat versus vertical? Why is the convention programming like this? Tell me about this or that legislation.' Then she would decide the same thing or change it to the way she thought was best.

"It took us weeks, literally, to go through that, but it was important," Jaynes continued. "I think one of the strategies for our successful transition was me downloading information about people and situations so that Beth at least knew how everything had been done and why it had been done that way. I had walked her through every facet of the organization with the exception of the staff."

> "One of the strategies for our successful transition was me downloading information about people and situations so that Beth at least knew how everything had been done and why it had been done that way. I had walked her through every facet of the organization with the exception of the staff."
>
> ~Betty Jaynes

Nora Lynn Finch capitalized before and after the hiring process on the relationship she and her predecessor at the ACC, Bernadette McGlade, developed over years of working together in the conference. "She could not have been more helpful in answering my questions about what to expect: 'How is John Swofford as a boss? How is Jeff Elliot as a boss? How is he on a day-to-day basis? What happens if you do mess up? How do people react to that?' She couldn't have been more candid. But my relationship with her enabled her to do that. And she knew that whatever she was telling me, I wasn't going to come back and share with anybody. It was just for my needs, not anything else, and I knew her well enough to be asking the questions.

"I had some questions about staff, but not many, really," Finch continued. "People weren't my concern. My concern was the logistics of planning the tournament, when the pieces needed to begin to be put into place, where the limitations with ACC properties were. They're kind of meaty topics. But she knew the answers to every one. I asked about the things I had familiarity about, and I asked Bernie to advise me on things I need to know that I don't know I need to know. She was perhaps too complimentary when she said, 'You're not going to be surprised by anything you can't figure out once you get in it.'

"I guess that's true. Naturally there are surprises. I couldn't know everything this office does: the timelines of when things need to be coordinated with the Greensboro Coliseum with the tournament, what needs to be coordinated with the properties, the marketing side, the media side, all of their timetables. It's further out than it is at an institution. At an institution, you're closer to the actual day of doing something when you announce things and get things rolling. But there are so many hands in the works that everybody has to be involved often. So there are meetings to plan meetings, meetings to plan agendas, meetings to go over the agendas, meetings to go over the handouts at the meeting. There are meetings that are follow-ups to the meetings, and meetings to review the minutes of the meetings, and I've had meetings on how to prepare my minutes and distribute them, because the conference has its own way of doing things and as a formality that is standardized in all of the correspondence that goes out of the conference. The formal correspondence we've adapted to well, but often my correspondence directly to individuals is my usual, casual, Southern way, so I don't put that on letterhead!"

Team and Staff

It takes time as an incoming coach to establish relationships with, build trust with, and get a handle on student-athletes. The outgoing can accelerate that process by providing background information about the players: their personalities, basketball skills, academic skills, off-court interests and issues, and motivational tips.

"She knows the players so well," Gail Goestenkors said of Texas outgoing coach Jody Conradt, "and when you're coming in new it takes time to get to know the players and how best to motivate them. She really was able to give me a jump start in that area in letting me know what the players' strengths and weaknesses were, not just as players but emotionally as well—the things they needed to work on to grow."

Kathy McConnell-Miller at Colorado also was eager to hear outgoing coach Ceal Barry's methods of motivating the players. "'Tell me about each student-athlete. What makes her tick? Does she like being called out in front of her peers or is she wanting me to go behind closed doors?' Things like that. Instead of through trial and error trying to figure it out, just go to the source. She coached her for two years. I'm not above constructive criticism or assistance."

The information Marsha Sharp shared with Texas Tech incoming coach Kristy Curry included but also went beyond the court. "We talked about the players' parents and the dynamics of their environment in high school or junior college," Curry said. "That's one of the first places you need to go."

Sharp recounted their conversations. "We talked about the year we just had, the players who were injured that were going to be back for her who were different from any people she was probably going to see on film that had played that previous season, where the players fit into our offense or defense and that kind of thing. But as far as, 'She's not a gamer,' or 'She's not a practice player,' or 'You're going to have trouble off the floor here,' not any of that took place."

Theresa Grentz stayed true to her mission and relayed information to Illinois incoming coach Jolette Law that would help them all reach their potential. "There were certain things I felt would be helpful for her: knowledge of certain players, an overview of the strong points and certain ways I think you can get players to respond. And then the idea of how I thought the players could go to the next level: 'I think these players can be better. Don't be afraid to push them.' Because the bottom line was, I wanted them to be champions. And I knew they had a great chance to be champions with Coach Law. Now I'm sure, being an intelligent woman, it didn't take her long to figure that out. But she had a little bit of a step up."

Beth Dunkenberger got an even bigger head start at Virginia Tech by virtue of her longtime friendship with outgoing coach Bonnie Henrickson. "I also got a lot of insight [from her about the program] through the years, because when you go through ups and downs with a team, you usually talk to friends about it," Dunkenberger explained. "Whether it was how well one player was doing or how she was having to discipline another player, I knew a lot of history that nobody else would have known, just because we were friends. The kids would look at me a lot of times, and they weren't sure what I knew and what I didn't know."

Recruiting

The importance of recruiting cannot be overstated. Discussions about the team inevitably start with or lead to discussions about recruiting: methods, specific prospects, coaches at various levels who had, have, or might have a line on a special player. Especially for coaches who have taken a position out of their previous state or region, an outgoing's perspective and briefing on his or her experiences and inroads can significantly impact the next couple of years of recruiting.

"We went through all of the high school players they were looking at in the state of Texas," Goestenkors said. "I was really only recruiting one or two while I was at Duke, but they were in on the top 20 players in the state. So we talked through every player—what she [Conradt] liked about them, what they needed to work on, if she thought they'd be a good fit for my style—and then I started making calls to their coaches and to them to continue that process. With the coaches, she said, 'You need to get in touch with *these* high school coaches. They know the area, they're good people, and they'll help you.' That was very helpful to me, because I didn't know many. We had recruited Texas, but not extensively."

McConnell-Miller fired off a string of recruiting-specific questions to Ceal Barry. "'What is it like to recruit to the University of Colorado?' That is mostly what we talked about. 'What was easy about it? What was hard about it? What were the challenges? Can you take an at-risk kid here? Is international an easy way to go? What's the state like? What's your relationship like with coaches in AAU and the high school ranks? What is the perception of Colorado basketball in the state? What do the players growing up think about Colorado basketball? How easy or how difficult is it going to be to attract the best players first and foremost in Colorado, and then nationally, and then internationally?' That was the gist of our first conversation. The most important thing that any coach wants to know is about the recruitment. That's the crux of what we do. That's what our job is based upon—our players."

Henrickson and Dunkenberger took turns filling one another in while playing leapfrog at Virginia Tech for much of their careers after both served as assistant coaches for the Hokies. "We talked every step of the way," Dunkenberger shared. "When I went to Florida, I helped her transition back to Virginia Tech because she'd been gone for a couple of years, like how the recruiting files were based. I spent a lot of time on the phone helping her make that transition, and when I came back she did the same thing. Whether it was picking up the phone to say, 'OK, we have a folder on Jane Doe. Can she play?' it was a big source of comfort to be able to ask a question about something from the past any time I needed to."

Other People

The process of sorting out who is who, learning whom to consult internally, and connecting with people externally is simplified with input from the outgoing employee. Who better will know the intricacies of interacting with such varied groups from such a high-profile position than the person who has been doing so for years?

From Dawn Staley talking with Tonya Cardoza about working with the administrators to Jolette Law learning from Theresa Grentz about "connections on campus and relationships with some of the key people who are going to be very supportive," the outgoing offers a perspective that is impossible to obtain otherwise.

Marsha Sharp places a priority on people, and Kristy Curry described how that transferred to Sharp's approach to the transition. "It's the people that make a place special," Curry said, "and Coach Sharp really made it a priority that I got to know them: everybody from the ticket office to the administration to the academic center; from the training staff to the strength staff; people on campus; where you can get the most help here with this or that; certain people in the community I needed to call or have breakfast, lunch, or dinner with; and she was glad to go with me if I wanted."

More than simply introducing Curry, though, Sharp worked to help her understand the dynamics and feel comfortable with the staff's skills. "We talked about basic things about Lubbock and our fan base," Sharp said. "We talked through our academic setup and who was best to go do that; anything you'd need to know in a university setting that changes from school to school. With all of her support people, like media relations, strength and conditioning, and trainers, I really wanted her to feel confident in their abilities, that she could trust [strength and conditioning coach] Tory Stephens to take care of her summer workouts or whatever it might be."

Be Yourself

Being yourself sometimes is hard enough when you're not replacing a beloved, legendary figure. But throwing that in the mix can cause a person to overanalyze every move, making it tough to find that balance between honoring the past but not living in it. Yet in successful transitions, the outgoing works to unburden the incoming from feeling the need to replicate their methods.

Grentz made that point to Law. "It was important for Coach Law to do things her way. She could not do them Coach Grentz's way and think she was going to succeed. And, yes, we would do things differently."

Joe McKeown understood that things would change at George Washington when Mike Bozeman replaced him, even though Bozeman had been an assistant for McKeown for three years. "We had a great run and won all these games, so there's going to be a natural comparison," McKeown allowed. "'Well, Coach McKeown did it this way. Why would you not do it the same way?' I think it's important to be your own coach, and I think Mike understands that really well."

Curry remembered Sharp's words and attitude fondly during that initial period. "She was just so consistent with her love and concern," Curry said. "She says I have to be me. The way her communication has been is not telling me what to do, or saying you have to do this or that, but saying, 'Here's the information, but you be yourself.' If you try to be anybody other than yourself, you're not going to be successful. You can't be somebody that you're not [for too long] before it catches up with you."

Not even if you're trying to be like someone who is like you, as Bonnie Henrickson, former head coach at Virginia Tech, explained about incoming coach Beth Dunkenberger. "Philosophically we are cut out of the same cloth as far as taking care of kids and working hard and treating kids with respect. But it's her program, and there were some things she wasn't going to like. There's plenty that she changed. She's her own person with her own style, and some of it she felt like worked for her, and I'm sure some of it didn't. But you have to be you, and you have to be comfortable with what you're doing."

CONTINUE STRENGTHENING THE RELATIONSHIP

The outgoing will impart the bulk of the details to the incoming during the first several weeks of the transition. But a richness and quality to the relationship can develop over time if both parties move forward with an attitude steeped in unity, mutual appreciation, and honesty—the same things coaches ask for in their teams. Communication should never end. It's not a short-term task or mid-range project.

Beth Bass knew that trust had to reign supreme for the transition to work. "I just remember saying, 'Betty, one thing I promise you, I will never, ever be dishonest with you, and I'll trust you until you give me a reason not to."

Sharp mentioned another important concept necessary to build a relationship that thrives beyond the initial fact-based phase. "You can't take anything personally, from her side or mine," she explained "There are going to be comparisons every day.

There might still be from time to time. But as long as she and I have that relationship, that just can't be part of. It can't be on our radar screens."

Present a United Front

A united front doesn't materialize at will, much like team chemistry doesn't just happen. It takes a concerted effort, intention, and dedication. It takes consistency, awareness, and desire. It takes respect, continued communication, and humility.

Betty Jaynes and Beth Bass handled what could have been an organization-crippling transition with aplomb at the WBCA. Both were proven leaders and innovators. Both were highly esteemed and successful professionals in their respective fields. Both were used to making decisions.

Wary witnesses referred to the arrangement as a two-headed monster. Staff tried to divide and conquer, or at least divide. A few colleagues succumbed to gossip and manipulation. "All of my friends were having a conniption fit," Jaynes chuckled. But Jaynes and Bass never waivered in their partnership.

"It was funny going out when I was first hired," Bass said. "Mostly women—administrators, people in the game, coaches—would say, 'You've got to be kidding me. Y'all are going to work together and she led the organization for how many years?' I want you to know we did the Obama fist bump before it was popular. 'Just don't ever let them wedge us,' was our motto.

"We had a tremendous trust and appreciation for each other," Bass continued. "I don't remember any kind of formal discussion. It just happened that way. She never disagreed with me in front of the staff, even when we'd be in a knock-down, drag-out, bloodied-locker-room, retreat-in-our-corners-for-a-while-'discussion.' But I think the proudest thing I can say about it is that, even with my senior management today, we never bring things outside the family of the WBCA, and we try to keep it behind closed doors and away from the staff."

Jaynes couldn't believe the number of people who subtly, and not so subtly, hoped for their demise. "What really began to bother us a great deal—and it took us many months before we said anything to the other about it—is, we would be traveling a lot together doing certain things, and people would split us up and want to know how we were *really* doing. The first four or five times it didn't bother me, but then it really began to get on my nerves. At one point Beth asked me, 'Did you talk to so-and-so?' And I said, 'Yeah.' And she said, 'You know what she told me? She wants to know how I'm getting along with you, or are we going to make it.' And I said, 'Isn't that funny? She's done the very same thing to me.'"

Use Each Other as a Resource

An outgoing's resourcefulness does not end once the minutiae is shared, as Texas Tech's Kristy Curry relayed. "The first couple of years, I could really ask Marsha [Sharp] questions about these kids that I didn't really know and ask her advice: 'Who is that? What is this? Where is that? What did you do here? What did you do in Houston?' Now, even though it's starting to be my own players, I can still seek her advice: 'What would you do in this situation? Do you know this coach in Dallas?'"

Jaynes and Bass worked so well together, Jaynes said her retirement has been on hold for years. "We were really planning on transitioning me out in 2000, but right as it began to happen, Beth said, 'Betty, I really want you to think about staying and advising me on this and consulting me on that. Something that was supposed to stop in 2000 is now still going on in 2010."

As Bass put it, "Some people fake their deaths. Betty has faked her retirement for years, which is great for us. Keeping her, her knowledge, and her passion in circulation helps the sport and me so much, so we'll keep Betty involved as long as she lets us."

Jaynes understands and embraces her role as consultant at the WBCA. "The great thing about consulting is you just tell people what you think," Jaynes said. "I do a lot of phone work, just a tremendous amount of phone work, with the coaches and other people. That gives Beth the freedom to see the big picture, be visionary, travel, form strategic alliances, and secure sponsorships. Marketing is such a huge role for her. And she has Shannon [Reynolds, chief operating officer] here to manage NCAA legislation and the staff of up to 21 members during our peak operational periods."

When Bowling Green head coach Curt Miller served on the WBCA board of directors, he commended Bass for continuing to keep Jaynes involved in the organization's operations. But from Bass's point of view, it would be ridiculous not to take advantage of what Jaynes offers. "She's seen everything come full circle, from deregulation of recruiting to being too regulated. She can always say, 'Beth, you can do what you want to, but let me just lay out when we tried this in 1987.' I take that and listen to it. What a marvelous safety net!

"She took the time to download for me whenever she got back to the office from a trip," Bass marveled of those early months. "I *never* got blindsided. She'd say, 'I talked to so-and-so, and they're probably going to call you. They hit me up at halftime and they're not happy about this, this, and this.' That's really considerate. It goes back to communication and trust.

"She definitely has a whole different skill set than mine, and she has a great temperament," Bass continued. "I think it's her wisdom that was so valuable to me as a rookie. She lived through so many wars and in my first battles would try to help me keep them in perspective. She's always so calming: 'I've been there before. This is how we handled it,' or 'I think I would have done this differently if I had a chance to do it over.' In essence that's good therapy. She was very inexpensive therapy in the early going. I'm not proud that I rent my mental health!

"She unequivocally made every single decision the way she thought was for the good of the game," Bass said. "It is unbelievable. She always says you're never bigger than the game, and I believe that. She was always a good barometer if I would go too far one way or the other, or if we were focused too much on this or that,

"Beth listened to Betty. You listen to people who have been there and done that. They can keep you from making a lot of mistakes, and I think Beth did that from day one."

~Sylvia Hatchell

or changing our priorities. Or if a president came in we'd say, 'Do you think he or she has their own agenda?' She'd say, 'I've seen this before,' or 'There was this time,' and 'This is what we did.'"

Then-president Sylvia Hatchell could see the collaboration from a state away. "They just had a special regard for each other. Beth used Betty as a sounding board. Beth would say, 'Here's what I'm thinking,' 'How have we done that in the past?' 'What about this person?' 'Have you met with this person before?' 'This conversation didn't go well,' and they'd talk. Betty would say, 'You have to understand, this is how you deal with this person.'

"They just communicated so well because they believed in the mission of the WBCA and loved the sport of women's basketball so much. Betty wanted Beth to be successful from day one, and Beth listened to Betty. You listen to people who have been there and done that. They can keep you from making a lot of mistakes, and I think Beth did that from day one. As far as new ideas and all, Betty knew what needed to be done. But she was wearing too many hats and she just couldn't get it all done, and so she was saying, 'This is something we wanted to do but hadn't been able to do.' So they were great at implementing and taking new ideas and running with them."

Keep Each Other Informed and Involved

The first step in communication is recognizing you or someone else has something to share. The importance of certain bits of information will be very obvious. But more often it requires a vigilant awareness, stepping outside of oneself and looking at the picture through the other's eyes. It is not surprising that the Betty Jaynes/Beth Bass and Marsha Sharp/Kristy Curry teams nailed this aspect of the transition.

Curry and Sharp have kept the lines of communication, and the opportunities for participation, open and flowing, as Curry reflected. "If something was going on that I felt like she needed to know with those kids, there wasn't a time I didn't pick up the phone and call, because Coach Sharp has her heart in the right place. I know she's not behind you stabbing you in the back.

"I want her at every game, at every function," Curry continued. "For the alumni day, for instance, the letters going out were from both of us. When [former Lady Raider] Alicia Thompson came back into town, I wanted Coach Sharp presenting that ball, not me. She played for Coach Sharp. Alicia knows I care, and she knows I'm going to continue the tradition, but you have to know when to step aside.

"And I want to know how I can help her. She has the Marsha Sharp Leadership Circle. How can I help with that? How could I help with the Kay Yow tournament in Dallas? She's tried to include me in events, whether it's charitable organizations at her house, or Leadership Circle events, or anything with the WBCA. She's always kept me informed of anything she might be aware of, and I've tried to do the same. There were even times she'd call me to communicate something she knew that maybe I didn't. It goes both ways."

Sharp appreciated Curry's openness and trust. "She's been awesome to me. We talk as often as once a week. Sometimes it's a little less just because it seems like between us we're usually out of town. But she's been terrific in trying to keep me involved in the program some and feel like I'm updated on things that have gone on, particularly as long as some of the players I had recruited were playing. If there was an injury that occurred or they were having an issue with something, she always allowed me to know about that. 'Coach, if you want to call them, they'd probably love to hear from you.' She was great about keeping me involved. I don't think that will be quite as important with kids from now on, because I don't know them as well. But with those kids I had a lot invested in and really knew—and had known for a lot of years through the recruiting process—I really appreciated her trusting me to do that."

HONORING

When you get right down to it, the elements of a smooth transition are as simple as the incoming and outgoing employees respecting and honoring each other and each other's position, whether in the spotlight or out of it. Both are tough places to be, with unique challenges, but each person has continual opportunities to make the other's life easier and better.

Honoring another person through words and actions shows respect. Honoring can occur at any time, in any place, under any circumstances. It requires neither money nor elaborate plans but only an acknowledgment of a person's right to be respected, a panoramic view of the situation, and a heart of humility.

Sylvia Hatchell's description of the relationship between Jaynes and Bass reveals a number of ways they honor each other, including respect, protection, and deference. "Betty and Beth have done a tremendous job, and we're very blessed and fortunate to have them running our organization. From day one, it's been about communication and being on the same page, that spirit of oneness. I said, 'Beth, you're going to be the boss, but you *must* take care of Betty.' And Betty has never felt threatened by Beth. In fact, she's almost like a mother to her. Betty has embraced Beth and done everything she could to help her be successful. Betty in many situations has made Beth look good.

"And Beth will tell you she could not have survived without Betty, because Betty would pick up the pieces, smooth things over sometimes, go in there and say, 'Beth, you need to think about this,'" Hatchell continued. "She'd never say, 'You have to do this,' or 'This is not good,' or 'You made a bad decision here.' But she'd say, 'You need to think about this, and this is why.' And Beth would. So a big part of their relationship is respect. Betty respects Beth's enthusiasm, her youth, her abilities. And of course Beth respects Betty's knowledge and what she's done for the organization."

Bass's quick implementation of a vision regarding the WBCA's headquarters is a prime example of the pair's determination to survive and use of humor to thrive. "Our offices were upstairs, and the whole downstairs was an orthodontist practice," Jaynes began. "And from the day Beth walked in here, she wanted to make the downstairs into our face to the community, to be more authentic and just speak basketball. She wanted people to open the door and see the conference room with the gym floor and the basket and go, 'Wow!'

"I wasn't that set on it, because we would have to borrow money, and I'm probably more conservative than she is," Jaynes admitted. "So Beth came in and said, 'This is what I want to do, and this is how we're going to do it. But the downside of it, Betty, is we're going to have to take half of your office, because that's where the stairwell has to go to be up to code. And you're going to have to cover up everything in here because the dust is going to be so bad.'

"And I said, 'Where am I going to go?' She said, 'Betty, it wouldn't take but three weeks. You and I can share my office.' Well, instead of three weeks it was more like six months. And we got a little irritated with each other because we had no space to ourselves. We could never have a private conversation. I think she felt the same way. There would be some mornings Beth would call me and say, 'I really think it's best if you work from home today.'

"But Beth has such a keen sense of humor," Jaynes laughed. "For example, I have DirecTV and would watch so many games, I wouldn't be able to hold my head up some days. Beth would come in, sit cross-legged on my huge desk, and pretend to give me a hard time about coming in too late, not being able to work. 'I'm going to turn you in to Sylvia Hatchell,' she'd joke. She was just so good at trying to make things work."

Bass marveled at Jaynes's ability to adjust. "Not many people could go from having the biggest office to sharing an office to being in a storage cubicle," Bass said. "But Betty did it and had a ball. She just keeps adapting and enjoying herself. I call her the godmother of women's basketball—she was instrumental in the growth of the modern game—and now she's obsessed with her Blackberry and Twitter."

The art of honoring isn't limited to the incoming and outgoing employees. Judi Henry described the scene at Texas Tech's final home game of the 2005-06 season, its first after news of Marsha Sharp's retirement became known just days prior. "With that last game being against [Oklahoma and head coach] Sherri Coale, it says a lot about who Sherri is in how she handled that," Henry said. "Her kids came out during warm-up wearing the special T-shirts we had made for the fans that read 'Thanks Marsha from Lady Raider Nation' on the front and listed all of her accomplishments on the back. It was special because it was Sherri and because she had kind of taken the leadership role in Big 12 women's basketball and even at the national level in understanding that there's a need to provide leadership for younger coaches in women's basketball."

BY INCOMING

Tightrope walkers don't look down when they're on the wire. They set their eyes on a fixed point ahead and, step by step, proceed toward the goal with an incredible balance based on practice and feel. The same approach—keeping the bigger picture in mind, taking each step with deliberation and grace—will steady an incoming's balancing act between paying tribute to the outgoing while maintaining a sense of self and making improvements to the program.

"The tough thing when you're a new coach of a program is sometimes you want to honor the past," Texas's Gail Goestenkors said of the quandary, "and certainly with Jody [Conradt] being a legend. But you also want to get your players pumped up and excited about the future. So sometimes it's a fine line that you have to walk with the media to make sure you're excited about the future while at the same time you respect the past."

Kathy McConnell-Miller at Colorado developed a saying by which she, her staff, and her team kept their objective at the forefront of their minds. "My philosophy throughout has been that we respect the past—the traditions and former players— we celebrate today, and we enjoy tomorrow."

Sometimes a sense of history helps. Texas Tech's Kristy Curry witnessed firsthand the development of the sport in the region, and the experience gave her a sense of peace about following in Sharp's footsteps. "Growing up in north Louisiana and having a chance to watch Louisiana Tech, Delta State, Texas, Texas Tech—I mean, those were the premier programs. That's how women's basketball became women's basketball in my opinion. I don't think there's anybody who has more respect or admiration or appreciation for what Coach Sharp has built here, and that's why it probably didn't scare me [to follow her]. I'm not afraid to walk in her shadows. I'm very honored and I consider it a privilege to carry on the tradition she has in place."

Temple associate athletics director Kristen Foley credited Tonya Cardoza's self-confidence and genuine respect for outgoing coach Dawn Staley for unyoking herself, her team, and the department from what could have been pressure-filled, awkward discussions about the direction of the program.

"Right from the beginning, in her interview, she paid tremendous respect for what Dawn and this program did, and she continued that with comments at the press conference," Foley explained. "You know you're going to get those questions: 'What's the difference [between Cardoza and Staley]?' And she doesn't hide that, doesn't forbid those types of questions. She's not afraid, and that makes the players unafraid. She openly talks about the change to more offense. We'll be the first ones to say, 'Gosh, we only shot 31 percent last year and now we shoot 40 percent.' She's very open and confident about what she stands for and what's different about her philosophy—her Xs and Os—than what's been done in the past. She

> *"Right from the beginning, in her interview, she paid tremendous respect for what Dawn and this program did, and she continued that with comments at the press conference. She openly talks about Dawn and isn't afraid of what she created, and certainly appreciates it and knows because of what Dawn did that she is going to be able to take it to another level because of her own experiences."*
>
> ~Kristen Foley

started that right from the beginning, and that really helped. She openly talks about Dawn and isn't afraid of what she created, and certainly appreciates it and knows because of what Dawn did that she is going to be able to take it to another level because of her own experiences. She just showed that respect from the get-go. She could walk that line, had that confidence, but has the same respect and makes the players know that as well. They're not afraid to talk about it—not afraid to talk about Dawn in front of her—which is great. A different coach brought them in and that's OK. You're still going to have a relationship with that coach. Tonya encourages that, and that's quite confident for a first-year head coach."

Pay Respect to the Past...

The past isn't the enemy, and the previous coach isn't the adversary. Regarding either as such is counterproductive at best and insolent at worst. Conversely, the benefits reaped when the incoming points the spotlight on the successes of the past are immeasurable.

Lisa Love credited Mick Haley's tributes to the history of the Southern Cal volleyball program under both Love and interim head coach Jerritt Elliott with softening any potential dissent about the way that unique transition played out. "He was very complimentary of the efforts, and that comes from being a very confident coach and having a confident perspective, which lent itself to a lot of respect for what Jerritt had done and even I'd done before Jerritt. It also helped warm him up to any constituents who maybe had wanted to extend their loyalties to someone else. He wasn't hesitant to extend compliments to past efforts."

Mike Bozeman so esteemed the past that he saw no need to revamp what had been done. "I didn't have to come in with all these demonstrative ideas of how I was going to make the program successful," he declared. "It already was. I didn't have to reinvent the wheels. I just had to keep the wheels rolling. It would have been a drastic mistake for me to downplay what Joe McKeown meant to the program. I think what helped with the smooth transition is that I accepted the fact that he established the program, he built the program, and my role now is to carry that on. I don't feel like I'm in competition with Joe McKeown's legacy. I can't compete with that right now. Now give me 20 years, and I still may not be able to compete with it, but at least you'd have some measure. I may change the curtains, put in a new chandelier, put some polish on some things, but I accept the fact that this is the house that Joe built.

"I think my peers were expecting for me to do it in a different manner," Bozeman continued. "So their concerns were, would I be able to carry it on without bucking the system? But I have so much respect for what he did. And sitting in this position now and seeing some challenges I face in recruiting, trying to get the top-notch student-athletes versus some of the schools that have amenities we can't compete with, sometimes I sit back and say, 'Wow! How did Joe do this for 20 years?' My respect for him was genuine. It wasn't something I was fabricating."

Curry's regard for her predecessor at Texas Tech could not be any stronger. "I can't be Marsha Sharp, but I can embrace the past with so much love and respect," she acknowledged. "Honestly, all I really care about is continuing to run this program with the class and integrity that she has, and hopefully she'll enjoy being a part of what we're doing and be pleased with what we're doing."

Judi Henry reflected the praise back to Curry. "I have never heard Kristy speak publicly, and particularly early on, without first acknowledging Marsha and her program, the things she'd done for this community and the type of people she turned out of the program," Henry said. "She never for one second lost sight of that in my mind. As excited as she was about the opportunity, it could have been all about her, but it wasn't."

Beth Bass at the WBCA couldn't help but honor Betty Jaynes. "That's how I was raised," Bass said. "You show somebody respect, and you appreciate what they've done for you personally as well as for the sport. You give back and you take care of those people who have given you the opportunities you have. I'd be venting about the job or work to my parents and they'd listen and then ask, 'How are you treating Ms. Jaynes?' That was the most important thing to them."

"I have never heard Kristy speak publicly, and particularly early on, without first acknowledging Marsha and her program, the things she'd done for this community and the type of people she turned out of the program. As excited as she was about the opportunity, it could have been all about her, but it wasn't."

~Judi Henry

The answer, according to Jaynes herself, was very well. "Beth was so great about mentioning me and acknowledging what I had done any time she spoke, whether it was at one of the board of directors meetings or in a speech or in an interview. She would say her number one priority was to make sure I was acknowledged and rewarded. She's been very instrumental in all of the awards that I've been nominated for, from Halls of Fame to the Distinguished awards. She's worked hard to make sure the nomination is there. I might not get it, but she always takes pride in the fact that Betty's name is in the hat. She often calls herself my 'pseudo publicist.' And she made sure everybody knew of our mutual friendship and admiration, which was apparent because she would do a lot of teasing."

...While Moving Forward

It's helpful for everyone to remember that the administration hired the new employee for a reason. They thought that person was the best choice to keep the program progressing. Each step creates a slightly different scenery, perspective, and subsequent plan for the next step, all in the name of getting better. That's what the outgoing was doing when he or she was in the position, and that's what the incoming strives to do.

Change is inevitable, but the manner—the process and the attitude—in which the incoming makes changes, implements his or her own philosophy, and interacts with others will determine how much momentum is gained or lost.

"I just want to embrace the past and build on the future, and make things even better," Kristy Curry said of following Marsha Sharp at Texas Tech. "When I say I want this to be better, it's not because the past wasn't really special already. That's what she would do if she was sitting here. She would want things to be better than they were a year ago, four years ago, five years ago, whether it's the support we get in the community, financially, or recruiting. Whatever we're doing, she'd want it to be better. I tell our team every day, 'We either get better or worse. There's no staying the same.'"

> *"I just want to embrace the past and build on the future, and make things even better. That's what she would do if she was sitting here. She would want things to be better than they were a year ago, four years ago, five years ago, whether it's the support we get in the community, financially, or recruiting."*
>
> ~Kristy Curry

Colorado was experiencing a tremendous amount of change when Kathy McConnell-Miller stepped into the opening created after Ceal Barry moved from coaching into athletics administration for the Buffaloes. Athletics director Mike Bohn described a department experiencing growing pains.

"Kathy was trying to emerge as a leader and the one who's driving the ship in women's basketball, and I think that was not easy because Kathy was so respectful and cognizant of the past," Bohn said. "Obviously there were a lot of things about the past that worked well, and why would you want to reinvent that?

"On the other hand, she recognized that with the talent in the league and the conference that we play in, she would have to change some things and begin to evaluate how we could put things together and really escalate the program," he continued. "We had to play catch-up in facilities, in the way we travel, and the way we do things to help these programs grow. So we were really in a growth mode for all of us, not only on the specific areas that Coach Miller was responsible for, but also Ceal's area and hopefully as the athletics director, too. As all three of us come together, then it really becomes contagious and all three legs of the stool, if you will, help the entire women's basketball unit become more and more prominent and successful."

A necessary part of integrating a new leader into the fabric of the university is branding that program with the face and personality of the incoming employee. That process is what can be so disconcerting to those close to the program or disruptive to the program's forward motion if done brashly. Barry's wisdom shows in her acceptance of that reality.

"Kathy has been nothing but respectful of the history and tradition of the program," Barry stated. "She makes a point to compliment or point out some of the strengths of the program in place before she arrived. But she has to establish a name for herself. It's not Ceal Barry's program anymore. It's Kathy McConnell-Miller's. I think she's savvy in terms of marketing and knows she has to brand it with the

McConnell-Miller brand and not the Ceal Barry brand, and she's done that very well."

In the case of the WBCA, the branding was less about who was in charge and more about the organization's presentation, image, and visibility among its constituents, corporate sponsors, and fans. When Bass became its executive director, she brought her marketing acumen to a burgeoning organization that Jaynes had nurtured beyond its current staffing.

"The first thing I did was assure her that I respected her and needed her [in order] to be successful, and that I would do my best to make good decisions and keep the association moving in the right direction," Bass revealed. "But with the kindest respect to Betty, part of my job was to come in and update the imaging and branding. I was really into the marketing and merchandising—that felt really natural to me and played to my strengths.

"The next phase was to get people more engaged and continue landing high-profile coaches on our board of directors," Bass described. "Then after four or five years we really started to gain some traction in impacting the governing structure of the NCAA, and key to that was the leadership of Donna Noonan and Sue Donohoe. Then when you start having an impact on access points that determine how our game is played, officiated, and administrated, you gain credibility not only with association members and the coaching community but also with administrators on campuses and in other organizations."

Despite Bass's eagerness to dive into her forte, she did so with respect, as Jaynes recalled. "Anytime she wanted to make a tremendous change, she always would tell me. It was somewhat hard, but you have to let it go. I've had to learn to do that, to understand that my opinion isn't always going to be the one that we go with, but she doesn't slam it down your throat."

Traditions are powerful tools to ground people, to preserve links to the past, to comfort people with familiarity. Traditions have their place, but they don't—and shouldn't—always survive a transition, as Gail Goestenkors explained.

"Texas had done things a certain way with boosters, like meeting with them after games, and those were some of the things that were different than what we had done," Goestenkors said of her Duke days. "So Jody told me why they had done it and I told her why we hadn't, and we talked about what might be best heading forward with the boosters."

Chris Plonsky elaborated, shedding light on the administrator's role in maintaining a program's customs without being held back by them. "There were some things she was going to change that we expected," Plonsky said. "She closes her practices, although she has a couple open for fans' sake. It's a different day and age. She eliminated some postgame opportunities that had been traditional here. That was something that we as a staff had to take on and educate our fans about. We felt that Gail was making the decision in the best interest of our competitive ability, that we had a group of student-athletes who had not succeeded. Technically, when you're up in front of fans and being able to publicly comport yourself, that is a reward, and it crossed our minds that maybe we were creating reward settings without earning them. Many of our fans were disappointed, but if we aren't winning, it doesn't matter how friendly we are, we're out of sorts with our mission. We asked that they let her get the kids moving in a different direction. They hadn't realized their potential. Let's make some progress, go through an entire competitive cycle, and then reevaluate."

BY OUTGOING

The more quickly an outgoing recognizes and fully accepts the basic concept that the goal still is improvement, the better he or she will understand and accept the inevitable modifications to the program. When the incoming says he or she wants things to be better, it's not an automatic dis.

Just as the authenticity of an incoming's actions depends on respect, the outgoing's hinges on humility. One general message to an outgoing is: "Your way isn't the only way, and even if it is, it doesn't matter, because you're not in charge anymore." It's that simple.

"When people leave jobs, it's time for someone else," former Illinois coach Theresa Grentz believes. "It's time to support them. When a lot of people leave jobs, they're bitter, they're upset, they wish bad things and hope they [their replacements] never do well. It's sad. I did what I did to the best that I could. Could I have done some things better? We all could do things better, but you do as well as you can. When Jolette Law came in, she was the new coach. It was not my program anymore. It was Coach Law's. It was my job to enhance her performance as the head coach. And I was going to do that as well as I possibly could so she could succeed. I was going to give her the information that I thought she should know, up front, so she didn't have to start looking for it. 'Here it is. You do what you need with it, but you have it.' And then get out of her way.

"I wanted it to be a very amenable bridge, that she knew she could call on Coach Grentz with anything she needed, if she needed it," Grentz said. "A lot of times with women that doesn't happen, and that's unfortunate. But I was determined as I made these moves that this is what I was going to do. I love Illinois. It was a great run. I loved working for Ron Guenther. I love the school. But in this case I look at the situation and say, 'It's time for someone else.' And I want that someone else to have every opportunity to be successful and to take care of the players that had come in under my tutelage."

Jaynes's grace in the transition with Bass at the WBCA was remarkable given her continued in-depth work in the organization. Most outgoings have the luxury of finality and distance to help them adjust to their new, greatly diminished role in what sometimes has been their life's work. But Jaynes remained in the office, not reporting to the new employee (Bass) but suddenly not in charge of all operations, either.

Her sense of her new role and Bass's was apparent in how she interacted with others. "In staff meetings, if Beth was gone and I had to run them, I would always say, 'Beth asked me to say this,' or 'By Beth's permission...,' or 'Under Beth's auspices...,' so they would know I wasn't on an island making decisions."

Be Appropriately Engaged

The line outgoings must walk separates support from suffocation, indifference from incessancy. The term "appropriate" is frustratingly nebulous, especially for outgoing employees who remain in the area. Should outgoings attend home games or not? How often do they engage the media? Do they saunter the halls of the department regularly? When should they send well-wishes or encouragement to the incoming?

Chris Plonsky remembered one line in particular Jody Conradt said to Gail Goestenkors: "'I'll be as far or as close as you need me to be,' because she did not want to intrude on the process. The time she spent with Gail was at Gail's request." In Goestenkors's words, "She's given the players and myself the space we need to grow together."

Four outgoings—Marsha Sharp (Texas Tech), Bernadette McGlade (ACC), Conradt (Texas), and Ceal Barry (Colorado)—had common, though still vague, thoughts on the subject.

SHARP: "I really just tried to stay underground. I tried to stay away and out of the way but at the same time not so far out of the way that it doesn't seem like I'm supportive. I don't go to all of the games, but I go to some of them. I've been to one practice since Kristy [Curry] has been here, just trying to be supportive without it appearing that I'm hovering over her shoulder. That's kind of a fine line to walk for everybody, not just me."

MCGLADE: "You need to be cognizant of stepping away. I believe it's always better for the new person to initiate contact: 'Hey, what about this or that?' And you do have to step away and let the new person feel their way a little bit. When they need a question answered, they're going to get around to finding you to get the answer."

CONRADT: "I really felt as if I needed to, once the hire was made, become invisible, and I tried very hard to do that. I was never visible at a game. I never lent advice unless asked. I just went about my new life. I think Gail always new I was available, but she needed to do things her own way and make her own decisions, and certainly I wanted to respect that."

BARRY: "For me, I felt like it was really important that I be invisible as much as possible. Now, if Kathy [McConnell-Miller] invited me to be at something, I tried to attend. But if you're going to have a reception for your scholarship donors, you don't want them talking to the former coach. You want the donors talking to the new coach and the new staff. I was respectful of the fact that she had to build this program. And I was really trying to adjust to a new job myself. So the early stages and my whole first couple of years were a blur because of the learning curve I had trying to do my job.

"Kathy asked for a few things she felt like she needed in those student services areas, which I think was a really good thing," Barry continued. "But as far as basketball, her style was different. I think what she wanted to do was establish herself and not have me looking over her shoulder. I don't know any coach who'd want to have the former coach coming to practice, evaluating practices, evaluating her recruiting, that sort of thing. It was really in the scope of my job where she asked for my support, which I was happy to give her.

"But I decided to go to the games my first year. I was an administrator, I had an interest in watching, I knew all the coaches and officials, and I said hello to all of them. I wanted to make that transition. Now it's much easier for me to walk into the gym to a practice or a game. The other day Kathy and I sat and talked for about 30 minutes prior to a game, and I think part of the reason we can do that now is because I decided to go from the beginning. I wanted to get to normal as quickly as I could."

McConnell-Miller offered a similar view of Barry's approach. "She tried not to cross that line. There were opportunities for her to come to some functions or things, where if she did come possibly the focus would have been on her and not necessarily me or what we were trying to do, because of the awareness of who Ceal Barry was and her relationships with all of these people. She was really good at stepping back and saying, 'This is Kathy's time. You need to get to know Kathy and her philosophy.' For her to come into certain arenas, meetings, parties, functions, whatever, there was the stepping back of saying, 'You need to get to know her style and her team.' That was the support that we both felt was necessary."

Sharp tried to lend some philosophical form to what exactly "appropriate" entails. "Try to put yourself in their situation," she suggested, "sensing when it might be time to make a call and see if there's anything you can do and when it's not necessary. I think that discernment is something you'll know."

Voice Support to the Team

Perhaps the most important way an outgoing coach can honor the incoming coach is by boosting the team's confidence in the successor. The players likely had the closest relationship with—and thus are most devastated by the departure of—the outgoing. They also have the most at stake in developing relationships with the incoming, relationships that are key to the success of the program.

Thus, a vote of confidence from that authority figure will go a long way toward the players having a positive attitude about the transition, as evidenced by those at George Washington and Virginia Tech.

"We had a couple of team meetings," GWU outgoing coach Joe McKeown said. "I told them, 'Obviously you know what you're getting with Coach [Mike] Bozeman. You played for me and I recruited you, but he's been with you every day, too.' They understood that. I think they were glad they got somebody who'd been with them."

Bozeman felt the gesture was key. "Joe called the recruits' families and explained the situation. He, the guy who was recruiting them, put the stamp of approval on me after I was hired."

Bonnie Henrickson did her best to assuage the fear and uncertainty in the Hokies before and after she learned that Beth Dunkenberger would follow her at Virginia Tech. "She let the team know they may hate her leaving, but they would be very happy with who they brought in, so just hang on," Dunkenberger said. "I think that reassurance from someone they knew and trusted—that they would be OK, that the new person coming in really was good—really helped."

Dunkenberger also credited Henrickson's blessing of the new staff with keeping a local recruit at home. "Brittney Cook is from about 30 minutes from Blacksburg," Dunkenberger said. "She's been a camper at Virginia Tech and committed very early in her high school career to Virginia Tech. Obviously she was very close to Bonnie and her staff, and she was devastated when Bonnie left, because all she knew and associated with Virginia Tech was Bonnie. Bonnie had called and told them they would be very happy with the choice, they would be fine, we would take good care of them. When we got the job, she and her family came to campus on our first or second day here and met with all of us. We have a great relationship, but it was one where a lot of Brittney's faith in our staff was based on trust because of the recommendation that Bonnie gave."

Tonya Cardoza of Temple spoke of the unselfishness that is required for an outgoing coach—Dawn Staley in her case—to advocate for the replacement. "When Dawn decided to take the job [at South Carolina], and some of the players were thinking about transferring or leaving, she said to them, 'Before you do anything you need to wait, because if Tonya gets the job you'll really enjoy playing for her.' That was probably the biggest help, that she was behind me and supporting me and letting them know everything was going to be all right and to just give me a chance, where someone else could have been like, 'Follow me. Come to my [new] school.'"

Theresa Grentz began her campaign for the incoming coach at Illinois before the administration had even hired one when she directed the team to give whomever it was their full support, and she continued doing so after Jolette Law was hired.

"Theresa did a good job of setting the stage, saying it's time for her to move on to another juncture in her life," Illinois athletics director Ron Guenther said. "Theresa communicated to them that things are going to be good, that things are good here, that they have an administration that's going to support basketball."

"She never said anything negative directly to the kids," Law noted. "She just told them, 'Trust and follow this woman. She knows what she's doing.' Whenever there was anything negative being said, she would always push the positive. She just told them they should be blessed to have someone who knows the game, who's been there, who knows what it takes to help them get to where they want to go."

Show Support Publically and Frequently

Public displays of support may not be as critical as support among the team, but communication with external parties about the incoming staff and the new direction of the program is so much more visible and open to interpretation that missteps could be as detrimental as poor team reaction to the staff.

"Every once in a while, people would start asking questions like, 'Do you like this? What do you think about this?'" Marsha Sharp recalled of questions she got after resigning from coaching at Texas Tech. "If I wanted to be involved in that, I'd still be coaching. There's nothing in me that wants to do those things or wants to make any judgments about the way she's doing it. That's not even on my radar screen.

"The most important thing is, every single word that comes out of your mouth has to be positive," Sharp continued. "I would never have gone out and intentionally said something negative, but you can't even say it in a way that could be translated that way. For instance, someone says, 'You know, they didn't play well tonight.' If my response is, 'They didn't play very well tonight,' all of a sudden it gets back that I'm up in the stands telling people we weren't very good. You just don't do that. You just can't."

Ceal Barry found comfort in working as a broadcaster for Fox Sports Net Rocky Mountain during Colorado women's basketball games. "Everything I say during the games is over the air, so it's easier than if I sit with so-and-so and say something. 'What's Coach Barry saying?' I may be saying I have to go to the bathroom, please hold my seat. So it was very helpful for me at the games."

What she did say about Kathy McConnell-Miller and the program, during those broadcasts and in other interviews, was very positive. "I actually think Ceal has gone overboard at times with recognizing what we're doing," McConnell-Miller considered. "We got the player of the year in the state last year, and Ceal would come out publicly and say, 'I never would have gotten that done.' Or she'll say, 'Brittany Spears could be one of the best freshmen to play at Colorado.' And to me, that's a pretty bold statement considering she's recruited the last 19 classes. So she's complimentary of the team when she speaks. She promotes our program, and she promotes me."

Grentz did the same thing in Urbana-Champaign—one-on-one and in groups, in person and in writing—to endorse Law and encourage the community to back her. "I sent the Cager Club and the Courtsiders notes, thanking them for their help," Grentz explained. "My comment was always, 'Make sure you take care of this next head coach as well as you took care of me. It's going to be a great team.' I would do the same thing when I was in the community. 'Support this coach and this team the way you've always done it.' That was my battle cry."

Law felt the affirmation even more personally. "With the breakfast that she took me to, she made sure that everyone knew this was going to be a smooth transition, that she believed in the direction of the program. She made it very, very clear that she was very supportive of me. So I think the community seeing us together, talking and sharing, made the transition smoother. I never felt that she didn't want me to be successful."

SPECIFIC WAYS TO HONOR

Incoming and outgoing employees can honor each other in more ways than simply choosing their words carefully. Specific actions and events, in conjunction with good communication, can create a culture of honor and respect that is impossible for the team and public to miss. That goodwill and collaboration can start an upward spiral, generating more of the same.

Grentz and incoming George Washington coach Mike Bozeman began the new chapters in their lives by bestowing small but heartfelt gifts to their counterparts.

"When I first got the job, I went and bought them a bottle of wine," Bozeman said of Joe and Laura McKeown. "I showed up at his house and had the bottle of wine, and his wife sees me first and started crying. We all talked. It was great. That was my small way of honoring them and thanking Joe for what he had done in helping me with this position."

In addition to the goal of leaving Law with information she might need to be successful, Grentz also wanted to set the stage for a smooth future with the Illini. "I had a book for her," Grentz remembered. "I wanted to give that to her and wish her well, let her know where I was coming from, and that this was ongoing. Because there will be times I go back to Illinois. There will be teams honored, players honored, and I want to be able to walk into that gym. I want to be able to acknowledge that coach and that team."

CHART 4.2: WAYS TO HONOR OUTGOING

_____   Acknowledge at public events, in media interviews

_____   Recognize at game

_____   Check in at significant times: first practice, first game, etc.

_____   Involve in fund-raising efforts

_____   Inform about issues surrounding players they recruited

_____   Include in correspondence for alumni day

_____   Be aware of traditions and records

_____   Keep significant décor

_____   Include in publications and posters

_____   Retain staff when reasonable and appropriate

_____   Present with a small gift

_____   Communicate

Law, in turn, honored Grentz in a number of ways, but perhaps none more revealing of her genuine feelings for Grentz than by a personnel decision. "I respected the former coach so much I kept her son, Kevin Grentz, as my manager. If I didn't respect her there's no way I'd have her son—her blood—as one of my family."

Bozeman also relayed an anecdote from a recruiting trip that emphasizes McKeown's down-to-earth nature and continued support of Bozeman. "You're on the road so much, you get your favorite people you're going to eat lunch with. There was an event here in the Washington, D.C., area, and I was sitting with some buddies that I always ate lunch with as an assistant coach. I refused to try to change or feel I needed to hang in different circles because now I'm a head coach. But Joe made a point to come out and meet with me there, with my buddy crew. And he sat with us and he was just one of the guys. I thought that was tremendously huge."

Gail Goestenkors at Texas incorporated the reverence due Jody Conradt into the team's promotional materials for the first two years she headed the venerated Longhorn program. "One way we did it [honor Conradt] was throughout our media guide and poster," Goestenkors said. "The quote we used was, 'Remembering the Past, Representing the Future.' We want to make sure that we never forget where we came from and how great it once was. And this year in our recruiting guide it says, 'History will repeat itself.' So we're determined to bring back the glory that was once here at Texas."

Beth Dunkenberger at Virginia Tech and Kristy Curry at Texas Tech continued long-standing events their predecessors (Bonnie Henrickson and Marsha Sharp, respectively) had established to great effect. "A lot of things we had in place, like an auction, a picnic, how we met with boosters, she didn't change much," Henrickson said. "It worked pretty well for us. Sometimes you want to come in and change everything, but if it's not broken don't try to fix it. I think she respected what we'd done."

Curry had the same philosophy. "They had a chili dinner every fall with the longtime Lady Raider supporters, and we continue to have a chili dinner. Little things that make a big difference. Why would you not continue to do those things? That's awesome."

But Curry went a step farther and made sure that Sharp, the person, also was honored and nurtured. "I'm so conscious of knowing you just don't walk away from the game without it hurting a little bit, so I want to be there for her and let her know I do care about that."

From Sharp's perspective, the treatment has been welcomed and reciprocated. "She's been awesome, trying to check on me to see if I'm doing OK. After the first practice they had, and the first time they played, she called to say, 'Coach, are you good?' They did a wonderful thing when they did the recognition day the very first game of the first season they were here. They brought the national championship crystal trophy here and put a banner up and those kinds of things. I really appreciated that, and I told her that was really special for me. Of course the [Marsha Sharp] Leadership Circle here gives us a little bit more of a way to stay in touch, because there are some things we can help with, like raising money for special projects like going to the Virgin Islands. And I in turn tried to make sure that every time there was a big moment for her, I'd send a note or a bouquet of flowers to say that I was still with her right there and wanted it to be good."

Kathy McConnell-Miller at Colorado made sure to honor Ceal Barry and her body of work on a number of levels. "We recognize the former athletes and coaches, and open up our door to them and make them feel very welcome here. That's a key component. All are welcome, regardless of what year you graduated or how many points you scored or who you played for. You are a Buff, and you're going to be a Buff for life. There is a complete respect on my part, my staff, and the present student-athletes in regard to the past.

"Secondly, we're aware of tradition, of records, of players who have done things in the past, and we recognize that. We draw upon that at times. For example, Jackie McFarland [one of McConnell-Miller's players] is the second all-time-leading scorer. Well, who is she behind? She's behind Lisa VanGore. Just having a knowledge of that is important. Lastly, there are things in our locker room that I'll never touch, from the record board to the stars for graduation."

Barry expounded on McConnell-Miller's respect for tradition and décor. "When I was in college, my coach, Debbie Yow, brought in the slogan, 'Cats Are One.' When I went to Cincinnati, we were the Bobcats, so I'd say, 'Cats Are One' When we got here, it was, 'Buffs Are One.' Just the other day I was watching practice. They huddled up five or six times, and every single time they said, 'Buffs Are One.' I think that was handed down from the players to Kathy. Kathy didn't get that from me, but they've been saying it.

"I had a lot of things in the locker room about the tradition of the athletes. I had plaques made for the top 10 in scoring, rebounding, assists, and steals. They have their names and totals at the end of their careers, and she's kept that up. Every player who graduated had a star in our Champions of a Higher Degree wall for any player who graduated, and she kept that going."

Beth Bass had a number of people from all walks emphasizing the importance of taking care of the face of the WBCA, Betty Jaynes—from her parents and mentors to the co-founders of the organization. But they needn't have worried.

CHART 4.3: WAYS TO HONOR INCOMING

_____   Be honest and forthcoming

_____   Stay out of the way, but be available

_____   Voice support to team, staff, fans, and public

_____   Be positive in all public communication

_____   Send congratulations at key times

_____   Present with a small gift

_____   Dedicate tournament

_____   Initiate special game-day activity

_____   Include perpetual ad and/or information in event program

_____   Communicate

"Everybody thought, 'Well after three years, surely Beth is just going to put Betty out to pasture,'" Bass said. "My friends couldn't believe I was OK with Betty still being around. And I thought, 'Are you kidding me?' Her knowledge plus my skill set are good for me personally and professionally. I want to have all of her experience because it helps me be successful.

"I don't think we do that well on the women's side," Bass lamented. "The men keep this brain trust, this continuous influx of basketball knowledge, from the C.M. Newtons to the Dave Gavitts to the Pete Newells to the Terry Hollands. When they retire they become administrators. They keep this perpetual learning and sharing of information. But it's almost like ageism in the women's game. If you're 55 or 60, you're shown the door, whereas with men that's when you start getting wisdom. I was learning and seeing the inequities, that administrators in women's basketball didn't get what the men got. So Betty was my laboratory, where I tried to change that paradigm one person at a time. She should have lifetime benefits. So that was one thing, to truly try to build a model to start doing the right things, or better, on the women's side of the house."

***

Preserving and utilizing the experience of those who worked so hard to advance the cause of women's sports is vital to the continued growth not only of the individuals taking up the mantle but of the movement itself. To refuse such momentum would be like a newly hatched butterfly crawling out of the chrysalis and attempting to take flight without waiting for the transfer of blood to its wings.

Teamwork in transition takes forethought and thoughtfulness, and it is essential to combating the "one-woman-in-the-room syndrome," as Bass calls it. "Many corporate boards are filled with men but have one token woman to 'prove' they aren't sexist. But if that one spot is taken, other women who are upset they weren't chosen often descend into cattiness and ankle biting instead of networking and banding together to make the most of that voice, whereas men will buddy up to people they know in influential positions.

"At the WNBA All-Decade Team luncheon in 2006, Madeline Albright gave an amazing keynote speech, and one of her quotes was, 'There's a special place in hell for women who don't support other women.' We need to do what we can to make sure that place is empty."

Chapter 5
PROGRESSING WITH CLASS: An Intentional Effort

Every living person moves forward in the most fundamental sense. Time forges on, tick by tock, pulling life with it. But just as creating a fulfilling, meaningful existence is a deliberate process, moving a program forward the right way—improving with steadiness and distinction—requires a concerted effort by each person involved.

It takes a village to raise a program, to paraphrase the African proverb. Some citizens of that village and their duties are obvious. The coaching staff guides the student-athletes and sets the program direction and tone. The sport's immediate support staff (academic advising, athletic training, compliance, life skills, media relations, strength and conditioning) make sure the student-athletes and, to a lesser extent, the coaching staff are healthy and nurtured on several fronts. The sport supervisor takes care of the coaching staff.

Others are less apparent but just as integral to the program's success. The players help care for each other. Departmental staff ensures the program functions on a business and procedural level. Coaching colleagues provide each other an understanding yet analytical ear, given that they are among the few who truly understand the rigors of the job. Athletics directors keep the entire operation moving in the same direction.

Fulfilling those roles effectively, and with excellence, requires great leadership, a common mission of putting the student-athletes first, teamwork, and each person staying attune to and meeting his or her own needs. The overarching effect is a classy program.

When Jerritt Elliott left the Southern Cal volleyball program for Texas's, his expectations of himself and his program reflected those of someone who had made two trips to the NCAA tournament and one to the Final Four as an interim head coach.

"I had had so much success with back-to-back [number one recruiting] classes, I thought, 'With so many more amenities and offerings, I can do this at Texas in three to four years,'" Elliott confessed. "But not until you're an established program do kids want to go there. It was great for Chris [Plonsky, athletics director] to be supportive and reach out when you take a tough loss, saying, 'It's OK,' and 'You've got time,' and 'You're doing it the right way,' and really reinforcing that. It's nice to have that kind

> *"But you can't lose sight of how you're going to build it the right way. You can unravel pretty fast as a coach if things aren't going your way. And when you unravel, then the whole progression to get to that point can really be affected. You have to stay task-oriented on how you're going to get there, stick with that blueprint."*
>
> ~Jerritt Elliott

of leadership available to me and looking out for me, because there were a lot of frustrating things I went through, and you want it to change faster than it can.

"But you can't lose sight within that time of how you're going to build it the right way," Elliott continued. "You can unravel pretty fast as a coach if things aren't going your way. And when you unravel, then the whole progression to get to that point can really be affected. You have to stay task-oriented on how you're going to get there, stick with that blueprint, and go on a run or go be able to vent to some people.

"We've had to make some changes over the years in terms of figuring out what's right, what's wrong, and how we can go about improving that. I think if you're always trying to strive to be the best, you're always looking for strengths and weaknesses in your program. We have interviews at the end of every year—what went well, what didn't—from the coaching staff on down, trying to figure out where we're strong and where we're weak and trying to improve in those areas."

The final phase of the monarch butterfly's metamorphosis is adulthood. About an hour after emerging from the chrysalis, its wings are full-size, dry, and ready for flying. Four to six hours later it is ready for mating, thus beginning the life cycle of the next generation. Reaching "adulthood" in a successful transition takes longer than 60 minutes, but the result is the same: a mature, fully functioning, soaring work of art that touches more people than imaginable with beauty and grace.

LEADING FROM THE TOP

As in any village, the chief makes a world of difference in its operations and style. How does the department act? What is its culture? Do the employees maintain a business-like facade or do they interact with warmth? Are they just there to do a job, or are they heavily invested in the success of each program? Are staff members co-operative or competitive with each other?

Though not impossible, it's tough to move forward with class if the leader isn't laying the groundwork, setting the pace, providing the example. The supportive infrastructure must be in place and an ethos of teamwork and togetherness rooted within for an organization to evolve with decorum. This is precisely what Mike Bohn described attempting to do at Colorado after various scandals and financial challenges rocked the university and athletics department before he came on board.

"We had just lost our university president, and we had an interim chancellor at the time," Bohn said. "So while the leadership at the top was very, very supportive, they had significant challenges as well. They were really counting on Ceal [Barry] and me to help support Kathy [McConnell-Miller] as much as we could, but Ceal was in a brand new role, and Kathy and I were new to campus. With the challenges the program had faced before, there weren't a lot of constituents lined up across campus saying, 'How can we help?' It was more like, 'Let's see what you guys are going to do and what you're all about.' There wasn't a well-established support base that we could really rely on.

"I'm still trying to establish that foundational support not only for coaches but any new employee, and for that matter any new major business that moves to the community," Bohn explained. "ConocoPhillips is moving into the Front Range with a major research initiative and a lot of prominent employees, and trying to be sure that we have all the tools—the game plan—to welcome people like that is no different than welcoming coaches."

SUSTAIN SUPPORT

An administrator offers initial support to a new employee in a number of ways discussed in Chapter 3, such as relocation assistance, procedural training, equipment issue, verbal backing, and introductions. But continued progress also demands of its leaders consistent, meaningful interactions to know what their employees are dealing with and how they're coping, to furnish in-the-moment professional and personal support, and to present genuine, big-picture perspective and encourage-ment. An administrator should provide a safe place for a coach to vent and vacillate when reacting to frustrating times while at the same time being a steady, calming presence when a coach is flailing in the wind.

"I meet with the men's basketball coach and the women's basketball coach over a cup of coffee every day," George Washington athletics director Jack Kvancz said. "Sometimes those meetings are 30 seconds, sometimes they are 10 minutes or 20 minutes if they have a problem. My feeling is, 'You know we're going to have it. If you've been brooding over something you want to bring up, bring it up.' If there's nothing to be brought up, I'm not Dick Tracy here. I'm not trying to make a problem where there's no problem. If everything is good, that's good!"

Lisa Love took a like-minded approach as she mentored interim volleyball coach Jerritt Elliott and new head coach Mick Haley at Southern Cal. "Jerritt and I spoke very, very frequently, and when Mick came on board, he was in my office every day. It was a regular line of communication of where we were and where we were going."

But regular communication doesn't qualify as support if it's not actually support-ive. It seems obvious, but transitions disrupt a program's stability and equilibrium. Just because a successful coach replaces a successful coach does not automatically mean the program will experience similar success right away. In the collective 24 women's basketball seasons represented in this book—from the first season after each transition through the 2008-09 season—only nine times did the incoming coach win at a 55 percent or better clip, and only *twice* did it happen in conference play. Administrators should not look for comet-like success, and they should make sure to communicate that clearly to their hires.

"I was really fortunate to have an administration that was willing to help," Texas's Gail Goestenkors recognized. "They understood when I was having a bad day and would say, 'It's going to be OK.' You're going to have days where you feel totally overwhelmed, and I had a great administration behind me."

In addition to coping with a transition, which is difficult under any circumstances, Jolette Law also was learning to be a head coach when she followed Theresa Grentz at Illinois. Two administrators in particular, senior associate athletics director Terry Cole and athletics director Ron Guenther, buoyed her spirits. "I call on Terry all the time," Law revealed. "When things are like, 'Oh, my goodness!' I just bounce things off of him. He always has something positive to say, like 'Coach, we have your back, we're there for you, keep plugging away, do what you're going to do, stick to your guns.' That means a lot to me, especially when I was going through [that first year]."

Specific acts of support by the administrator, reinforcing his or her belief in and commitment to the new regime, will ease a coach's mind. When Goestenkors felt strongly about closing practices and discontinuing a few opportunities for fans to mingle with players, athletics director Chris Plonsky took action on her behalf.

Judi Henry at Texas Tech didn't limit her support of Kristy Curry to Lubbock. "I traveled [with the team] early on, because a lot of the places she was going were new to her, and I knew the places where there were most likely to be glitches," Henry explained. "There are certain things that are important to different coaches. Things that would have been a major glitch to Marsha [Sharp] were a non-issue for Kristy, and there were other things that might be the reverse."

Dawn Staley appreciated the Temple administration taking time to provide a second voice about the program to recruits. "Temple did a tremendous job being very supportive both budget-wise and with the athletics director being accommodating in the climate we recruit the parents in. I think it's very necessary for prospective student-athletes and their parents to meet the athletics director and ask the questions they always ask us during in-home visits to make sure things line up."

FOSTER TEAMWORK

Teamwork within the athletics department and across campus is just as important as on the squads themselves. And just as on an individual squad, collaboration must be cultivated through actions and words consistent with the mission of the group at large. It's up to the leader to establish the culture of genuine teamwork—its value and principles—so that each person buys into the ideal. Mike Bohn spent much of his first years doing this at Colorado, not only in relation to Kathy McConnell-Miller filling Ceal Barry's shoes but for the entire athletics department.

"We were spending a lot of time as a department in town meetings, trying to educate people with issues associated with the entire department," Bohn said. "I'm trying to really establish the sense of where the athletics program is, not only on campus but with the media, the community, our donor base, the season ticket base—all of those constituents. It was really all of us trying to keep our ankles taped and focused on trying to make all of that go at once, because we really didn't have anything established we could stand on other than Ceal's good name and the accomplishments she had over her tenure.

"I think the neat thing is, and I hope Coach [McConnell-Miller] believes this, I feel like we're all in the trenches together: the new chancellor, Ceal in her role and increased influence in the department as SWA, our compliance officer, Kathy's operations staff. Everybody stayed in the trenches helping each other.

"The most important thing now is you've got coaches and other people in the department on a team, recognizing the importance of being able to pull all of that together," Bohn continued. "So teamwork is huge. That starts with the central administration on campus, your booster support group, your senior staff in the athletics department. All of those efforts are unified, and that fabric in the community, on campus, and the department becomes tighter to the point that it becomes easier to support people and know where you can get quick answers and get things moving rather than say, 'I don't know where to go with that. I'll have to get back to you.' And that's a huge difference. We didn't have a lot of those things in place, but we certainly tried and worked hard to make that happen. In the end, I think it helped us be a better teammate across campus, in the community, in our own department, and it helped pull that sense of team together. The slogan of the Colorado Buffaloes right now, and has been since I've been here, is 'Your Team.' And team is an acronym for Together Everyone Accomplishes More. We're trying to instill that.

"So I think in transitions, you have to have that sense of teamwork so that coaches know that whether it's admissions, the courtesy car program, your insurance benefits—all those things that are intricate to people—there is a great sense of team, and they know that [those people] are on their team rather than having to fight or struggle to get information to the point where it's frustrating for them. As I said, I think we're better—we're dramatically better than it was when we were all new—but yet we're still trying to improve that as well."

Bohn described how two of his mentors have influenced his ideas, first with (president of the University of Idaho) "Bob Hoover's model for teamwork on campus and collaboration with the faculty: how athletics can be an integral part of the campus, instilling a sense of pride and emotion and energy in the campus, really being the heartbeat of a campus and providing the resources to us to do that, and also providing the access into deans and into the strategic plan of the university.

"I think the neat thing is, everybody stayed in the trenches helping each other. The most important thing now is you've got coaches and other people in the department on a team, recognizing the importance of being able to pull all of that together."
~Mike Bohn

"And now to have [Colorado] Chancellor Bud Peterson come to campus as a former student-athlete and reinforce those principles," Bohn continued. "It's kind of interesting how his style and his expectations and attention to detail really pull into that sense of focus but also that sense of teamwork as a campus so that athletics is in the fabric of the university."

The result of such integration is a sense of family, a unity within the university and athletics department that makes the place special for newcomers and longtimers alike, as related by Jerritt Elliott about Southern Cal, Gail Goestenkors about Texas, Bonnie Henrickson about Kansas, Jolette Law about Illinois, Sharon McCloskey about Virginia Tech, and McConnell-Miller about Colorado.

ELLIOTT: "There were a couple of people within the department who didn't have a role with the team, like event management, who were really excited for me and were always showing up and helping me. And then my second year, Pete Carroll [Southern Cal football coach] was a big part of it. He came in to watch practice and I thought, 'Great. I've got Pete Carroll coming in to watch practice,' because his daughter came to play for me. The first day he got the job he came running in my office and jumped on the couch and said, 'What can football do to help you out?' So it was just creating an energy. It was great. I used a lot of the other coaches that I got close with."

GOESTENKORS: "The other coaches [at Texas] have been through it and understand what you're going through when it's your first year."

HENRICKSON: "Coach Self [men's basketball coach] is an unbelievable guy."

LAW: "Personally, I think I have the most positive administrators in the country: Terry Cole, Ron Guenther. They have really helped me navigate my way through making my transition [easier]. Even the coaches here: Bruce Weber [men's basketball], Ron Zook [men's football]. They called when we got here and said, 'The first year is going to be tough, but hang in there.' We have such a sense of community here, and it starts with the direction of my administrators."

MCCLOSKEY: "The building up of our fan base for women's basketball has been helped by a collaboration between football and women's basketball. They've always had a good relationship. Our football coach [Frank Beamer] comes to every women's basketball game when he's in town. He's an alumni of the school, so he supports every one of our teams. He stopped in to talk to Bonnie's team when they were getting ready to go on a football trip. It was Bonnie's first game, and he said, 'We really wish we could be here to support you, but we'll be thinking about you and listening to the score.' And that means a lot to those kids, and definitely to the staff."

MCCONNELL-MILLER: "Everybody just opened up their arms to us: Gary Barnett in football, Ricardo Patton in basketball, Jon Burianek in the business office. I never felt like an outsider even though Ceal was always in the room. At senior staff meetings with the head coaches, Ceal was there and the rest of the head coaches were there, but I never felt like an outsider in this department."

John Swofford, commissioner of the ACC, has created a culture of teamwork among his staff, which Nora Lynn Finch fit into very well when she replaced longtime associate commissioner Bernadette McGlade. "By her very nature and by the nature of the staff here—it's a very inclusive place to work—it has worked out well," Swofford said. "It wasn't like a mass staff changeover by any stretch of the imagination, so there were people here who were involved in the nuts and bolts who were ready and very capable of showing Nora Lynn the ropes. Our staff is very interactive. She was welcomed right into the fabric of the organization internally. Externally, she was already a well-known and established figure nationally and a well-known name with our schools. People at our institutions had worked with her at N.C. State and on various conference committees."

FOCUSING ON THE STUDENT-ATHLETE

One of the initial challenges of a transition is for the outgoing coach to convince the student-athletes that the impetus for the change is not about them. Like many people, players tend to think the world revolves around them, and when their leader leaves, it's hard not to take it personally. But in fact, college athletics *is* about the student-athletes. The coaches, the department, and the university all are working to help them learn, grow, and mature through discipline, teamwork, and competition.

"The student-athlete is the center of the universe," Lisa Love stated as she began to explain why the unique, two-year transition with Southern Cal volleyball—from her to interim head coach Jerritt Elliot to head coach Mick Haley—progressed so smoothly. "Everybody stayed focused on the fact that that was the most critical element. It was just a student-first environment. Any frustrations, any changes anyone may have wanted to make, any way anyone felt about wishing for a different result, they weren't wearing that on their sleeve. The character of these two men was the primary reason for success, on behalf of the students. The student-athletes did not feel any kind of negativity or friction, even though it's perfectly natural to have opinions and dialogue about all of it. That's healthy—very healthy—and invited, as a matter of fact. Opinions are certainly respected, but it was just a matter of having the well-being of those students in mind that helped people lead in a healthy, teacher-like direction. I make it sound like it's all tiptoe through the tulips, but it required a lot of character strength from everyone involved. But everyone realized that the greater good was going to help everybody involved."

The transition from Marsha Sharp to Kristy Curry at Texas Tech transpired admirably, not because the coaches were similar in their mannerisms or styles but because their underlying philosophies matched. "They're totally different people and totally different personalities," senior associate athletics director Judi Henry explained, "but they had the same mission and goal: taking care of the student-athlete and the legacy of the program, and carrying that on in the same classy manner, with integrity and fairness and keeping it all about the student-athlete."

REMEMBER: IT'S ABOUT THEM

Making decisions with the student-athletes always in mind sounds like an elementary principle, but in the heat of a collegiate coaching tenure, it becomes tempting, subconsciously, to begin swerving from that noble path and blazing a trail that forks toward winning and professional advancement at the expense of player experience and education.

Part of what the student-athletes are learning is how to survive and thrive in change, and their example comes from the adults leading them through it. Much like a child does not wake up one day with a full vocabulary, players cannot learn every lesson at once. Change for change's sake can overload their circuits and hinder their growth. At the same time, maintaining the status quo simply because the players are used to it can be detrimental if the status quo isn't constructive.

Curry applied that tactic when she analyzed how to proceed with each facet of the program. "My challenge was to figure out: if this is good, and these kids are used to it this way—maybe I had done it another way—don't be so hardheaded, don't have such an ego, and do things the way the transition would be easier for them," Curry asserted. "It may be harder for me. But you know, why we do what we do every day is those kids. I tell my staff all the time that the reason they have a job—my sports information director, my trainer, my strength coach, my assistant coaches, our secretary—is because of the kids. Otherwise we wouldn't be here. So why do we do what we do every day? To put them in a position to be happy and successful. There is more than one right way to do it. You can't be afraid to realize that things have been done really well. If it's not broken, why are you going to try to fix it? There's not any fixing. You're going to be wasting your time."

Love praised Haley for how he handled his arrival at Southern Cal in the middle of the 2000 volleyball season, Elliott's second year as interim head coach. "What was most important for him was the player experience during that period of time," Love said. "If there was awkwardness, it perhaps could have been felt by Jerritt because Mick was around. But Mick didn't take part in any coaching duties. He did not dictate anything. He said, 'This is Jerritt's season. Jerritt's the coach, and this is how it is.' He did not attend all the matches. He did not attend practices regularly. The reins were in Jerritt's hand, and Mick felt that was most important for the success of the team in that particular year—not to confuse the matter."

Jack Kvancz, athletics director at George Washington, is passionate about his beliefs that college athletics is about the student-athletes, not about winning, but that success will follow when well-established priorities, talent, and hard work meet.

"We have been very, very, very successful," Kvancz started. "So one of the things I talked to Mike [Bozeman] about after he was hired was: 'I understand we play Tennessee, we play Texas A&M and Rutgers away. Those are scheduled games before you took over. So don't worry. Wins are very important. I hired you to win. However,

I don't want to be built on sand.' He's not that type of person, but I didn't want him to feel the pressure. I want to win, don't get me wrong, but I'm not going to mortgage the house just to win. I'm not going to do that.

"I want him to understand that the pressure he has is his own pressure. I understand that, and that's just coaching. 'You want to win national championships. But you have to understand that when you and I sit down to talk, there are things that are just as important.' Because you can't be hypocritical. You can't say, 'I want you to graduate all your players and have a great APR,' but then fire you because you didn't win enough. You have to say, 'Winning is important. We're paying you to win. But we're also paying you to take care of these kids.' And whenever we have any kind of evaluation, it's going to be based on winning, yes, but how successful are the kids? Are they getting the experience they need at the university? Are they getting themselves qualified to go into the real world? Are you making decisions based on that, or are you saying, 'They can't read or write, but I'm going to take them because they're a great player?' I don't buy that. The best way I can describe it is, build it on concrete, don't build it on sand. And actually that's what we had, because Joe [McKeown] did that, and year after year after year we were good. Again, this is me. So you lose 8, 9, 10 games? So you're 18-10? That's fine! What's wrong with that? Now, if you look in the past, you're 26-4, 26-3. I understand that, but that's with seniors. Now you have a bunch of young kids. I want them to be sophomores. I want them to be juniors. I want them to be seniors. I want them to have a good experience.

"We're in Washington, D.C.!" Kvancz exclaimed. "I'll give you an example. We don't practice Tuesday. It's the inauguration. So Mike told his kids, 'You better get down to the inauguration, because history's being made.' To me, that's really big. We had the Million Man March. It's six blocks away! Are you going to stay in your office? Are you crazy? That's part of all of what I think you should take part in if you go to a school in D.C. Why not be involved in that stuff? At least be part of what's going on. That's what intercollegiate athletics should be about.

"The truth is, they're only going to have those experiences once in their lives, and they should have them. Hopefully that's why they came to Washington, D.C., to go to school. And if they don't take advantage of that, shame on them. Sometimes there's more to be learned outside of books. And Mike did it on his own volition. It's not like I have to take him every day and say, 'Take the garbage out.' He understands that. And Michael is also a native of the area, so he understands some of

"I'm of the theory that if you get good kids, you treat them OK, they take advantage of everything the university has, and you're a good coach, you're going to win. But don't sell your soul, because it's not worth it in the bigger picture."

~Jack Kvancz

the things they have. Now, when it comes time to play between the lines, let's play to win, but I think there are other things you have to look at. I would like to think every school does that, but I understand that perhaps some schools don't.

"I'm of the theory that if you get good kids, you treat them OK, they take advantage of everything the university has, and you're a good coach, you're going to win," Kvancz continued. "I haven't, fortunately, been in a situation where they've done all of that and lost. I don't know how I'd react. But the games will take care of themselves. 'You're going to be all right. But don't sell your soul, because it's not worth it in the bigger picture.' That's what I said to him. The advantage I had is he already knew that, because he's been around. And that's what Joe had done for us. And we won! I don't think you should have a coach who's overly demanding and who doesn't want to listen to your problems. I don't mind being demanding, being a tough coach, but if a kid comes in with a big problem, you should try to help that kid out. Because where else are they going? You're the coach! They spend all their time with you. If you just do that, I think your relationship with your players is going to be better. And I think the relationship between the players and all the administrators is going to be better, because they're not going to feel bad coming in and saying, 'Hey, I've got a problem.' We don't want to sweep them under the rug. Deal with it. You'll feel better. Everybody will feel better. You might hurt a little bit more now, but in the end you'll feel better.

"So that's what we believe here. Anybody who says they don't care about winning is lying, but I'm just as happy if we're 15-14 and the kids have had a good experience and everything is fine—I'm happy—as opposed to being 23-and-whatever and have all kinds of problems. To me, it's not worth winning at all costs. Life is too short."

OUTGOING: KEEP COMMUNICATION APPROPRIATE

It is amazing how a relatively small group of very successful, very esteemed coaches—those involved in this book—can have such varied opinions about such a crucial aspect of transitions as whether the outgoing coach continues to interact with former players. It seems like the best of the best would agree on that, much like they believe basketball players must communicate on defense.

But if nothing else has become clear, it is that situations and personalities dictate a great deal in transition. (After all, coaches may claim they would *never* run anything but a man-to-man defense, but even that can change depending on personnel and opponent.) Has the outgoing coach retired or moved to another school? Was the parting amicable or strained? How well do the incoming and outgoing coaches know each other? What is the nature of the interactions?

Regardless of the details, outgoing coaches should share how their relationships will look with former players moving forward, which necessarily will change given the outgoing's minimized role in the players' lives. The players have new leaders, and their focus should be on assimilating with the new coaching staff rather than clinging to the old. What does help players understand, or at least become aware of, the new roles is clear communication with the outgoing before he or she leaves.

Talking Points

Just like toddlers understand more than adults realize, student-athletes can digest and adapt to very difficult situations better than they're sometimes given credit for.

And that understanding happens more quickly and thoroughly when they're given the information clearly and in a variety of settings and forms. Making a quick speech in the locker room that blindsides a team immediately before jetting off to a new job may be all the coach has time for in that moment, but individual conversations and written communication can help get the players through the transitions much more smoothly. Regardless of how, when, or where it takes place, making very clear how the next phase of the relationship should look will sidestep a great many headaches and heartaches.

"It was hard, but one of the things I tried to do for Mike's sake is not call the players, not return their calls, try to let him get his feet under him," Joe McKeown said of Mike Bozeman at George Washington. "But I talked to every player, explained my decision, wished them the best, and told them that anything I could do to help them when they graduate, I'd be there for them the rest of their lives. So I tried to separate myself a little from the team coming back, because I thought that wouldn't be fair."

Jolette Law made sure the Rutgers players she left when she became head coach at Illinois knew how she felt and how she would proceed. "As much as possible I just tried to tell them, 'I love you guys. I love you to death. I'm just trying right now to build my program here, and I want you guys to start building relationships with the staff there. I'll always love you and I'm loving you from afar, but I'm needing to let go a little bit. If you ever need me, I'm here. But the little things you were pulling on me for when I was there, you're going to have to do that with other coaches. I have a brand new team myself, and I have new personalities and different things I have to learn about them. We both have to make some adjustments, and we both have to adjust to change.' It was hard. You're used to talking to the kids all the time, then all of a sudden you kind of have to cut the umbilical cord. They understood."

Boundaries

As much as is asked of college student-athletes, and as anxious as they are to grow up, it's sometimes easy to forget they are drudging through the marsh between adolescence and adulthood. Sometimes adolescence swallows them like quicksand; sometimes adulthood pitches them forward. But very few college students are consistently mature, fully formed adults, with grown-up perspective, wisdom, and emotional wherewithal. Therefore, the outgoing coach must set the expectations of what is appropriate and inappropriate, just as parents set rules and limitations for their children.

"When you recruit a player and you coach them and you're successful like we were, you usually have a pretty positive relationship with your players," noted McKeown. "When you do leave, they still expect that same type of relationship, and when you separate that it's really hard. I had a couple of players cry. They were really upset because I left, and they felt like I deserted them. But they're 20 years old and I told them, 'Hey, you're going to play college basketball at GW again for a great coach, but you won't have me yelling at you!' They also appreciated that I was pushing them and challenging them and trying to get them to do the things they're supposed to do as a college student-athlete."

Virginia Tech's Beth Dunkenberger believes the boundaries should be pretty narrow, to which players naturally will adapt. "Kids get their feelings hurt, but they are pretty resilient and will adjust to who's there for them," she said. "I don't think you have to lose touch completely. I see former players I coached from time to time, and I've had former players come up to Virginia Tech to watch our team play. But you have to let them go on with their careers before you can re-engage."

Bonnie Henrickson, who preceded Dunkenberger at Virginia Tech, agreed. "I'm very respectful that there are boundaries once you leave, and sometimes people don't understand that," she explained. "They are young adults, but they're kids still, and emotionally they're kids in that transition. It was hard. There were a lot of tears shed in that locker room. I had worked hard to build relationships with those kids and took care of them. As much as I wanted to [stay in touch], it wouldn't be the right thing. If I had to do it all over again, I wouldn't do anything differently.

"The staff, dealing with adults—we can all handle that," Henrickson continued. "You just have to be careful about the kids. Some people get caught up. They have egos and they want their former players to tell them how much they hate their new coach and how much they loved you. They are kids. Leave them alone. When they graduate, if they want to have contact—e-mail or whatever, come see us play—that's wonderful. But I don't ever feel bad or regret that I undermined anybody. Even if it's all, 'Beth's great! Beth's great!' if Beth heard they were talking to me, even though we're dear friends, human nature says, 'What were y'all talking about?' I wouldn't want that.

"Do unto others. Would you want anybody to do that to your kids? All of us would say no. As much as that's hard, you have to be mature enough, have the character and integrity to understand it's not right to do that. And that's in recruiting and everything else. If you're not getting it right in one lane, you're probably not getting it right in another."

Virginia Tech endured a very difficult situation when a player contracted meningitis in 2002. When Henrickson left for Kansas, Rayna DuBose was only halfway through with school. "I would communicate with Rayna because she wasn't playing," Henrickson clarified. "I was just so worried to make sure she would graduate. She'd been through so much, and I felt like I'd been such a big part of talking to her family and just being there and being strong for her and her family, but I knew Beth would take that on and could handle that. It was more talking with her about graduating and getting her degree, and 'What are you doing? How are your classes going? What are you taking?' I would talk to Beth about what we'd been able to do for her, what I felt like she needed, connect her with her parents. That was life-changing for everybody."

Part of being a great coach is having good instincts about people and then acting on those instincts in a way that advances the player or team without one's own biases, needs, and wishes muddying the water. It goes back to determining what is best for the student-athletes. Will they benefit emotionally and athletically from a continued relationship, or will it divide or distract them? If there is *any* hint or possibility of the latter, all contact should be discontinued until the student-athlete is no longer on a collegiate squad.

Texas's Gail Goestenkors knew that the line between maintaining contact with her Duke players and cutting them off was a very fine one. "It was really tough, because I didn't get to spend a lot of one-on-one time with them," she began. "A couple came over to my house while I was moving, so I spent time with them there, but it was extremely emotional. Once I got to Texas, we e-mailed back and forth some, and even throughout the season when someone would have a tough game, they might e-mail, and I would continue to encourage them. They knew and they know that I'm always going to be there for them. Always. But the communications are fewer and further between now. And I've encouraged that as well. I knew I couldn't be as much a part of their lives because they had a new coach, too, and they needed to buy into a new system as well. So I was just going to be there for support, but at the same time I knew they needed to make their own way and form their new bond with their new coach."

Jolette Law at Illinois had the same attitude about her former Rutgers team. "It was hard initially, because I had such great relationships with all of them. I didn't want it to be where I'm gone and new coaches were there, that they didn't give them [the new coaches] the opportunity to get to know them. I had to sort of transition and limit my contact with them, because I'm at a new place and I'm trying to get to know my new group and build relationships with them.

"I loved them from afar," Law continued. "Whenever Rutgers was playing I'd watch them and support them, but I tried to limit my texting and e-mailing to them because I wanted them to be able to grow under the assistant coaches that were there and build relationships with them. It was good to see a text from them if they had a big win or we had a big game: 'We're winning! We won! We're rooting for you in the Big Ten tournament!' It feels good that my former players are pulling for the success of my team at Illinois. I did go to the regional game when they [Rutgers] went to the Elite Eight once our season was done, but they didn't know I was coming. I didn't want to be a distraction."

Tonya Cardoza tries to be an upbeat presence in the lives of the UConn players she left even as she leads Temple. "I still have interaction with them," she acknowledged. "I still talk to them on IM or a phone call—not all of them, but the ones I was closest to, because I still want to be part of their lives and help them grow, just making them stay positive and being that other ear of someone away from the program they can talk to and feel comfortable with. And I check the stats and check the box scores, and if I see someone not doing what I know they're capable of doing, I might send them an IM or text to try to push them forward."

Marsha Sharp made it clear how she would communicate with her former Texas Tech players after Kristy Curry replaced her. "My deal with those kids was: 'I'll tell you what we're going to do. I will help you with anything, if it's to get through an injury or you need a job recommendation or you need something to do in the summer or you're having trouble trying to figure out what direction you're going to go here, or there's a family issue—absolutely! But basketball is *completely* off limits. We are *not* going to talk about basketball.' And I think Kristy knew that and trusted that. But I really appreciated her allowing me to at least know what was going on with them and if they needed help or not."

Curry was equally straightforward in revealing how she felt about Sharp's continued contact with the players. "She helped with that transition with the kids," Curry shared. "She may do this this way and I may do that that way, but the biggest thing was communication with those kids, and me not being afraid. I can remember certain times with injuries or issues, or anything good, when I found out, I called Coach. I felt like she should know that, and I wanted to seek her advice, keep her in the loop, let her know what was going on in their world. I don't mind if she calls them or if they call her. How can you be a good person and keep them from having a relationship? I want that. So, to me, in any transition, why would you be so selfish that you would not allow them to have a relationship with who recruited them, with who brought them here? But you have to trust that person, that they're not going to hinder what they as individuals on the team are trying to accomplish, and I totally trusted her. So it's about trust and communication."

But Curry herself felt it best to make a substantial break from her Purdue players. "What I tried to do, for the best for those kids, is step away and cut ties," she explained, unless "it's a birthday or something's happened. It's never been anything about basketball more than, 'Good job.' That's how I handle it. Now I have a whole other group that needs me, and I need them, and we need each other. My kids at Purdue were feeling the same way these kids were feeling, so I tried to jump in and sink my heart and soul into these kids, and be there and give them a chance. Coach Sharp [said to the players]: 'Give her a chance.' And that's what I wanted those kids at Purdue to do: give [incoming coach] Sharon [Versyp] a chance. And I think in order to do that, sometimes it's good to step away."

Perhaps the most important rule for an outgoing coach to institute, as a few touched on, is to refrain from engaging in conversations with former players about team drama or anything sport-related. "I think it is unprofessional when coaches leave a program and continue to interfere with those players and that program," Theresa Grentz asserted. "When they graduate, then you pick up those relationships. The last thing I wanted were for those players to be calling me and saying, 'Well, Coach Law doesn't do it this way.' That's not what we needed. I wasn't going to get in the middle of that. I don't want to be in those conversations. I don't want to give those kids that opportunity."

Permission

One tactic that can help ensure a smooth, reverential transition is for the outgoing coach to ask for approval from the incoming coach to speak to players—it is now the other coach's program, after all, a fact that cannot be forgotten. Dawn Staley used this approach when she left Temple.

"I'm not going to be able to connect with them on a daily basis, but I made a commitment to them as people," Staley said. "I just wanted them to know I'm still going to be here for them. I know that fine line of bringing in a new coach, and I don't overstep my bounds when it comes to other people's kids. Those are Tonya's kids now, and I don't contact them unless they contact me, and if I contact them I will let Tonya know. That's just how I operate."

New Focus

A potential hazard for outgoing coaches who have been the rock for their players is to mistake the need that those young adults have for a leader with the notion that *they* are the essential element. It's easy to inadvertently make the relational dynamics about the coach instead of the players. It's natural to want to be needed, and it's a nice stroke to the ego, but what those student-athletes usually need more than the safety of the outgoing is to develop a relationship with the new coaching staff.

Learning to figure that out and adjust is part of the growing-up process, as Kathy McConnell-Miller at Colorado recounted about her conversations with her former players: "'You know what? You need to talk to your coach. You need to deal with your coach.' That was a very significant piece to the puzzle in how the student-athletes handled things."

Joe McKeown imparted similar wisdom. "I think the main thing is, as you get older and a little more experienced, you get a better feel for these things, and you want to give the person coming in a chance to build their own program, to do it their way instead of your way."

Conveying that concept to the former players and following through with it is part of the continued leadership process of the outgoing, as Bonnie Henrickson at Kansas explained. "Transitions by far are hardest on the kids. I tried not to have contact with them afterward, and I think that's the right way to do it. There was no texting—at that time instant messaging was big—but I promised Beth [Dunkenberger] I wouldn't do that. Because if they were talking to me, even if it was five minutes, that was five minutes they needed to be talking to their new head coach.

"It was really, really hard, but I told them, 'You need to work on developing a relationship with your new staff,'" Henrickson continued. "'I love you, and it's not that I don't care about you, but it's not healthy if you're calling me because you might be struggling with the transition. If you are, then you need to be having conversations with the new staff.' If it were switched, I would hope someone would do that for me. That was the most important thing.

"Now, when they graduate, yeah, I've had contact with players now that they're done, but not while they're playing. That's not fair to Beth. I think it's selfish that people do that. I don't want them to still like me and not like her. I recommended her for the job. But they need to work on a relationship with her and the new staff. That was important to me."

Dunkenberger handled her departure from Western Carolina the same way. "I was very careful when I left. I loved those kids. They were like my own kids. But when I left they had a new coach, and they needed to know that was the new coach, and they didn't need to come to me with their problems. They needed to go to her. They needed to build that level of trust there. While it may have seemed cold and painful, I cut that relationship with those players because that was what was best for them. And that's just out of respect for what Kellie [Jolly Harper] was trying to do."

TAKING CARE OF SELF

The student-athlete reigns supreme in athletics departments, no doubt about it. The concepts of rigid boundaries and "leaving the office at the office" don't apply to a career in athletics. But in the 24/7/365, very public, high-pressure profession in which success and livelihood depend on young adults (who by their very nature of maturing do immature things), at some point it *must* be about the employee in order to remain sane, grounded, and fresh.

Taking care of others and making selfless decisions—doing what's best for others and not subconsciously meeting your own latent personal needs—requires that coaches and administrators keep themselves in a good place mentally, physically, emotionally, and spiritually. This is even more important during transitions, when mayhem and angst are heightened. Spend time really pondering something other than out-of-bounds plays. Remain active and fit. Stay connected with trusted advisors, long-time friends, and family. Develop relationships inside and outside of sports. Seek out professional counseling. Understand how your spirit is filled, and fill it regularly.

UTILIZE A SUPPORT SYSTEM

Creating and cultivating a network of friends, colleagues, and mentors is imperative to surviving in the coaching profession. Not every person in the network has to be a coach in the same sport or even at the same competitive level, but the more similar the background, pressures, and experiences of people in that network, the more specific the feedback and forewarning they can provide.

Jerritt Elliott, Texas volleyball coach, said, "The biggest thing is being able to have those peers, whether it's in your sport or other sports, who you can reach out to and say, 'Hey, this is the situation I'm in. How did you handle this?'"

When Mike Bozeman moved from assistant to head coach at George Washington, he knew he needed a strategy for weathering the inevitable pop-up storms a first-year head coach faces. "One of the things I did is talk to some coaches who had already been through the first-year dramas," he revealed. "When things come up, you've already talked about it with your circle of colleagues. You're prepared for that, or at least you know the possibility that it's going to come. It helps you to be able to handle it smoothly, and you're not so panicked about it.

"It's almost like watching film for the game you're about to play," Bozeman explained. "If you see something in the game and you've already scouted it, it doesn't surprise you. But if you weren't prepared for it, it does surprise you. I tell my team all the time, 'It's the punches you don't see that really hurt you.' If you see a punch coming, you can brace for it. But if you don't see a punch coming, it can knock you out.

"I just think rallying around colleagues who've had similar experiences helps," Bozeman continued. "You become wiser by their experience. One in particular was Julie Rousseau at Pepperdine. I also talked to Coquese Washington at Penn State, and she gave me some tidbits, but Rousseau recommended this book—and I really should be contacting this guy, because I've been promoting this book like his agent: John Maxwell's *Talent is Never Enough*. I'd called her about some things about coaching. She shared some of her stories, and she said, 'You have to get this book. It's crucial.' I pulled into a bookstore and bought it while we were talking. Of course she didn't tell me the book cost $30, but it's a great book and touches on everything from coaching to running your own business. It relates to the coach, it relates to the player, it relates to the fan."

Jolette Law reached out to peers and mentors when she transitioned into her first head coaching position at Illinois. "I have those people that, when I didn't have people here, I could pick up the phone and call to help me in my transition, coupled with my best friend, but she never coached," Law said. "So I called some coaches, some legends, people who have been there and made it, just to bounce ideas off them. When you're going through transition and it's your first time, it's difficult."

Young head coaches aren't the only ones who need that reinforcement from close associates. Joe McKeown had 22 years of head coaching experience, but he sought advice and reassurance during and after he made the unlikely move from George Washington to Northwestern. "I lean a lot on my friends in the profession," McKeown said. "Gary Blair at Texas A&M is one of my best friends, Jim Foster at Ohio State, people like that who made changes when they were 50 years old, too. Gary went to A&M from Arkansas, Jim went to Ohio State from Vanderbilt, and they didn't do it when they were 25 or 30. I've leaned on them a lot, and some other people I've known a long time have helped me get through some things they dealt with, too."

CREATE BALANCE IN LIFE

Coaches are always impressing upon their players the importance of balance: balance in training, balance in diet, balance in activities. So why is it so hard for coaches to follow their own advice?

"You have to have a balance in your life," Kathy McConnell-Miller emphasized. "I love where I live. I love what I do. When I recruit, my student-athletes recognize that, and they know they're going to have a pretty balanced life here as well. I think balancing your life is really important, whether it's spiritual or social or professional. You have to have good balance to be successful.

"How that applies to me is, my student-athletes know that I have a family," McConnell-Miller explained. "They know I absolutely love my job, that I'm passionate about what I do, that I want to be the best, that I want to be great. But they also know I have three children who are very much a priority for me. So I understand there is more to life than putting that ball through the basket, and there's a respect for the student-athlete when they want to have a life. I'm not saying Party Girl or Sorority Girl. I'm just saying a balanced life."

The product of that balance can take a lighthearted slant, as Texas's Gail Goestenkors related. "I worked for Lin Dunn for five years at Purdue as an assistant. She taught me to be able to laugh at myself. In this business, if you take yourself too seriously and can't laugh at yourself, you're going to be in for a short career. She's a tremendous motivator, and she taught me the Xs and Os. She studies, studies, studies film, and that's something I learned to do with her, but she also probably has the best sense of humor of anyone I know."

KEEP LEARNING

Personal care involves not only balance but also growth. Regularly stoking the fire of education and enrichment keeps the mind and spirit engaged and energized, both prerequisites to passing on that passion for the sport and life itself. Learning can take on a number of forms. Clinics, webinars, books, videos, game film of other teams and leagues, networking, and skull sessions are but a few. Elliott took advantage of the rich resource of head coaches when he was at Southern Cal.

"I used to go to a lot of practices, whether it was women's basketball or football," Elliott remembered. "I wanted to watch how they handled transition, how they handled coaching, how they handled personnel, the management within the practice and the organization of that. And Pete [Carroll] was phenomenal at it. The energy was the best I've ever seen. The level of what he would bring every day to practice was just beyond my comprehension, so it was nice to have somebody like that to be able to rub elbows with."

Dawn Staley realized early on that simply staying observant can furnish a quality education in and of itself. "For coaches who will transition from assistant coaches to head coaches, you just have to keep your eyes open," she said. "You can learn a lot of things just by watching people, by listening to the way they talk, seeing the way they handle themselves. For me, Pat Summitt is one you could look at and say, 'She's in it for the right reasons.' She's very professional in her approach to the game and to young people. I know her just through playing against her and maybe having a few conversations, but I watch her. I watch how she handles situations. I think she's a good example of how coaches should be. I know she's experienced, and she's been around the block a few times, and that's what you need when you're starting. As a young coach or a first-time head coach, you get so caught up in the things you want to do because it's your program and you get possessive, and sometimes you don't see all the angles that you need to see."

"You can learn a lot of things just by watching people, by listening to the way they talk, seeing the way they handle themselves."

~Dawn Staley

***

For an athletics department and team to be fully and brilliantly functional, like a monarch butterfly, requires an advancement through the natural growth stages of a transition. It requires true leadership from the administration supporting the coaches. It requires coaches who are mature and self-actualized, able to put the student-athlete's well-being ahead of their own. It requires all adults demonstrating the character traits of discipline, respect, and teamwork they preach to their players.

In short, each person will be marching ably toward the same goal: an excellent experience for the student-athlete, which requires an excellent experience for the coaches and staff. When these benchmarks are consistently met, the department will exude excellence on all fronts.

Chapter 6
PREPARING FOR GREATNESS: Young Head Coaches

All new hires create additional work within an organization. From the interview and relocation efforts to introductions and procedures, administration and staff spend dozens if not hundreds of hours making sure the new employee becomes integrated into and comfortable with the structure of the department.

While all transitions go through each stage of a metamorphosis, coaches and administrators who enter the transition from an established position similar to their new role move from the figurative chrysalis—that protected cocoon where dramatic changes occur—to maturity relatively quickly. The time they spent going through that growth spurt earlier in their careers serves as a shortcut the next time around, allowing the employees to focus more on transitioning into that particular team and organization rather than splitting their attention and emotional energy with an occupational transition as well.

But young coaches require extended time in the cocoon to develop more fully on a professional level. They bring with them unique opportunities—energy, freshness, eagerness, malleability—in exchange for the necessary hands-on guidance related to the details, management, and duties required of the position.

That time of mentoring is well-spent, benefitting not only the employee and the program but also the person investing his or her time with the employee, according to Theresa Grentz. "In our profession, we need to take care of the younger coaches, because the job is getting more and more difficult," she said. "We can provide information that helps them continue moving forward instead of three steps back. Whenever you have the opportunity to help someone, you should do it, because it raises the quality of your life and the lives of others."

In some respects, this chapter is a microcosm of the rest of book. The topics—interviewing, seeking advice, managing a team—have been covered, but the dynamics, issues, solutions, and results can be quite different when the employee has not yet gained experience in the role.

MOVING UP FROM WITHIN

Familiarity can breed contempt, sure, but it also can breed comfort. Promoting an employee from within an organization is not a slam dunk solution to a vacancy, but in many situations—when the candidate has established strong relationships, stockpiled respect from years of solid performances and work ethic, and proven sufficiently mature and equipped for the position—that employee will feel as reliable and comfortable as a pair of broken-in shoes.

Certain early aspects of an inside job, though, can be touchy, misleading, and uncomfortable: the application process, comportment during the interview stage, the determination of when the familiarity is a positive or negative. Knowing what those critical times are and being prepared for how to handle them can prevent a promising inside job from going bad.

Longtime George Washington head coach Joe McKeown surprised the women's basketball world—most notably his team, staff, and administration—by accepting Northwestern's offer to head its program in the summer of 2008. McKeown and athletics director Jack Kvancz knew that assistant coach Mike Bozeman would be interested in the position, and the manner in which they all handled the vacancy is laudable.

"He assured me that if I didn't get the GW job, I could come with him to Northwestern," Bozeman said of McKeown, "but he had already had preliminary talks with the AD and some people on the board about me. He told me up front that he was going to endorse me, but that they were going to open it up. He didn't know exactly what they would do, and he didn't know how much influence he would have, but that he was going to endorse me.

"I touched base with Jack Kvancz," Bozeman detailed. "In that conversation—and there was only one about this—I told him I was definitely interested in the job. I took my resume packet and put it in his mailbox. That, to me, was submitting it. And then I went about my duties, talking to our recruits and their parents and staying in the office wrapping up what we had done. It was an awkward time for me because I was wondering, 'Am I doing this work in vain?' not knowing if I was going to be there or not. But I felt like I should be diligent with that. I didn't really talk to Jack a lot, and when we did it was about other issues.

> *"I took my resume packet and put it in his mailbox. And then I went about my duties, talking to our recruits and their parents and staying in the office wrapping up what we had done."*
>
> ~Mike Bozeman

"I definitely talked to Coach McKeown," Bozeman continued. "He was my mentor for several years before this. He told me to be low key about it. He advised me to just submit my resume. My name was already in the area of interest, so his advice was to just sit back and keep doing my duties while they went through the process of narrowing down the list."

McKeown also warned Bozeman about over-engaging the team during that period. "I thought it would have been a mistake to have the players go in and recommend him," McKeown explained. "I've seen that backfire. I think that could work against you. I think he handled it very professionally."

Bozeman took the counsel to heart. "From that point, my own thoughts were, I wanted to stay away from the players. What I didn't want to do is get them intertwined. I didn't want them rallying for me, because if it went the other way, which I felt like it could, I didn't want it to hamper their connection to whoever the new coach was. I wanted them to be successful most of all, so I stayed away from them. I got a few calls from some alumni, ladies who had just graduated, so I fielded those calls, but I didn't talk to the players at all. I thought that was crucial, because I wanted to keep them neutral. I didn't think that, one, I needed them to politic for me, and two, I just didn't think that was very ethical."

From Kvancz's viewpoint, input from the players was important. "I really, really tried to involve the players as much as I could, because in the end that's who's playing," Kvancz reasoned. "Now, I didn't take the eighteenth person on the team. I took the ones who were playing, and I was up-front: 'Listen, you have to understand, one of the candidates is someone you're very, very familiar with. Just understand one thing. In the role of a head coach, he says, 'Sally, you go in. Sally, you sit down. That's a lot different than an assistant coach, whose job is to pump you up and get you ready. So you have to factor that in, too. If you think he's a real human being or a real person you can talk to, that's all I'm interested in.'"

Bozeman appreciated senior associate athletics director Mary Jo Warner staying up front about the process. "She wanted to make sure that every candidate was going to get the same consideration, which I felt was fair," Bozeman said. "I had my packet, and I made copies for each member [of the board]. The advantage I had was having been there for three years. I was very familiar with the people who were on the board. They were very familiar with my approach to the program and my diligence to the excellence that Joe McKeown had started.

"First I met with Jack," Bozeman said about the interview itself. "The panel took me on a tour. Shoot, I'd been giving the tours, so that was a little awkward. We talked about renovations planned for the arena. I went to lunch with Jack and then came back and met with the board. The days the other candidates were interviewing, and I knew them, I stayed away from the university, because I didn't want to bump into them."

The intimacy developed during the previous three years obviously helped Bozeman, as Kvancz admitted. "We were successful, and he was part of our success. So my question was only, did I think he could run the ship. Because I think there's a big difference sitting in that chair than sitting in the chair next to him. Subliminally I said, 'I know him. When it gets hot and tough, I know how he's going to react. I've seen him under fire.'

"That to me was a big plus. I knew Michael, but he also got to know the development guy, the admissions person, the president and vice president. He already knew those people, and he got to know the fans. I have to say, that was clearly an advantage. Because if I'd hired somebody from somewhere else, I'd have had to go through all that stuff."

From Bozeman's perspective, the players and staff being accustomed to him also was a benefit. "It helped that those returnees were very familiar with my passion for the game, and our training situation didn't change. I guess what helped me most with that was that I already had a relationship with those guys. I had a respect for them, they had a respect for me, so that was easy."

If a viable internal candidate indeed exists and presents a logical choice for succession, it's hard to underestimate the goodwill created by hiring that person. "There was a certain feeling, at least in my mind, that they had hired someone from the family, and that they had not gone outside," McKeown acknowledged. "It's a great program. You're talking about back-to-back Sweet 16s and all these players coming back, so it's an attractive job in a great city. George Washington could have gone out and hired any number of great coaches. They kept it within the family, and I'm happy about that. There are a lot of people who played for or coached with me out there. I'd have been happy with anybody from within the family. I'm glad they didn't hire someone from the outside."

MENTORING AND BEING MENTORED

The practice of mentoring can be very empowering for both parties involved. A mentor can take pride in developing another professional, just as a parent does with a maturing child. The individual being mentored gains skills, confidence, knowledge, and the leeway to make decisions and mistakes.

Mentoring can take place at any time of a person's life or career: in an entry-level position just out of school, in an assistant role that is progressing in responsibilities, and throughout a head or director position.

IT STARTS BEFORE THE JOB DOES...

If a young professional is lucky, the mentor relationship begins before the promotion, thus preparing him or her for the added duties and pressures of the new job. Bozeman and Jolette Law at Illinois are among those who benefitted greatly from relationships with their mentors prior to landing their head coaching positions.

"He was preparing me to be a head coach," Bozeman said of McKeown, "but not necessarily at George Washington, because I don't think he knew he was leaving until [he did]. But he was always preparing me, sharing experiences he was going through. We always had those conversations. He'd bring me in on situations and tell me, 'When you're a head coach, you'll have to deal with this,' so we'd go through the whole process. He was always telling me that he was preparing me, by the conclusion of that first year, and that he knew I was going to be a head coach. He did that with his other assistants, too."

Kvancz agreed. "Joe didn't hide assistant coaches. They were out and about, you could talk to them, you knew what their philosophy was."

McKeown himself touched on the idea. "With the administration, with the higher administration, with the board of regents, and some of the bigger donors and boosters, I had tried to introduce Mike to those people over the last couple of years."

Law felt similarly groomed by C. Vivian Stringer at Rutgers. "Coach Stringer prepared me in the last four years with her, allowing me to do some things that she knew I would experience in my first year: budget, running this, making decisions.

'OK, Jolette, handle it. Make this decision.' I thank God daily for her and those experiences as an associate head coach. She allowed me to really make decisions and be able to stick to them, to be able to say, 'OK, this is what I think and this is why.' She'd say, 'Do not bring me a problem without a solution.'"

...AND CONTINUES AFTER IT STARTS

Once the shift is made to the corner office, so to speak, new employees not only must consider things they never had to consider before, they aren't even aware of what all to consider. On top of that, the notion and emotion of the new position are facets of a job that aren't necessarily instinctual or easy to master. The mentoring can continue with the original mentor and should begin with the new supervisor

When Lisa Love moved out of coaching and into full-time administration at Southern Cal, Jerritt Elliott continued learning from her as she explained the changes and challenges he would face as interim head coach.

"It was more the conceptual, psychological perception of moving from the second chair into the first chair," Love explained, "and therein he was getting on-the-job training to prep him for being a head coach at some lucky institution. In talking to him on a regular basis through the volleyball season, I worked with him on the relationship of an administrator to a head coach. So whether it was budget management or facility management or scheduling discussions, strategizing about where the program is and what the next round of needs is, I was working with him strategically, administrator to head coach."

Elliott appreciated the continued education. "It was great because I was able to go to her a lot and ask some questions like, 'Hey, how would you handle this situation? Here's what I'm doing. Can you give me some insight? Am I making the right decision or the wrong decision?' Ultimately I had to pick what decision I would go with, but it was nice to have that to factor along with it. Again, that's what made the transition a little more unique, because I still had someone I could go to to ask questions, or how to go about this, or how to fight for certain things within the program where we needed it."

Illinois athletics director Ron Guenther helped Law with, among other things, the all-important task of compiling an outstanding staff. "There's a learning process, and we spent a lot of time with Jolette learning about what she's looking for in assistants," he began, "because their success is going to be dependent upon making the right kind of decisions as to who that staff is going to be. She started out with one profile in her mind, and as we worked through that profile, it changed. As much as Jolette was ready, I think it's important that we participate, come up with pluses and minuses, strengths and weaknesses for her, what gaps are we trying to fill, how did she see that all unfolding. I think that was the next part of the transition that was going very, very well here, and I'm very pleased with how things ended up."

Mike Bozeman valued the time he spent talking with Jack Kvancz once Bozeman became George Washington's head coach. "Jack had meetings with me," Bozeman said. "He told me some of the challenges he thought I was going to face recruiting-wise. We just had sit-down conversations, I guess to make me feel more comfortable, which it did. He shared some of his stories. He has a storied history in basketball himself. He played in the Final Four at Boston College, he played against Kareem Abdul-Jabbar, those kinds of things.

"He would talk to me about scheduling, about his philosophy," Bozeman continued. "One of the funniest things we joke about still, in talking about planning games, is he said, 'You know, 73 percent of games are won by the home team.' And we talked about making sure I avail myself to the community and the college community."

Kvancz elaborated on their discussions and his rationale for them. "One of the things that happens when you have a coach who's been here a long, long time like Joe [McKeown] had, is you allow that person to do an awful lot of things on their own. They're going to schedule what they're going to schedule. Joe's comment about all the candidates was, 'You're going to have to be much more involved than you were with me on little things, because those little things I took care of. These people are going to be first-time coaches.' So consequently, Mike and I do the scheduling together. With Joe I'd say, 'Hey Joe, are we all set with the schedule?' He'd say, 'I'll run it by you next week.' That's fine. I trusted him enough that everything was going to be fine. And it proved to be a good trust, because everything *was* fine. But he said about Mike, 'Some of the things you let me run with you're going to have to sit down with him,' and scheduling is a prime example.

"And I tried to tell him [that first year], if you look at the schedule, I don't care if Joe was still coaching, or if Jesus Christ was coaching, Joe got out at the right time, because he got all those teams at home. Now we have to go on the road, and I do think our women's basketball fans understand that 73 percent of all games played away from home are going to be lost," Kvancz said, proving Bozeman's comment. "So I don't think they necessarily were going to give him a hard time about the A&M loss or the Rutgers loss or even the Tennessee loss.

"Now, that being said, Mike's got some games in the league he should win, and I would assume that we will win," Kvancz continued. "That's easy for me to say because I'm not coaching the team. On paper you're always going to win. The problem is, as I told Joe, 'You're too good.' They [the fans] don't realize the work that goes into beating that team. You're going to win some games and you're going to lose some games. It's not automatic that you're going to win just because you work hard. The other team's working hard too. They're not lying down for you."

Itineraries for road trips are another topic on which Kvancz mentored Bozeman. "I meet with Michael about away trips and how many players he has [traveling] and what time they're leaving and if it involves [missing] classes, and he's really good at that. But in Joe's case I'd say, 'Are we all set with the trip?' because I knew the only reason he'd leave early is if there was only one flight out. If you're going by bus, he was going to let the kids go to class and leave later in the afternoon. I knew that. But that's the point Joe brought out to me: 'There are a lot of things that, at least for a year or two, you're going to have to talk to him about.'

"In all fairness, when you have someone come in like that, they didn't know what was going on," Kvancz explained. "So it behooves you to tell them what's going on. And once you do, he's fine. But in Joe's case, after all those years, it just happened. In Mike's case, we sit down and talk about it. And 9 times out of 10, it's fine. But I'm just more active in trying to do that with him. I think we'll get to the point where he knows where I'm coming from, he knows what he has to do. But you have to point it out, because they never thought of those things. And he's fine with it. He handles it all.

"Sometimes I say to him, 'I want to talk to you as a basketball guy. I'll tell you when I want to talk to you as your AD.' The majority of the cases have all been basketball. 'Let's talk basketball. Why are you doing this or that?' And he has reasons. That's really important to me that we have those kinds of conversations. That's why we meet every day, just to talk. 'How did you do? What are you doing about that?' I go to all the home games and some of the away games, so I can ask him, 'How's Sally's jump shot? Has she improved? Is she working on it?' So he knows I'm talking to him about a game he loves and a game that I love. And we can go into other things, but we haven't really had to do that.

"Now there are things with coaching," Kvancz went on. "I think personally, and I told him this, you can take advice from your assistants. That's what they're there for. However, when you're saying, 'Sally, go in,' *you're* saying, 'Sally, go in.' You have to be the head coach, because in the end you get the Ws and the Ls. That's a big thing. A lot of times with a young coach—now he was a high school head coach for many years, but he's been an assistant everywhere else—you have to understand that you can take all of that information, and you should, but then *you* have to decide what you're going to do. They give you advice: 'I think we should do this.' And sometimes it's good, but you have to synthesize and decide what you want to do taking that into account.

"Just certain little things. I think a young coach who comes in, you don't want to stifle them, but you say, 'I have a lot of gray hair. One, the sun will come up tomorrow. I guarantee you.' And if you try to hammer into the kids something and don't have success, one of the things you have to look at is, 'Maybe they can't do that. Maybe I'm asking them to do stuff they can't do.' I think a lot of times younger coaches don't understand that. 'If you don't do what I ask you to do, then I'm going to look bad as a coach.' The truth is, players play. Put them in positions that they can do the things they're supposed to do. And if they can do that, that's fine. That's good!

"I knew a guy years and years ago. He was a very good coach," Kvancz recalled. "I'm from Connecticut. He was at Sacred Heart. October 15 was his starting date. October 15-20 he would sit in the stands, and his theory was, as crazy as it sounds, 'I recruited all of these kids, but I don't know if they can do what I'm going to ask them to do. So I'm going to see them all play together and then I'm going to decide what offense I'm going to run, what defense I'm going to run.'

"Stupid. However, there's a little bit of truism in that. 'I'm going to take you and fit you into this peg because that's what we're going to do. But what if you can't do it?'

He was a good player, but he was running up and down the floor, and now you're going to put him in this slow-down offense? Maybe he can't play that way. Or maybe he's a good player, but he's a great player if he plays that way. The point I was trying to make to Mike, because every assistant in my book has all the answers: 'Understand you're not the assistant anymore. You're calling the shots. So if you say you're going to play zone, you better make sure they can play zone. If they like one out-of-bounds play better than an elaborate one you drew up, run the one they like best. They will execute the one they like better than the one you like."'

Not only are coaches themselves making transitions, but their families are, too. The spouse, especially, has a role and persona that is different from that of an assistant coach's spouse. Bozeman understood that and respected Laura McKeown for helping his wife, Wendy, make the transition.

"She really set an example of a coach's wife," Bozeman said. "She helped my wife formulate how she's going to conduct herself and really realize there's a role for the head coach's wife, a pertinent role. I think Laura did a great job of that, and I thank her so much for that. Because it wasn't just me. The transition wasn't just Joe to me. It was more like Joe and Laura to me and Wendy."

MANAGING PEOPLE, PLACES, AND THINGS

There is a reason supervisors command a higher salary than their employees, who sometimes perceive themselves as doing all the work. Managing people is difficult. Humans are unpredictable creatures who haul baggage around with their disparate competencies, all of which supervisors must learn to handle. Likewise, coaches have the arduous task of keeping competitive yet unequal players pushing each other to be better while at the same time developing chemistry among them.

But people aren't the only aspects of managing a team, as Jerritt Elliott was fortunate to experience on an interim basis. "I learned a lot about coaching and what it means to wear the head coaching hat," he said. "Any top coach will tell you, 'You can recruit, you can coach,'—and there are a lot of them [coaches who can do both]—'but it's the management of the personnel within the program on a daily basis'" that separates coaches and their programs.

"You always have issues with players," Elliott explained. "Being able to define everybody's role really set the ability for the team to be successful as a whole, and trying to identify and get my assistant coaches to identify when the players are having a hard time and when they need a meeting. It's different coaching women, too. If I walk by them and I'm thinking about practice and I don't say hello, they may think I'm upset at them, so I make sure I'm always clear on where they stand with me."

Managing people starts with the manager. Elliott learned that the hardest part is "figuring out how to manage your emotions and being able to put on a front as the head coach and the leader of the program that everything is going in the order that you want, and never losing sight of that. Once you lose your players in that area, that is the biggest downfall that can happen to a program. You can be stern, but you can't lose sight and you can't unravel. You have to be the rock as the leader. There are a lot of hard times you go through. You have to be persistent and believe in your vision, and hopefully you'll get to the point where you want to be. This is our eighth year, and we just got to the Final Four for the first time. I thought we'd do it in four. We had opportunities the two years before but just missed. It's unpredictable. You have to embrace that change, and you have to know things are going to happen and have your support group you can really trust and vent to and talk to."

PLAYERS AND TEAM

Managing the dynamics of the team on and off the court takes intuition and practice. So many facets and nuances, along with the fluid dynamic that involving people creates, keep the task from being anywhere near clear-cut. When Elliott looked back on his experience at Southern Cal, he recalled the thought processes, strategies, and decisions he used to prepare himself and his team for his first shot as a head coach.

"Coaching is trying to be two steps ahead of your players and know what they're about to get themselves into," Elliott said. "You go through the first preseason and they're all invigorated, because the practices were great and they're going to be great. They have no idea they're going to fall flat on their faces. How are you going to get them to rebound, to build that confidence on a day-to-day basis?

"If you're just going to go in and kind of coach, it's going to make it difficult," Elliott continued. "There has to be a blueprint of what you're trying to make happen in the program so they understand what we're trying to do, from recruiting to the daily training habits to the weight lifting and what the standards are going to be. That was the big focus: what are the standards of the program, and how are we going to improve this program on a daily basis?

"Kids are always trying to push and take: 'Oh, I'm hurt,' and going to the training room. But the trainers and the strength coaches are on the same page knowing that these are the standards, and knowing who could practice and who couldn't by the trainer sending out something every day saying what they can do lifting-wise and who can practice. Having everyone that was involved talk about the same philosophies, about what we were trying to do as a program, was a big key to being successful in such a short period of time, and then really letting them embrace this whole process of developing a program to be a national championship program, showing them a road map of how we were going to go about doing that.

"We were all on the same page and looking out for each other, because I think the hardest thing of coaching is, if one person gets away with [something], then their standards are let down," Elliott said. "When everybody has to live up to a certain expectation and do it a right way, it's a lot easier to build team confidence in those areas. So those were the ways we went about creating really strong, united support services from every area to make sure they were doing that. And if they weren't, there was punishment we called Breakfast Club. If they were late to study hall, or if they tried to get out of something, or there were certain standards [they didn't meet], they had to go do Breakfast Club. Everybody was treated the same way. They understood the blueprint of what we were doing and why. They knew why they had Breakfast Club, because they understood that it was building trust. If someone was getting away with it, someone else might do it, and it kind of deteriorates.

"We tried to get the leadership to buy into it by training the captains, because coaches are only around about 20 percent of the time. The captains are around more. We wanted to get them to understand they were an extension of the coaching staff and really have open forums where they bought in—they like what we're doing, they understand what we're doing so they can have ammunition of their own, so when they were with the players they could hold up the standards of the program.

"I had a captain I got on pretty hard one day in practice," Elliott explained. "She walked in the locker room—I heard this a couple of weeks after it happened—and one of the freshmen walked up to her and said, 'What was wrong with Coach today? Why was he picking on you?' And she turned to her and said, 'Hey, I didn't live up to the standards of the gym today. It was my fault, and I let the team down, and he was right on for it.' Those kinds of little comments are big in terms of boosting the team's confidence and understanding that there is actually a vision of what the standards are.

"I probably had meetings every day with two or three players so they understood their roles, what they were getting themselves into. When they were good, I was making sure to be positive. When they were bad, I was trying to meet with them to explain these were standards we were looking for as a program and trying to get better as a whole."

PROGRAM

Many coaches dream: "If we only had to deal with the players and the team…" But athletics at all levels has mushroomed in breadth and complexity, such that perhaps more time is spent away from the players, practice, and competition than with those energizing aspects of the job. With departments like marketing, academics, compliance, business, and game management, balancing the needs of the program takes an adept, steady hand.

"The thing you don't understand as an assistant coach is how many hats you have to wear," Elliott admitted. "As an assistant coach, you report to the head coach and you have a lot of the day-to-day operations of the program, but it was the overall management of the program [that makes the scope of the head position surprising]. You're not dealing with marketing or the academic counselors or compliance or the financial part of it, and how to balance the books.

"As a head coach, you're dealing more with confrontations within the department, and trying to get those people to see your vision and how to go about making that happen," Elliott pointed out. "There are so many different areas you have to report to. The key to transitions is to make sure you know every support service that you have, to extend your arms to create relationships and make sure they feel welcome. Be very connected and involved with the heads of those programs to make them understand what your vision is and to allow them to be a part of the program, to see where you want to end up.

"I had meetings with my strength coaches and my trainers—I believe we also had my psych person, Mike Voight, who was working with us at the time—trying to come up with a philosophy and new things we would try to incorporate, and make sure my outside forces who have day-to-day interaction with the athletes knew there was going to be a change and this was the way we were going to go about it. So there was unity amongst us all. They were clear in terms of the vision and direction I wanted to have."

Dawn Staley recognized the importance of the head coach managing the staff as well. "You have to have your ego in check," Staley said. "You have to allow people to help you. You can't do everybody's job. You have to be able to delegate and not micromanage. If you have to micromanage, you probably have the wrong [assistant] coaches. And you have to make all of your coaches feel like they're your right hand, no matter if they are or they're not. They want to feel important and like they're contributing in a way that leads to success.

"You want everybody to be a head coach who works with you," Staley continued. "And I think sometimes we tend to forget that we're shaping lives. We're shaping players' lives and we're shaping coaches' lives. And sometimes I think you lose sight of that because of the pressure of wanting to win and making sure things are done the right way when they aren't done the way you want them done. But you can get all of that accomplished with keeping in mind that people want to feel a part of it."

Another startling component of a head coach's job is the amount of time spent speaking to others and promoting the program. That type of interaction rarely comes naturally, and young coaches generally have much less experience relating with a more established, powerful, influential population than with recruits, parents, and team members.

As much grooming as Illinois's Jolette Law received in her 12 years at Rutgers, she didn't realize the extent to which she would be out in public. "Being a head coach is much more than coaching a game: the media, all the speaking engagements, selling myself on a daily basis. Taking the job, I knew I was going to have to speak, but every day my calendar was booked, being pulled here for the community to find out more about me, about my vision, and all the things I had to do. The opportunities were so great to be that voice, that mouthpiece, to sell this great university. I didn't think it was going to be as intense as it was. I tell people every day that the Xs and Os part is the easy part."

***

Getting a break and landing that first head coaching job can be tough. But actually having the job is vastly tougher. Having been involved in the game for years makes the Xs and Os like breathing to most who step into the leadership position. But many young or first-time head coaches are amazed at the amount of time and energy spent on the management of the individual players, the collective team, and the program. They are dumbfounded at the number and variety of tasks expected of a head coach every day.

The mentorship of an up-and-coming coach is absolutely invaluable. Oprah Winfrey once said, "A mentor is someone who allows you to see the hope inside yourself." An equally wise but unknown person defined a mentor as "someone whose hindsight can become your foresight." It takes time, respect, and trust on both sides, and it rarely can be forced. But when the chemistry is right, the mentor is skilled and selfless, and the mentee is sponge-like and respectful, the payoff is tremendous for both sides.

Chapter 7
UTILIZING A LONG-TERM INTERIM COACH: A Dialogue

In 1999, the University of Southern California initiated an atypical transition within its volleyball program. Lisa Love, who had served as head coach since 1989 and associate athletics director since 1991, made the difficult announcement on March 24, 1999, to relinquish her coaching duties and focus solely on her administrative career.

After a three-month search, Southern Cal introduced Mick Haley as its new coach on June 23, 1999, but with an unusual twist. Because Haley at the time was serving as head of the USA women's volleyball team, the culmination of which would be the 2000 Sydney Olympics, the school announced that Jerritt Elliott, a four-year assistant for Southern Cal and a candidate for the vacancy, would serve as interim head coach until Haley arrived in October 2000. Five-year assistant coach Paula Weishoff remained as Elliott's top assistant.

What could have been a disastrous arrangement instead is a model of how interim positions can be handled to the benefit of all. What follows are outtakes of conversations with Elliott, Haley, and Love regarding their thoughts and experiences, which provide a glimpse of how the trio collectively put program success above personal attention, and how each reaped breathtaking achievements as a result.

BIRTH OF A UNIQUE SITUATION

Lisa Love moves from the dual job of head coach/administrator into full-time administration. Assistant coach Jerritt Elliott applies for the head coach opening. Southern Cal hires Mick Haley as the head-coach-in-waiting until the 2000 Olympics are over. In the meantime, Elliott serves as interim head coach.

ELLIOTT: "During the [interview] process, they brought in other coaches. Ultimately they decided on Mick Haley. I think there's no question they made a good decision. I understood their decision-making, and I got a wonderful opportunity. They came and presented me with a two-year opportunity to be the interim head coach."

LOVE: "As it turned out, Mick was a strong candidate for the job, was offered the job, and accepted the job. While Mick was finishing his tenure as the Olympic coach, we asked Jerritt to serve as the interim head coach.

"My biggest role with Jerritt, as a candidate for the head position, was to have him understand psychologically that the position was offered to somebody with a very powerful resumé and proven talent as a collegiate head coach and an Olympic head coach, and helping him understand—and it was not hard—that he was being given a very powerful opportunity to lead the Trojans as an interim head coach."

THE PLAN

Love, Haley, and Elliott worked together to establish a cohesive strategy, laying the groundwork and ground rules for making the transition smooth and effective over the next 16 months.

HALEY: "Once the announcement was made, I went to Los Angeles and spent a full day with Jerritt and Paula. I wanted to make sure they knew what my expectations were for the program, because many times schools want to hire people with a name, and you better get it then because after that you're just going to get what you get. So I went in and we solidified that [after I joined the staff] Paula was going to be the second assistant and Jerritt was going to be the first assistant, and we talked about him being associate head coach if we could get along well. And Erica, who was the second assistant, would be the operations director. She wanted to be coaching, but she was willing to go along with it. We all got in a room with Lisa, and I tried to round up sports information and a few other people, and we went through developing a three-year plan, which was to get the program updated, and a five-year plan, which was to win a national championship."

ELLIOTT: "He came in within two weeks after he was hired and we spent a good day-and-a-half, two days meeting, getting his advice, informing him of what players we had, how many scholarships we had, trying to make sure what he inherited was going to be better by the time he got there with some young talent.

"We just discussed where we wanted the program heading. He was kind of out of touch with who the new recruits were, because within two years you can start losing that if you're out of [college athletics]. So I was just communicating with him what we were doing, trying to identify the game plan of what recruits I was going after and how that was going, things we were doing within the program, and where we wanted to head to build it the right way so it would be a smooth transition for him."

HALEY: "We developed the plans, and everything that Jerritt was to do the next two years was to fall into the framework of that. So he would call me from time to time, but not very often. I gave him carte blanche. I didn't care as much about [who he hired as coaches]. All I wanted was final approval on who he offered scholarships to. I just didn't want him signing people I didn't think were good enough.

"With Jerritt having the five-year plan and the three-year plan and me going on and focusing on the USA team, he went out and did the recruiting. He would call and say, 'Well, I have so-and-so committed,' or 'I'd like to offer so-and-so.' I might say, 'Well, maybe her grades aren't very good,' and he'd say, 'Yeah, but we can take care of her here.' And if that was a 'No' by me he would reconstruct it as, 'Well, I can sign her, but…' And he did a good job. He got those kids in and he would use me as, 'The national team coach is coming and we're going to have this and we're going to have that.' And so it worked pretty well."

EVERYBODY WINS

The trio made an impressive—and successful—effort of teamwork, always putting the program ahead of self, and therefore they all came out ahead.

LOVE: "How I believe you could make this work, especially with someone internally who was a very strong candidate for the job—in all three cases, it was advantageous to all parties concerned. You had three people who stood to gain from this type of transition, all with their eyes on the fact that if the University of Southern California was successful, it would be successful for all people concerned. So the better the volleyball team performed, the better it would be for Jerritt, for Mick, and for me, as far as reward, as far as focus, as far as goals and objectives. Ultimately what it led to was, Jerritt recruited two back-to-back number one recruiting classes. After incorporating one of those classes, he advanced that team as we dreamed and hoped beyond regionals into the Final Four and did a fantastic job. And he coached again the following year very successfully.

"What could have been a natural challenge was player loyalty. You could have, in three phases, all sorts of player loyalty: some degree of player loyalty to me, a significant degree of player loyalty from those recruiting classes to Jerritt, and you could have had some dissention relative to someone else—Mick—being selected as head coach. That didn't happen, at least publicly, because people were dedicated to playing well and because the table was set appropriately and admirably to make the transition a smooth one. A lot of that had to do with very wise council from Paula Weishoff, who was supporting the program as an assistant coach for me and then Jerritt, and then Jerritt's approach to creating the appropriate bridge for players to be successful under the next coach.

"It was advantageous to all parties concerned. You had three people who stood to gain from this type of transition, all with their eyes on the fact that if the University of Southern California was successful, it would be successful for all people concerned."

~Lisa Love

"The only thing that players witnessed, appropriately so, was the respect that all three parties showed each other. There's a tremendous amount of respect for Mick and all he accomplished, and the opportunity he was being provided at Southern Cal. Where there could have been natural friction of who was selected for the job versus who wasn't selected for the job, all that was set aside—I never witnessed that kind of friction. I have no doubt there would have naturally been some level of frustration, but the program and the student-athletes always came first, and the kind of character displayed by Mick and Jerritt toward each other was very, very respectful. Jerritt respected Mick for his accomplishments, for his very successful tenure in coaching, for what he was doing with the Olympic program. Mick was very respectful of Jerritt for what he was doing and his significant contributions to Southern Cal, for two back-to-back number one recruiting classes. And Mick was quick to acknowledge Jerritt's contributions. I think it's safe to say there did not seem to be a need for grabbing the limelight. There did not seem to be a need for, 'I need to take credit for this,' and 'I need to take credit for that.' There was simply a very transparent reality that was in play, and people addressed it for what it was, and if the program was successful, all three parties would be successful.

"I will say this, though. With this particular group of three people, if we were going in the wrong direction on planning or with the wrong view, both for the program and for each person individually, we would have addressed it. We would have resolved it and pulled everything back into focus if it started to get blurry. There was very open dialogue, and I served as a sort of conduit between both coaches, and that was not a difficult job because of their character."

ELLIOTT: "A lot has to do with personalities and confidence. The ultimate goal—what Lisa left behind with me taking over and Mick coming in—was for all of us to be able to create something so Southern Cal could be successful. Coaches come and go, but you're employed by the university. There was no animosity. Understand, step back from the situation, and say, 'What is the most important thing that is going on right now?' And that is the players involved in the program. They don't need to know what's going on on the outside. We can take care of them. We can work well with adults and really communicate our issues we're having, meet and talk or make sure we're trying to be on the same page. And that's where Mick was really good about that. I tried to work with him as well as I could with what he wanted.

"I knew at some point I was going to be a head coach. It wasn't going to be at Southern Cal, and I was OK with that, but I understood every move I made was above the line, doing it the right way, knowing that the AD from another school would come over and look at me and ask, 'Hey, how did he do this?' I was very conscientious of not rocking the boat at all. I wanted to be a catalyst to push that forward and make that happen."

LOVE: "He [Elliott] had a year-and-a-half experience to feel what it was like to work with the administration as the CEO of a collegiate volleyball program—in other words, to move into the first chair and get a feel for that around the internal mechanisms of the department, the external roles of being a head coach as opposed to an associate head coach, and all of the workings that go along with becoming the CEO of a program."

INTERIM SEASONS

Elliott stepped in as interim head coach, recovering from the disappointment of not winning the job to lead the team to new heights by understanding the triple role of honoring the past and making the most of the present while selling the future of the program.

ELLIOTT: "It [the new role as head coach] was obviously a change. I was the good cop as an assistant coach. I was the one always there pumping them up after a bad day if a head coach gets on them. I just tried to explain to them, being in my [new] seat, how my role would really change. So they understood that I had been an assistant coach, but now I had to be stern, to put my thumb down, to help them really be able to understand the roles of a head coach. And I tried to let them see that they have roles as players—whether they become starters or nonstarters—and that as a head coach: 'Here are the things it's going to take for this program to be success-ful, and here are the things I'm going to have to be able to take over for Lisa, and I can't always be the good cop anymore.'"

HALEY: "USA Volleyball was such a difficult job and such a stressful thing for me. In the summer before we went to Sydney for the Olympics [before Jerritt's second season], Jerritt came to my house and said, 'I want to coach the team for the whole year.' And I said, 'I can do that,' because I knew how tired I was going to be, and I knew it was going to be his team, and to come in the middle of the season and try to make it my team would be like trying to put a square block into a round hole. I just know how this works enough to know it doesn't work like that. So I said, 'Yes,' and I think that's what allowed such a great effort by him, because it gave him a chance to really prove himself. I thought that was only fair. He did all the recruiting. Sure, he used my name, but it was never a competition or anything. It was all for the better-ment of the program."

LOVE: "In Jerritt's second season [as interim head coach], Mick was involved in periodic meetings, was moving his family to southern California, was in transition from the Olympic team. Periodically he would join Southern Cal at home matches, but the season was completely engineered and led by Jerritt Elliott, with Mick in preparation in the wings and me providing administrative oversight and the conduit for all parties. Mick was able to evaluate talent, the program, Southern Cal, what he was moving into, and think about how he might set things up. But he did not assert himself when he arrived on campus in a coaching role. He was in more of an obser-vatory and supportive role.

"Mick was introduced [to the public] very politely and wonderfully but not with pomp and circumstance. We didn't create an event to introduce him. He was certainly introduced to very dedicated fans when he was attending matches. He was intro-duced, if you will, on a more singular, personal basis, and then he was introduced being up in front as the leader of the volleyball program. Then he stood front and center in front of donor audiences and groups after that last season. It was one step at a time."

HALEY: "October 1 was the first day of my job at Southern Cal. And you know how everybody tries to pit you against each other. They'd say, 'Jerritt, how can you let that happen?' Or, 'Mick, how come you don't take over right away?' And I would say, 'I just need to work into this. It will take a while.' And the guy who hired me kept saying, 'When are you going to take over?' Basically I wanted to tell him, 'Just be quiet and let me do this.' I told them I wasn't going to take over for Jerritt until after the season was over, and I would have input and would be helping out but that nothing changes. But it was his ego. He wanted the person he hired to be in charge because he didn't want the other guy to do well, because he didn't want to hire him. So he had a dog in the fight. And I just didn't think I could do that to Jerritt. I didn't think it was fair, and it would have been really unreasonable, stupid.

"It was very difficult for me on one hand and, as I said, very easy on the other hand. I was so burned out that I didn't have the intestinal fortitude to get in there and try to change things. On the one hand, I couldn't believe we would practice so little. On the other hand, I was so glad to get out of there and go home. So I'm just being real honest here. I don't know if anybody ever admits this stuff, but I just wanted to be like Rip Van Winkle and just sleep until my beard grew down to my ankles. I was really, really tired. But when I got here, it just felt like everybody was flying by the seat of their pants, and it was amazing to me that we were doing as well as we were doing. But all I needed to do was rock the boat a little bit and I think that would have knocked them off-kilter. They were cruising and they had a good feeling and the coaches were dealing with things as they were and so I just went to work."

ELLIOTT: "It was October. We were playing UCLA. I think it was his first match on the bench. We had gone undefeated, and that was the first time we actually lost a game. It was just different dynamics. I think they wanted to impress him and play well for him and just weren't comfortable with that process. But we had meetings [afterward] with the players, saying, 'Hey, he's going to be here. You're going to have to get used to him. He's going to be your coach through your career, so he's always going to be on the bench.'

"Mick and I had talked about that, and he was very good. Lisa, myself, and Mick had met and gone over all this stuff, and that I was still going to be there and I was still going to be their fan, and that was part of it, but we still have an opportunity to do something special, so let's not mess these next two months up for these players.

"And he was really good because he was pretty much hands-off. He was trying to get organized with the move, and it was so late in the season that he didn't know a whole lot of the systems and what we were trying to implement. He knew some of them, but he tried to be more of a mentor-type, giving me suggestions of what he would do and how to go about this process. It was nice to have that, but it was good too because he didn't disrupt it during the season."

HALEY: "We got through it in great shape, and that was the best part of it. I stayed out of the way. I stayed down at the end of the bench. Actually, I made Jerritt really nervous down there, and he wanted me to get up closer so he could hear if I said anything to the athletes. I don't view that as negative. When you're the coach, you want to be in control of that stuff. It doesn't matter if it's somebody who's going to take over for you. You're still the coach.

"It just felt that my way was so different that I'd really screw it up. And I learned at Texas that when you get them [the players] going, you get back out of the way and let them be responsible for their team. Because if you can empower them, they will take on the world. The last thing I wanted to do with this team is try to get into the mix. There were little things. I felt like I could make a difference with the blocking right away, so I gave little individual pointers and stuff, but I think that was driving the coaches crazy, so I finally stopped doing that.

"I always felt like everybody was watching to see if I was going to get in the mix, and I was very careful to move slow, not say much, just try to be a fixture so they could get comfortable seeing me. You know how you tell people, 'Be seen but don't be heard.' That's what I was trying to do. A couple of times I think I got a little mouthy, but I think for the most part I was able to do that. And I know Paula and the other coaches were walking a tightrope, trying to look like they were for me, but being loyal to Jerritt, too. It was probably really difficult for them also."

LOVE: "What was most important for Mick was the player experience during that period of time. If there was awkwardness, it could have perhaps been felt by Jerritt because Mick was around. But Mick didn't take part in any coaching duties. He did not dictate anything. He said, 'This is Jerritt's season. Jerritt's the coach, and this is how it is.' He did not attend all the matches. He did not attend practices regularly. The reins were in Jerritt's hands, and Mick felt that was most important for the success of the team in that particular year—to not confuse the matter. So he was in a position where, if Jerritt sought any type of feedback, Mick was available for that."

THE END AND THE BEGINNING

ELLIOTT: "As soon as the season was over, it was his to take over, and he could implement everything he wanted to do. But he was very good and respectful, and I think that was a lot of the reason we had success, because it was a smooth transition there. And the players could see that. They understood from day one that we were both on the same team, that I was OK with it. I think that was the hard part. It's a change for the players. They lose Lisa, and then they get this person who they had a very positive relationship with before and they loved playing for me—over two years we were able to create a bond—and then they think, 'Gosh, what are we going to get next?' So there's a fear, and those are the kinds of things you try to foresee and be two steps ahead of the players.

"In this kind of situation, you have to put the players ahead of your own ego and what you want. If it was Bobby Knight, I don't know if it would have worked. But also, I was a young enough age, too, I wasn't set in my ways. I think it would be a completely different scenario if I took over at an older age knowing what I know."

HALEY: "When he got over the slaps on the back and everything, that's when it crescendoed on him that he wasn't going to be the head coach. That's when I thought the outside influences got heaviest on him. It was easier for me. If I had been Jerritt, it would have been very difficult, and I had an appreciation for that and I understood that and I tried to be sensitive in every way I could. I tried to show appreciation as much as possible, always trying to include him in everything, always trying to ask his opinion. But it seemed like the more I did that, the more people thought, 'Maybe he doesn't know what he's doing,' meaning me. Everybody was waiting for me to take over and run with it, and I was probably being too sensitive and not really grabbing hold of it, not saying we're going to do this or that. I finally got around to it around April, and I think Jerritt leaving really helped me have to take charge.

"I think everything was really different. We were like night and day. He was cool and I was Midwest. Styles were different. But that's just the way it was. The great bridge was the players who could recognize that both coaches had something to give. The group of players who were there was the special entity. They just wanted to win. And they had known all along there was going to be a new coach, so it wasn't like it was sprung on them. They had two years to get used to it, and they came to school knowing that the people recruiting them might not be there. They wanted Southern Cal and they wanted to play together and they wanted to win championships.

"I always have felt bad for Jerritt even though I recognize it was a great thing for him. I thought there were some good things that would be coming for Jerritt. But it still made me awfully uncomfortable. I didn't like the feeling and wished I could have fixed it better. I just tried to do it as well as I could do it. But it's like my women's team: It's not about how well you played, it's about how well it felt. And it just didn't feel that great.

"But I think in the long term it's been really good for both of us, and maybe that's Lisa's foresight. I don't know, because I'm not privy to all sides, but I never really felt good about replacing Jerritt because he did an awfully good job. But given all of that, it is my job now and I do it the best I can do it, and I enjoy it. I enjoy going to work every day."

ELLIOTT: "The question I probably get most now is, 'Am I upset I didn't get the head coaching job there?' because I had back-to-back recruiting classes, we went to the Final Four, I was able to prove my worth within those two years. And I say, 'Absolutely not.' That was the door that opened for me and I was able to take advantage of it. I was never negative about the situation. I was never negative going into it saying, 'I wish this was my job.' I took it as an opportunity to develop what we had and build on that and to learn a lot about coaching."

***

And he did. Following an incredible two-season run—in which Southern Cal went 50-12, advanced to the NCAA Final Four for the first time in 15 years, claimed its first-ever share of the Pacific-10 Conference title, and landed two number one recruiting classes—Elliott landed the head coaching job at the University of Texas in 2001 and advanced to the national championship game in 2009. Ironically, that's the program Haley left for USA Volleyball in 1997. Haley went on to coach Southern Cal to the national championship in 2002 and 2003. Love was named vice president for university athletics at Arizona State University in 2005.

ABOUT THE AUTHORS

BETH BASS became chief executive officer of the Women's Basketball Coaches Association (WBCA) on Nov. 1, 2001, after serving the organization as executive director since January 1997.

As chief executive officer, Bass administers all operational affairs for the WBCA, which boasts more than 5,000 members, including coaches and leaders in women's and girls' basketball both nationally and internationally. Bass oversees all marketing endeavors; manages the non-profit organization's $3 million annual budget and all programs and services; and supervises the national office staff, which consists of 15 full-time staff members and six interns. She also is charged with overseeing the WBCA's external affairs as she takes on a more active role with affiliate organizations such as the National Collegiate Athletic Association (NCAA), Women's National Basketball Association (WNBA), Women's Sports Foundation (WSF), and USA Basketball.

In 2007, Bass spearheaded the launch of one of the most successful grassroots marketing campaigns for breast cancer awareness with the WBCA's "Think Pink," now known as the WBCA Pink Zone™. The campaign grew from 120 participating institutions in 2007 to more than 1,600 in 2010, when more than a million fans were reached and participants raised more than $1 million for breast cancer awareness and research. This breast cancer initiative created one of the largest movements in women's basketball history and served as a conduit to start the Kay Yow/WBCA Cancer Fund on December 3, 2007, in partnership with The V Foundation for Cancer Research. It serves as the WBCA's first health initiative on record.

Bass previously was a highly successful executive in the sports marketing industry. With experience as a women's basketball and women's sports marketing executive at Converse Inc. and Nike, Inc., Bass has been a catalyst for corporate support of women's basketball since 1986 and sits on several boards and committees, including the Naismith Memorial Hall of Fame board of trustees, the National Association of Collegiate Directors of Athletics (NACDA) executive committee, the Atlanta Tipoff Club board of directors, the USA Basketball board of directors, vice president of the Women's Basketball Hall of Fame, the iHoops advisory board, the Kay Yow/WBCA Cancer Fund board of directors, the McDonald's Girl's High School All-American Game advisory board, and the ex-officio for the NCAA Women's Basketball Issues Committee.

A native of Hartsville, South Carolina, Bass was a four-year women's basketball letter winner at East Tennessee State University, where she graduated with honors in 1984 with a Bachelor of Science in her double major of public relations/advertising and political science. She completed her master's degree in recreation administration from the University of Tennessee, Knoxville, in 1986, where she served as a graduate assistant for marketing and promotions in the Lady Volunteers athletics department.

***

BETTY F. JAYNES has been a leading figure in the sport of women's basketball since the mid-1970s. Currently the WBCA consultant, Jaynes functions with CEO Beth Bass in handling advisory assignments, including finances, programming, advocacy and special projects.

Named the WBCA's first chief executive officer on September 1, 1996, after serving 15 years as its founding executive director, Jaynes has cultivated and developed the growth and prosperity of the WBCA since 1981. The WBCA blossomed from its 212-member infancy into a 5,000-member-plus national organization and a leading resource, voice, and advocate for women's and girls' basketball at every level.

Among her numerous awards are the 2006 John Bunn Lifetime Achievement from the Naismith Basketball Hall of Fame (the highest award given next to induction into the Hall of Fame and only the second woman to receive the award), the 1997 Women's Sports Foundation's President's Award, the Georgia College and State University Alumni Heritage Award (2009), and inductions into the National Association of College Directors of Athletics Hall of Fame (2006), the Women's Basketball Hall of Fame (2000), the Virginia Sports Hall of Fame (2008), and the Georgia Sports Hall of Fame (2007).

Jaynes was head women's basketball coach at Madison College (renamed James Madison University in 1977) from 1970 to 1982, and she chaired the U.S. Girls' and Women's Basketball Rules Committee from 1979 to 1981.

A native of Covington, Ga., Jaynes lettered four years in basketball at Newton County High School, where she earned all-state honors as a junior and senior. She earned her bachelor of science degree in physical education from Georgia College in 1967 and her master of science degree in physical education from the University of North Carolina-Greensboro in 1968

***

JANA HUNTER assists others in writing, developing, editing, and publishing their expertise, ideas, and stories. Her career includes stints in college athletics media relations, sports publishing, and the non-profit sector.